# Business Valuation and Bankruptcy

# Business Valuation and Bankruptcy

IAN RATNER
GRANT STEIN
JOHN C. WEITNAUER

WILEY

John Wiley & Sons, Inc.

*Library of Congress Cataloging-in-Publication Data:*

Ratner, Ian.

Business valuation and bankruptcy / Ian Ratner, Grant Stein, John Weitnauer.

p. cm. — (Wiley finance series; 521)

Includes index.

Summary: "An essential guide to business valuation and bankruptcy, *Business Valuation and Bankruptcy* helps you—whether you are an accountant dealing with a troubled company, a lender, an investor, a bankruptcy and restructuring lawyer/financial advisor, or a private equity player—to focus on solving everyday and case determinative disputes when creditors, lenders, and debtors have differing views of value. Introducing valuation issues early on in the restructuring/bankruptcy process so you can plan accordingly, this book offers many real-life case examples and case descriptions. *Business Valuation and Bankruptcy* includes a review of the various approaches and methods to value a business and insight into when to apply each, a description of the life cycle of a troubled company and the various stages of a restructuring, an analysis of the valuation issues that confront practitioners in the real world of troubled companies and bankruptcy, and the application of business valuation issues to bankruptcy law. *Business Valuation and Bankruptcy* is written in terms that are common to bankruptcy professionals and is essential, timely reading for players in the bankruptcy and restructuring environment"—Provided by publisher.

ISBN 978-0-470-46238-6

1. Business—Valuation. 2. Bankruptcy. I. Stein, Grant.
   II. Weitnauer, John. III. Title.
HG4028.V3R37 2010
658.15—dc22                                    2009025212

Printed in the United States of America

10 9 8 7 6 5 4 3 2 1

# Contents

# Preface

This book is an integrated reference source for those involved in the valuation of a business in a commercial environment, with the focus on formal bankruptcy proceedings and distressed situations. It has been written by practitioners who have practical experience in the commercial courtroom, and the insights and analysis it contains are reflective of their collective substantial experience.

Ian Ratner is a CPA accredited in business valuation by the AICPA and the American Society of Appraisers. He is also a Certified Fraud Examiner and one of the founding members of GlassRatner Advisory & Capital Group LLC. Ian is a nationally known bankruptcy advisor and forensic accountant who regularly performs business valuations and deals with complex valuation issues in commercial disputes and bankruptcy-related matters. Ian regularly acts as a trial preparation consultant and expert witness in commercial disputes and bankruptcy cases. Kit Weitnauer and Grant Stein are senior partners with Alston & Bird LLP who practice commercial bankruptcy law and try commercial cases throughout the United States, including cases involving valuation issues. Mr. Stein began working on valuation issues in the distressed debt environment while at business school at Emory University in the mid 1970's, and has carried that through into his legal practice having tried numerous commercial valuation disputes in the federal bankruptcy courts, federal district courts and state courts. Mr. Weitnauer was one of the two trial lawyers for the plaintiff in the $1.35 billion fraudulent conveyance jury verdict obtained in *MAN AG et al. v. Freightliner LLC et al.* MAN was tried in Oregon under Oregon's version of the Uniform Fraudulent Transfer Act. The verdict included $350 million in punitive damages. This constituted the largest jury verdict in the United States in 2006. Mr. Weitnauer's primary responsibilities at trial was to direct the cross-examination the of all of the valuation experts. The authors were assisted by Leanne Gould, Prashanth Setty, and Wayne Weitz, all qualified and experienced professionals in the area of financial statement analysis and business valuation.

The bankruptcy process is a judicial process that is not always well understood by the noninitiated. For the accountant and business professional, this book provides background on the bankruptcy process, acts as a basic tool in the area of business valuation, and demonstrates the connection between these disciplines.

For the valuation expert, this book highlights the application of the business valuation discipline to the bankruptcy environment. It covers the key principles in practice, and explains both the legal environment in which the valuation testimony is received, and how the testimony is evaluated to determine its admissibility. Plan confirmation, preferences, fraudulent conveyance, adequate protection, timing issues on each of these, going-concern values, liquidation values, and the *whens*, *whats*, and *whys* are all explored. Valuation professionals will do a better job for their clients with a full understanding of the context of their work and the issues facing the trial lawyers.

For the lawyer, the book is a concise compendium of valuation standards and legal principles, including an outstanding discussion of *Daubert* principles dealing with the standards for admission of expert testimony applicable in the valuation context focusing on bankruptcy and insolvency questions.

# CHAPTER 1

# Introduction

## THE TROUBLED COMPANY CONTINUUM

Companies can have four stages in their life cycle: the start-up or development phase, the growth phase, the maturity or stabilization phase, and in many cases, the disruption or decline phase.

Start-up or development-stage companies are early stage companies seeking financing for product development and market testing. In many cases commercialization of the companies' products or services is not fully established. During this early stage of development, proof of concept is the goal. Once companies live through the start-up stage, they move on to the growth stage, where they have gained momentum in sales and market acceptance. During this stage, companies hire experienced management, and some form of permanent financing has been obtained. Mature companies have an established customer base, vendor network, business processes, and products or services. Mature companies often expand to new regions or attempt to grow in a horizontal or vertical manner both organically and through mergers and acquisitions. During this period, private companies often deal with wealth and ownership transfer issues.

If all companies followed the process just described and the economy maintained a stable growth rate, business would be less complicated, and there would be no need for this book. However, there is usually a disruption or period of decline either at some stage of a company's development, or as part of a general economic cycle that affects companies in the same industry or region. Business professionals and economists agree that it is highly unlikely for any company (or the economy) to maintain an upward trend indefinitely. This truth is playing out in the current downturn of the global economy.

Not all problems are similar or have the same level of severity; troubled companies move along a continuum. The continuum goes from a short-term liquidity crunch to the realization that the existing business model is simply

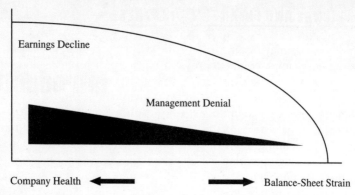

**EXHIBIT 1.1**  Business-Decline Curve

no longer viable. When this happens companies are faced with the challenge of restructuring or being liquidated.

The business-decline curve (shown in Exhibit 1.1) is a graphical representation of challenges faced by troubled companies along the continuum. When faced with financial or operational stress, even experienced managers often assume that the impairment is temporary and that performance will return to the norm. During this denial phase, management is more likely to focus on tracking performance for signs of expected recovery than to investigate and correct the root cause of the decline. This reaction is akin to treating the symptom of a disease without addressing the cause. The time wasted during the denial phase often allows the root cause to manifest itself in the form of balance-sheet strain. Continued losses, or even reduced margins in the case of a high-growth company, can quickly result in increased leverage and working-capital shortages. As the financial strain increases, management becomes more reactionary than proactive and typically lacks the time and resources necessary to resolve the root causes that brought on the decline. Unfortunately, the further down the curve management allows a company to travel, the less control management has over the outcome. Ultimately, as the situation evolves, control may be taken from the company and placed in the hands of other stakeholders or proceed in a judicial setting such as a bankruptcy.

The most controllable variable on the business decline curve is the time spent in the management denial phase. Excessive time spent in the denial phase makes the remainder of the trip down the curve almost inevitable.

Typically, troubled companies have roots in either operational stress or financial stress and most of the time some combination of both.

## OPERATIONAL AND FINANCIAL DISSTRESS

Operational stress may occur for a number of reasons, including competition from other companies, competition from replacement products and services, the departure of key employees or management, rapid changes in raw material quality or availability, changes in cost structure that cannot be passed on to consumers, or a change in the demand for the company's products or services. Whatever the reason for the operational stress, the financial outcomes are typically declining revenues or market share, increasing operating expenses, decreasing operating margins, and liquidity constraints. If the troubled company is unable to address the business issues causing the operational stress and react to reduce expenses, increase revenues, raise capital to meet short-term requirements, or some combination, then the business will soon inevitably experience financial stress and possibly insolvency.

Financial stress is likely to occur when the company's existing leverage is excessive, and the company finds it hard or impossible to make scheduled debt or principal payments. This is often the case when a company has been subject to a leveraged buyout transaction or other leveraged transaction. Financial stress is also evident in companies whose capitalization ultimately does not support its operations going forward. One common example of this type of capitalization is a company that has financed long-term assets, such as plant and equipment, through short-term financing, such as accounts payable and short-term lines of credit. When this happens, the business will starve for working capital because all the working capital sources are being consumed to sustain the long-term assets.

The expression, "good company with a bad balance sheet," is often used to describe a company that has a strong operational base but is in financial stress. If the troubled company is unable to refinance its existing debt or to divest noncore assets to cover its interest expense, then the company may face insolvency.

Operational and financial stresses are not mutually exclusive, meaning that a company with a strong financial position may be struggling operationally, and a company with strong operating activity may be struggling financially.

## THE TROUBLED COMPANY RESPONSE

### Prebankruptcy Options for the Troubled Company

Troubled companies do not immediately file for bankruptcy. Instead, once the operational or financial distress is recognized, the troubled company can take corrective steps.

Sometimes, instead of promptly analyzing and addressing operational problems, management is unwilling or unable to face the problems and make the hard choices necessary to tackle the problems. As a result, creditors concerned about the company's future will often require, as a condition to any forbearance agreement or loan amendment, that the company retain an outside consultant. Many companies can and have accomplished a successful operational turnaround outside of bankruptcy.

Financial distress can sometimes be relieved by one or more techniques, such as:

- Sale of part of the company
- Strategic acquisitions by the company
- New equity investments in the company
- Tender offer for debt
- Recapitalization of the business
- Interim forbearance by lenders
- Exchange offers, either debt for debt, debt for equity, or debt for debt and equity

Valuations are often needed by a troubled company before bankruptcy as part of the efforts of the company and its creditors to solve operational or financial distress. For instance, if operational distress has caused a company to miss financial ratio covenants contained in its loan agreements, as part of an amendment or forbearance, lenders may obtain or require the company to provide a valuation of its business. Similarly, efforts to sell the company or portions of the company's business will be preceded by a valuation of same as part of the due diligence process.

In some cases, deleveraging transactions can be achieved only through a Chapter 11 bankruptcy case.

## Bankruptcy and Similar Remedies for the Troubled Company

When the troubled company cannot correct its operational or financial distress it may have no choice but to (1) surrender its assets to its secured creditors (or be subject to foreclosure by the secured creditors) and/or (2) cease operations, liquidate its remaining assets, and satisfy its debts to the extent possible. Where foreclosure or liquidation is the only option, many companies will choose to file a Chapter 7 bankruptcy case and allow the liquidation to be handled by a court-appointed trustee pursuant to the applicable provisions of the Bankruptcy Code.

In cases in which a company's financial distress can be addressed through the reorganization provisions of the Bankruptcy Code, the troubled company may file a Chapter 11 case. The goal of a Chapter 11 case is the confirmation of a plan of reorganization, which results in the business that filed Chapter 11 continuing to operate postbankruptcy and being successfully reorganized. The fundamentals of a Chapter 7 and Chapter 11 bankruptcy are discussed in Chapter 6, Overview of U.S. Bankruptcy.

## VALUATION IN REORGANIZATION OR BANKRUPTCY

Regardless of whether a troubled company can successfully reorganize prior to bankruptcy, or in bankruptcy, or is ultimately liquidated, there is significant need for business valuations at different points during the continuum.

Valuations prior to bankruptcy will be required on many occasions for different users. Equity investors considering an investment in a troubled company may require a valuation to determine the impact on value that their investment could make on the company and assist them in developing yield expectations on their potential investment. Lenders may require a valuation to assess their loan-to-value position. For example, during the workout process, a lender will make decisions based on the value of the business versus the amount of debt outstanding. Management contemplating the divestiture of a portion of the business will require a valuation to assess the viability of the potential divestiture and the impact it would have on the company's financial situation. Entities or individuals acquiring troubled companies prior to bankruptcy also require a valuation to assist them in their decision-making process. Finally, any prebankruptcy global reorganization will require a valuation.

At many times during the bankruptcy process, valuations of the debtor's business (or specific assets owned by the debtor) are necessary. For example, valuations are needed in connection with a motion to lift the automatic stay (discussed at Chapter 7), to obtain adequate protection (discussed at Chapter 7), to seek or oppose confirmation of a plan of reorganization (discussed at Chapter 7), to prosecute or defend actions to recover preferential transfers (discussed at Chapter 8), or to recover fraudulent transfers (discussed at Chapter 8).

Often, the valuation question is, What is the value *now*? When answering that question, the expert delivers his or her opinion of *current* value (the valuation date) at a court hearing (the opinion date), and the court decides the *current* value of the business or asset. In this situation, the valuation date and the opinion date are the same.

In other situations, the valuation question is, What was the value *then*? When answering that question, the valuation date is a specific date *in the past*, but the expert gives his or her opinion now, at a court hearing or the date of his or her report. Then, the valuation date and the opinion date are different.

## CONCLUSION

The valuation discipline is equally important in the troubled company space as in any other phase of a business's life cycle. Business valuations for troubled companies or companies in the bankruptcy process present a unique set of challenges for professionals involved with them. This book will delve into these challenges and the business valuation environment in the context of troubled companies, both before and during bankruptcy.

# CHAPTER 2

# Industry Practitioners and Standards

**V**aluations are performed by a wide variety of practitioners for an even wider variety of purposes including solvency opinions, plan confirmations, and other matters that arise in bankruptcy cases. These practitioners may be certified in business valuation or appraisal by a professional organization or may simply have experience in negotiating and executing transactions. Regardless of who prepares business valuations, the reliance on judgment and the art of financial analysis is central to the process. As such, a valuation of a specific business by two different practitioners may produce widely different results and be the subject of contention between interested parties. Understanding the need for generally accepted business valuation or appraisal practices, various organizations have adopted developmental and reporting standards and certification programs. These programs and standards provide guidance and training to member practitioners but more importantly provide users a level of confidence in the valuation approach and conclusions reached.

This chapter will describe who is preparing valuations for bankruptcy purposes, the various professional organizations that have established business valuation standards, what those standards are, how they differ, and why standards are important to the valuation industry and to interested parties in a bankruptcy.

## PROFESSIONAL ORGANIZATIONS AND BUSINESS VALUATION STANDARDS

Each of the credentialed valuation practitioners identified in the sections that follow are affiliated with a professional organization and must adhere to the professional, ethical, and procedural standards established by that particular organization. Credentialed valuation practitioners who hold multiple designations must be careful to apply the standards appropriate to the purpose and/or subject of the valuation as standards may differ between organizations. This section begins by providing a brief history of each of the professional organizations involved with setting valuations standards and credentialing practitioners.

## Professional Organizations

**American Institute of Certified Public Accountants**   The origination of what is today the American Institute of Certified Public Accountants (AICPA) dates back to 1887. The AICPA is a national organization of Certified Public Accountants (CPAs) with international reach. The AICPA's over 350,000 members practice not only in public accounting but also in business, consulting, law, government, and education.[1] Members of the AICPA agree to be bound by the AICPA's Bylaws and Professional Code of Conduct and, if active, comply with certain continuing education requirements and practice-specific standards. These practice-specific standards cover a wide variety of specializations including audit, tax, and more recently, business valuation.

In 1998, the AICPA instituted the Accredited in Business Valuation (ABV) credential program as valuation services became a more prominent practice area for its members. One of the objectives of the ABV credential program was, and is, to enhance the quality of business valuation services provided by CPAs. In 2004, the Forensic and Valuation Services (FVS) section of the AICPA was created to further support valuation practitioners through education, news, advocacy, access to practice resources, and other benefits. In order to improve the consistency and quality of valuation services provided by its members, to promote transparency, and establish generally accepted best practices, the AICPA issued the Statement on Standards for Valuation Services No. 1, "Valuation of a Business, Business Ownership Interest, Security, or Intangible Asset" (SSVS No. 1). The SSVS No. 1 became effective for engagements accepted on or after January 1, 2008 and applies to all AICPA members regardless of specialization unless specifically exempted. In addition to SSVS No. 1 and AICPA Professional Standards, members are encouraged to look to the Uniform Standards of Professional Appraisal Practice (USPAP), guidance from the IRS, any relevant case law, and other guidance that may be applicable to specific valuation engagements. Furthermore, to enhance communication between valuation practitioners and users of valuation services, the AICPA adopted the International Glossary of Business Valuation Terms, which is discussed later in this text.

**American Society of Appraisers**   Originated in 1936, the American Society of Appraisers (ASA) is an international organization representing all appraisal disciplines, including machinery and technical specialties, real property, and business valuation. The ASA currently has 5,000 members in the United States and more than 40 other countries. Regardless of discipline, members are required to pass the ASA's Ethics Examination and a course and examination on the Uniform Standards of Appraisal Practice (USPAP).[2] Furthermore, each member is required to uphold the ASA's Principles of Appraisal Practice and Code of Ethics and to comply with established continuing education requirements.

In 1981, the ASA recognized business valuation as a separate appraisal discipline and began accrediting members. Designations held by ASA members include Accredited Member (AM), Accredited Senior Appraiser (ASA), and Fellow Accredited Senior Appraiser.

In 1987, the ASA and eight other appraisal societies founded The Appraisal Foundation, a national nonprofit organization created to establish uniform criteria for professional appraisers, the USPAP.[3] In 1992, the ASA's Business Valuation Committee adopted the ASA Business Valuation Standards, which incorporated certain portions of the USPAP.[4] These standards "provide minimum criteria to be followed in developing and reporting the valuation of businesses, business ownership interests, securities and intangible assets" and "a structure for regulating the development and reporting of business valuations through uniform practices and procedures."[5] The Business Valuation Standards are categorized into nine sections, and incorporate related clarifying statements, advisory opinions, procedural guidelines, and a glossary of terms, many of which are included in the International Glossary of Business Valuation Terms.

**The Canadian Institute of Chartered Business Valuators** The Canadian Institute of Chartered Business Valuators (CICBV) was established in 1971 and is the largest professional valuation organization in Canada with approximately 1,200 members. Members of the CICBV include individuals with backgrounds in commerce, accounting, economics, and finance. Members meeting the experience, training, and examination requirements of the CICBV are awarded the Chartered Business Valuator (CBV) designation. Members of the CICBV are required to abide by the organization's Code of Ethics and Practice Standards. The 12 standards and related appendices cover topics including valuation for financial reporting, fairness opinions, advisory reports, expert reports, and limited critique reports. The CICBV also publishes practice bulletins to provide members additional guidance, and it has adopted the International Glossary of Business Valuation Terms.

**National Association of Certified Valuation Analysts** The National Association of Certified Valuation Analysts (NACVA) was founded in 1991 as an association of CPA and non-CPA valuation practitioners. Recently, the organization expanded its membership to include financial forensics and other related advisory services. The NACVA has approximately 6,600 members of which 6,300 practice in the business valuation area. Members meeting the educational, training, and examination requirements of the NACVA for certification may obtain a designation as an Accredited Valuation Analyst (AVA). Those members holding a valid CPA license may qualify for the Certified Valuation Analyst (CVA) designation. Members of the NACVA holding the CVA and AVA credentials are required to comply with the organization's Professional Standards and Ethics Policies and Procedures and are encouraged to refer to the USPAP, IRS Business Valuation Guidelines, and other authorities for additional guidance. Furthermore, credentialed members must also comply with the NACVA's continuing education requirements for recertification.

In 2005, the NACVA executive advisory board, and other interested parties, provided comments to the AICPA's exposure draft outlining proposed valuation standards for AICPA members. Upon issuance of the AICPA's Statement on Standards for Valuation Services No. 1 (SSVS No. 1), the NACVA Professional Standards were revised to "eliminate conflicts and draw parity between the two."

**Institute of Business Appraisers**   The Institute of Business Appraisers (IBA) was established in 1978 and is the "oldest professional society devoted solely to the appraisal of closely held businesses."[6] In addition to offering its 1,300 members education, credentialing opportunities, and other benefits, the IBA maintains one of the largest transactional databases of sales of small to midsized businesses. Members agree to abide by the organization's Code of Ethics and Business Appraisal Standards, and those members meeting established educational and appraisal experience criteria may obtain one of the following credentials: Master Certified Business Appraiser (MCBA), Certified Business Appraiser (CBA), or Accredited by IBA (AIBA). Additional credentials offered by the IBA include Business Valuator Accredited for Litigation (BVAL) and Accredited in Business Appraisal Review (ABAR). The IBA Founding Standards Committee has recognized the contributions of individuals associated with The Appraisal Foundation and the ASA in the development of the organization's Business Appraisal Standards.

**Association of Insolvency & Restructuring Advisors**   The Association of Insolvency & Restructuring Advisors (AIRA) was organized in 1984 to support accountants, financial advisors, attorneys, workout consultants, trustees, and others involved in business turnaround, restructuring, insolvency, and bankruptcy matters.

The AIRA offers its over 1,700 members continuing education and certification programs leading to the Certified Insolvency and Reorganization Accountant (CIRA) and Certification in Distressed Business Valuation (CDBV) designations. The CIRA program was developed in 1992 and has accredited over 725 members. Course content for both the CIRA and CDBV designations include valuation analysis with more advanced topics and application covered in the CDBV curriculum. The CDBV experience requirement also includes submission of a formal valuation report or other materials demonstrating the analyses performed. Outside of the curriculum established for the CIRA and CDBV accreditation, the AIRA has not established its own valuation-specific standards.

**CFA Institute**   The origins of the CFA Institute and its predecessor organizations date back to 1925. Although the CFA Institute as it is organized today was incorporated in 1999, its Chartered Financial Analyst (CFA) accreditation program has existed since 1963. Today the CFA Institute boasts over 96,000 members in 134 countries and territories. CFA Institute members are employed by a variety of organizations including investment companies, mutual funds, broker-dealer/investment banks, banks, consulting firms, insurance companies, pensions and foundations, and research and academic institutions.

In order to become a CFA Charter holder, candidates must pass three levels of examinations covering the CFA Institute Code of Ethics and Standards of Professional Conduct, Investment Tools, Asset Valuation, and Portfolio Management. The Asset Valuation curriculum includes analysis of equity investments, fixed income investments, derivatives, and alternative investments such as real estate, closely held companies, distressed securities/bankruptcies, and private equity investments. The CFA Institute recommends, but does not require, continuing education of its members. While the CFA Institute has not published business valuation-specific standards, the organization has set a variety of practice-specific standards and guidelines for its members, including creation of the Global Investment Performance Standards (GIPS®), "a set of standardized, industry-wide ethical principles that provide investment firms with guidance on how to calculate and report their investment results to prospective clients."[7]

## Other Standard-Setting Authorities

**The Appraisal Foundation**   In 1987, The Appraisal Foundation was formed in response to the instability in the real estate and mortgage lending industries caused by the savings & loan crisis of the mid-1980s and the need for a uniform standard for valuation practitioners charged with valuing real estate assets held by federal agencies. Title XI of the Financial Institutions

Recovery, Reform, and Enforcement Act of 1989 (FIRREA) enacted by Congress established the following requirement:

> *at a minimum - (1) that real estate appraisals be performed in accordance with generally accepted appraisal standards as evidenced by the appraisal standards promulgated by the Appraisal Standards Board of the Appraisal Foundation; and (2) that such appraisals shall be written appraisals.*[8]

In January 1989, the Appraisal Standards Board approved and adopted the Uniform Standards of Professional Appraisal Practice (USPAP). The USPAP has evolved over the past 20 years to include Statements on Appraisal Standards and Advisory Opinions to assist practitioners and end users to interpret and apply the standards. As a result of its required use in federally related transactions, the USPAP have been adopted or are recommended standards to be followed by most professional valuation organizations. Specifically, USPAP Standards 9 & 10 relate to business appraisal development and reporting.

**The Internal Revenue Service**  The Internal Revenue Service (IRS) released business valuation standards in 2006 to provide examiners specific guidance in the valuation of businesses, intangible property, tangible personal property, and real property. It is important for valuation practitioners to be familiar with these standards.

## The Importance of Standards

Standards serve an important role in the practice of business valuation. Not only do standards provide structure and guidelines to the practitioner in the development and reporting of value, but standards also provide end users with a level of confidence that the valuation conclusion was developed using generally accepted and recognized approaches and methods by competent and ethical practitioners.

Although the requirements and backgrounds of credentialed valuation practitioners vary, efforts are being made in the industry to establish a common language and educational opportunities. The American Institute of Certified Public Accountants, American Society of Appraisers, National Association of Certified Valuation Analysts, The Canadian Institute of Chartered Business Valuators, and the Institute of Business Appraisers adopted The International Glossary of Business Valuation

Terms to offer uniformity and consistency to valuation practitioners with differing affiliations. As further evidence of the cooperation among professional organizations, the FVS section of the AICPA has a strategic partnership with the American Society of Appraisers to explore joint educational, training, and technical-writing opportunities.[9]

Internationally, business valuation standards are being adopted as formerly North American professional organizations expand membership and form partnerships and alliances. The NACVA, for example, is a charter member of the International Association of Consultants, Valuators and Analysts (IACVA), which provides accreditation in business valuation. The ASA serves members in 40-plus countries including China, Japan, Argentina, and the Philippines.

As valuation issues gain more prominence in the public eye (for example, fair value accounting, mark to market, impact of current credit crisis on the value of businesses and business interests) and across the world, the more important uniformity of standards and certification become.

The volume of private companies that are owned today through hedge funds and private equity firms further underscores the need for some level of uniform valuation standards. The value of these investments is aggregated with other investments to determine the Net Asset value of these investment vehicles; to ensure that capital can be available to these industry participants there has to be some level of confidence in their financial statement reporting, which includes record keeping and reporting of their investments and related valuation.

## Basic Reporting Standards

Although the approaches and methods used to value a business or business interest are similar across professional organizations, certain developmental and reporting requirements may differ. Notwithstanding these differences, which often tend to be subtle, any written report by an expert should include at least the following items:

- Client
- Subject or business interest being valued
- Valuation date
- Report date
- Type of report
- Standard of value
- Premise of value
- Purpose of the valuation
- Nature of the business being valued

- Sources of information disclosed
- Site visit or lack thereof disclosed
- Economic conditions, present and future outlook
- Past, current, and future prospects of the business and industry
- Financial analysis of future earnings/dividend capacity
- Past sale of interest in the business being appraised
- Ownership, size, nature, restrictions, and agreements
- Extent the interest has or lacks elements of marketability
- Valuation approaches and methods used
- Valuation approaches and methods considered
- Valuation approaches and methods rejected and rationale for rejection
- Conclusion of value
- Signature and name of primary appraiser

## BUSINESS VALUATION PRACTITIONERS AND CERTIFICATIONS

Just as each business is unique, each bankruptcy case is unique and offers its own valuation challenges. A single case may require the valuation of a large number of individual subsidiary companies, substantial real estate holdings and securities, as well as hard assets such as machinery and equipment. As such, a single bankruptcy case may employ several different valuation practitioners: a business appraiser to value the operational business, a real estate appraiser to value the nonoperating property, and/or a machinery and tool appraiser to offer a potential liquidation value. Because this book focuses on business valuation, this chapter discusses business valuation practitioners rather than those who value real estate and other hard assets.

### Credentialed Valuation Practitioners

Credentialed valuation professionals are those practitioners who have undergone training and/or have demonstrated experience prescribed by a professional organization. The following section gives a summary of the requirements to obtain the respective qualifications from each of the listed governing bodies involved in business valuation.

#### American Institute of Certified Public Accountants (AIPCA)
Certified Public Accountant (CPA)

- Holds a valid and unrevoked CPA certificate issued by a legally constituted state authority (requirements differ by state or other issuing authority)
- Passed the Uniform CPA Examination

- Completed 150 semester hours of education at an accredited college or university earning a Bachelor's degree or equivalent
- Completed 120 hours of required continuing education, or equivalent, in each three-year reporting period

## Accredited in Business Valuation (ABV)

- Member of the AICPA in good standing
- Holds a valid CPA certificate
- Successfully completed the eight-hour ABV Examination, the four-hour ABV I Examination for those holding an AM, CBA, CFA, or CVA designation, or holds the ASA credential
- Met business or full-time teaching experience requirements in specified areas of practice as measured by number of engagements and/or hours worked (a minimum of six engagements or 150 hours of substantial business valuation experience are required)
- Met Lifelong Learning requirements as measured by continuing professional education credits, university/college coursework, attendance at business valuation trade conferences, presentations, lecturing, and authoring (a minimum of 45 qualifying hours are required)
- Continue, to obtain 60 hours of Lifelong Learning in each three-year recertification period

## American Society of Appraisers (ASA)
### Accredited Member (AM)

- Member of the ASA in good standing
- Successfully completed 4 three-day courses, 3 half-day exams, and a one-day exam, or successfully completed a one-day challenge exam (certain business course prerequisites apply)
- Successfully completed the ethics and USPAP (Uniform Standards of Professional Appraisal Practice) exams
- Submitted an appraisal report satisfying the requirements of the Board of Examiners
- Possesses two years' full-time or equivalent experience in business appraisal (one year experience is granted to professionals holding a CPA, CFA, or Certified Business Intermediary (CBI) designation with five years of practice in that field)
- Holds a college degree or equivalent
- Continues to obtain 100 hours of continuing education (40 hours minimum) and organizational participation in each five-year reaccreditation period

### Accredited Senior Appraiser (ASA)

- Met all of the requirements for the AM designation and a total of at least five years' full-time or equivalent experience in business appraisal

### College of Fellows of the American Society of Appraisers (FASA)

- Met all of the requirements for the ASA designation and voted into the College of Fellows based on technical leadership and professional contributions

## Institute of Business Appraisers (IBA)
### Certified Business Appraiser (CBA)

- Member of the IBA in good standing
- Successful completion of 90 classroom hours of upper-level course work or 10,000 hours' active experience as a business appraiser
- Successful completion of a 16-hour report-writing course
- Successful completion of a six-hour written exam or holds a ASA, ABV, CVA, or AVA designation
- Submission of two business-appraisal reports demonstrating professional level of competence
- Continues to obtain 24 hours of continuing education for reaccreditation every two years, or accredited by IBA (AIBA)
- Successfully completed an eight-day workshop (course work may be substituted for journeyman level designation in business valuation from organizations recognized by the IBA) and a 16-hour report writing course
- Successfully completed written exam and submited one demonstrative report

### Master Certified Business Appraiser (MCBA)

- Met all of the requirements of the CBA designation and held the CBA designation for at least 10 years
- Has 15 years of full-time business appraisal experience
- Holds a professional designation such as an ASA, CVA, or ABV
- Possesses a two-year postgraduate degree

## The Canadian Institute of Chartered Business Valuators (CICBV)
### Chartered Business Valuator (CBV)

- Member of the CICBV
- Successfully completed six distance education courses (approximately 60 hours) and exams (certain exemptions to coursework are allowed for professionals holding an ASA or CFA designation)

- Successfully completed a four-hour membership entrance examination
- Possesses suitable practical experience in business and securities valuation (1,500 hours total) attested to by a sponsoring CICBV member

### National Association of Certified Valuation Analysts (NACVA)
### Certified Valuation Analyst (CVA)

- Member of the NACVA in good standing
- Holds a valid and unrevoked CPA license issued by a legally constituted state authority or the Chartered Accountant designation as issued in Canada
- Possesses two years of work experience other than in business valuation—no experience necessary in business valuation
- Successfully completed training, exam, continuing education requirements listed for the AVA designation that follows

### Accredited Valuation Analyst (AVA)

- Member of the NACVA in good standing
- Successfully completed a five-day training program or holds a business valuation designation from another business valuation credentialing body
- Successfully completed a five-hour proctored exam and submitted either a take-home case study (40–60 hours) or a client business valuation report (case study may be substituted for a client business valuation report only if the applicant has more than 10,000 hours or more experience in business valuation) meeting the requirements of the NACVA's Valuation Credentialing Board
- Possesses two years of substantial work experience in business valuation or performed 10 or more business valuations
- Possesses a business degree and/or MBA or higher business degree from an accredited college or university
- Continues to obtain continuing education (36 hours), work experience, and professional development for recertification every three years

### Association of Insolvency & Restructuring Advisors (AIRA)
### Certified Insolvency & Restructuring Advisor (CIRA)

- Member of the AIRA in good standing
- Holder of a CPA, CA, or CMA license or a Bachelor's degree
- Possesses 4,000 hours of specialized business turnaround, restructuring and bankruptcy experience
- Completed five years of accounting or financial experience
- Successfully completed three 20-hour courses and a four-hour exam

- Possesses a Bachelor's degree
- Continues to obtain 60 hours of related continuing education in each three-year period of which at least 20 hours must be completed in non-employer-related educational programs

### Certification in Distressed Business Valuation (CDBV)

- Member of the AIRA in good standing
- Successfully completed three multiday courses and related exams (certain coursework waived for holders of the Certified Insolvency & Restructuring Advisor (CIRA), ASA, CBA, CFA, ABV, CVA, or AVA designations)
- Demonstrated significant experience with valuation of companies and/ or assets in bankruptcy and other distressed situations
- Completed five years of accounting or financial experience
- Possesses a Bachelor's degree

### CFA Institute
### Chartered Financial Analyst (CFA)

- Member of the CFA Institute in good standing
- Successfully completed the Level I, II, and III exams sequentially (minimum preparation of 250 hours of study per exam)
- Possesses a Bachelor's degree or equivalent, is in the final year of Bachelor's degree program, or completed four years of qualified professional work experience
- Although not required, the CFA Institute recommends 20 hours of continuing education each year

It is important to note that several appraisal organizations waive certain educational or training requirements for certification if a candidate currently holds a business valuation designation. These waivers recognize the similarity in training and experience requirements across organizations.

## Other Valuation Practitioners

Although credentialed valuation professionals are more commonly associated with business valuation, there are others who, because of expertise and experience in the structure and negotiation of business transactions or the enforcement of government regulations and policies, may also value businesses or business assets. Although some of these practitioners may also hold valuation credentials, the primary focus of their work may differ from business appraisers. These individuals include:

- Business brokers
- Investment bankers
- Hedge fund managers
- Venture capital and private equity investors
- Various government agencies
  - Internal Revenue Service
  - Securities and Exchange Commission
  - Department of Labor
- Employee Benefits Security Administration

In some cases in which the business in question is either a large public company or a public company that has gone through a significant number of corporate transactions prior to bankruptcy, it is more typical to find an investment banking professional offering valuation opinions than a CPA.

## CONCLUSION

This chapter is evidence of the volume of work that the finance, accounting, and valuation profession has undertaken in the form of self-governance and education. The profession's actions improve the reliability and credibility of the valuation opinions developed for any purpose, including bankruptcy matters. Notwithstanding these professional advancements, there is no substitution for logic, sound thinking, and an independent mindset. In fact this is evident in bankruptcy courts around the country where the standard that matters most is the opinion of the trier of fact, the judge behind the bench.

## NOTES

1. www.aicpa.org/About the AICPA/Understanding the Organization/Membership Figures.htm. Includes Retired, Associate, Student Affiliate and International Members.
2. See Section 8.3.
3. www.oldappraisers.org/about/index.cfm.
4. ASA Business Valuation Standards, General Preamble, American Society of Appraisers, 2008.

5. ASA Business Valuation Standards, General Preamble, American Society of Appraisers, 2008.
6. www.go-iba.org/.
7. CFA Institute website, www.cfainstitute.org/centre/codes/gips/index.html.
8. Sec. 1110, Functions of the Federal Financial Institutions Regulatory Agencies Relating to Appraisal Standards [12 U.S.C. 3339].
9. http://fvs.aicpa.org/Memberships/Overview of BVFLS Section Benefits for Prospective Members.htm.

# CHAPTER 3

# The Basics of Business Valuation

## THE PURPOSE OF THE VALUATION

Any discussion of business valuation begins with one basic question: "What is the purpose of the valuation?" Valuations are required for countless reasons and from different perspectives in the business world as they provide interested parties, including the courts, with valuable information necessary to the decision-making process. For example, a lender may require a valuation of a business to support loan-underwriting decisions, whereas the owner-manager of a business may require a valuation for tax and estate planning purposes. Some other instances in which a business valuation would be required are

- Reorganizations and recapitalizations
- Due diligence related to acquisitions and divestitures
- Litigation support in which the value of a business or business interest is in dispute, such as buy/sell or partnership disputes

As discussed in more detail in this book, although the basic financial and valuation analyses remain the same, business valuations performed in the context of a bankruptcy or reorganization come with a unique set of challenges. For the most part, courts direct valuation professionals to use the same valuation approaches and methods they use in other contexts. As will be seen in Chapter 8, however, sometimes a bankruptcy court has suggested methods or particular applications of the methods that are unique to the particular case or the requirements of bankruptcy law.

That said, the bankruptcy process is a fluid one with substantial interaction and negotiation between the parties; therefore, although decisions are based upon information provided by the valuation, the resulting outcome may not be driven solely by the valuation conclusions of the experts retained by the interested parties.

Value often differs depending on the purpose, standard of value, and key assumptions. For example, the value of a business unit on a standalone basis could be different than the value of a business unit included as part of the overall corporation. The difference may be a result of several factors, such as the ultimate cash flows being valued. As a standalone entity a business unit may not receive the benefit of certain shared expenses with the parent such that cash flows could be lower. There could also be higher perceived risk to the operation of a business unit on a standalone basis, which would drive the value lower. Or, there could be other sales and operating synergies that are not available to the standalone business unit that could be obtained while part of the larger entity.

Just as in the preceding example, valuations in the bankruptcy context may differ depending on the specific situation, purpose of the valuation, and even the timing of the valuation during the bankruptcy case.

## STANDARD OF VALUE

It is important to define the *standard* of value and key assumptions to be used in the valuation of a business or business interest. One of the most common standards of value is *fair market value*. Fair market value is generally defined as the cash amount at which the business or business interest would change hands between a hypothetical willing buyer and a hypothetical willing seller when the buyer is not under compulsion to buy and the seller is not under compulsion to sell and with both parties having reasonable knowledge of relevant information and facts.[1]

This definition, however, would not apply in the valuation of a business by parties contemplating a specific transaction. In this case, the buyer and seller are known, and one or the other may, in fact, be under compulsion to ensure the transaction is completed, particularly if the business is in distress. In this situation, the more appropriate standard of value may be *investment value*. Investment value is the value of the business or business interest to a specific investor. Because the investor is known, this standard of value takes into consideration his or her expectations of future cash flows that could be generated by the business, synergies, and other factors specific to the investor. Investment value may or may not be the price paid to acquire the business or business interest.

*Fair value* is another standard of value used in valuation. Fair value is typically used in the valuation of businesses and business interests in a legal context and, therefore, the definition will be different based upon applicable state statutes and case law (generally, the term *fair value* in this context does not carry the same definition as used in public accounting). Fair value may be equal to the interest holder's pro-rata share of the business being valued without the application of discounts for minority interest and/or lack of marketability, and may include a pro-rata share of the value of the control premium.[2] In some instances, case law may even suggest the valuation approach to be used in determining fair value. Therefore, it is important to obtain legal advice when conducting a valuation using this standard of value. For example, the standard of value of a shareholder's interest in a shareholder oppression remedy matter may be fair value, whereas the standard of value of the same interest under a consensual transaction would typically be fair market value. Fair market value in the shareholder oppression remedy matter would not be appropriate because the discounts applied to the individual's interest would reward the oppressor. For example, a company wants to enter into a merger agreement whereby the interest holders would receive their pro-rata share of the proceeds. For a variety of reasons a group of minority shareholders disagree with the merger and are forced out. If the courts allowed the buyback of the minority interests at a reduced price (through the application of minority discounts, for example), the company/majority shareholders would reap the benefit of the ownership of those shares in the merger transaction and the resulting payout without penalty for their actions. Not only would the minority interest holders be forced out and unable to participate in any upside, but they would also be penalized by having to redeem the shares for a discounted price.

Section 506 of the Bankruptcy Code, U.S.C. §506, provides that "value shall be determined in light of the purpose of the valuation and of the proposed disposition or use of such property, and in conjunction with any hearing on such disposition or use or on a plan affecting such creditor's interest." Thus, valuation bankruptcy is not fixed or static.

## PREMISE OF VALUE—GOING CONCERN OR LIQUIDATION

The *premise* of value is as important as the *standard* of value and its selection will drive most of the detailed analysis thereafter. The premise of value is the overriding valuation assumption about the likely set of circumstances that apply to the subject company being valued. For example, are market conditions such that the most likely future circumstance for a business is liquidation, or do market conditions exist that a business can be considered a going concern? Therefore, the two primary premises of value are going-concern value and liquidation value.

In determining which premise of value is more appropriate, the valuation analyst typically considers the following:

- The market conditions and outlook for a business segment, industry, or economy as a whole
- The competitive environment for a business and industry
- The financial history of the company
- The historical operations of the company
- Management's track record
- The ability of a business to secure adequate capital to move forward as an ongoing entity

If these factors are generally favorable, the business may be valued as a going concern. If not, liquidation value may provide a more appropriate value conclusion. There may also be situations where a liquidation value is required for a particular business unit and a going-concern value is required for the remaining business entity.

As discussed in Chapter 8, bankruptcy courts lean toward using a going-concern valuation premise. Circumstances must be fairly extreme before a bankruptcy court will conclude that a liquidation analysis is appropriate.

In terms of liquidation value there are two distinctions that can easily be made: orderly liquidation and forced liquidation. The value of a business or assets in an orderly liquidation assumes a reasonable time period for the liquidation of the assets at market prices under normal market conditions. The value of a business or assets in a forced liquidation assumes that all assets are sold as quickly as possible and, therefore, value may be significantly reduced. The forced-liquidation scenario might best be described as a fire sale. Even if the appropriate premise of value is a going concern, liquidation value can be useful in establishing a floor value of the business in question.

In the bankruptcy context, *liquidation analysis* typically refers to the sum of the net proceeds of the sale of assets and recoveries on bankruptcy claims, net of any expenses to recover those funds (such as legal expenses, commissions, or transaction fees).

Generally speaking, the going-concern value of a business will be greater than the liquidation value. If not, then the liquidation of the business should be considered in order to maximize returns to creditors and other interest holders.

## VALUATION APPROACHES

There are three core valuation approaches generally accepted for use in determining the value of a company as a going concern: the asset approach, the income approach, and the market approach. In addition, several valuation methodologies are available within each approach. From time to time, hybrid approaches are used; however, these three core approaches and related methods, as illustrated in Exhibit 3.1, are the backbone of the valuation theory.

When valuing a business as a going concern, all of the aforementioned approaches should be considered prior to choosing the most appropriate valuation approach (or approaches) to use. Entities that are going concerns are typically valued using the market approach and/or the income approach. However, depending on the industry, the asset approach may also be appropriate. For example, asset-intensive businesses with low profitability relative to their invested capital may be more appropriately valued using the asset approach under a going-concern assumption.

The use of more than one methodology is encouraged when developing a valuation opinion. Many times the use of varying approaches and methodologies will provide a clear indicator of the value of the business or business interest being valued by producing similar value indications, or the expected differences will give insight to the appropriate weighting of the different approaches (e.g., a comparable company approach based on current Earnings Before Interest, Taxes, Depreciation and Amortization (EDITDA) will often result in an indication of value lower than the indication of value from a Discounted Cash Flow (DCF) that is based on an optimistic management forecast). Other times, the values indicated by the different approaches and methods will diverge. In those instances it is

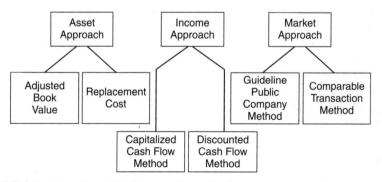

**EXHIBIT 3.1** Overview of the Business Valuation Process

appropriate to reexamine the inputs (such as management's projections or choice of comparable companies) of each valuation approach or methodology to see if errors have occurred. If not, or if after correcting any errors that were discovered, an unreasonable discrepancy in value still exists, it may be appropriate to consider whether it is appropriate to assign weightings to each approach or methodology reflecting the valuation analyst's confidence in the value indicated by each approach or method. For instance, an indication of value based upon a single market transaction may or may not be an appropriate measure of the value of the subject business. A low weighting would indicate a lack of confidence in the opinion, which may result from the fact that the sample size of comparable transactions was too small to place much weight on the result.

The courts generally agree with the use of weightings in the conclusion of value.

> *The standard valuation practice to calculate value using all three methodologies, and then reach an ultimate opinion by assigning weight to the value associated with each method, based on the methods suitable to the case at hand.*
> —*In re Nellson Nutraceutical, Inc.*, 2007 WL 201134, at *20 (Bankr. D. Del. Jan. 18, 2007)

> *[E]ach method should be weighted and then all methods should be considered together.*
> *In re Exide Techs*, 303 B.R. at 65

> *In many situations, multiple methodologies are used to eliminate outliers and derive as accurate an estimate of values as possible given that valuation is an inexact science.*

It is, therefore, important to understand each valuation approach and method, and associated strengths and weaknesses, in order to effectively assess the reasonableness of the values indicated by each approach or method. Ultimately, even if only one approach is relied on in the conclusion of value, the other approaches can be used to confirm or support the valuation derived as a reality check. The following sections provide an overview of each approach, and related methods.

## Asset Approach

The asset approach estimates the value of the equity of a business by examining the assets and liabilities of the business at a point in time—generally using the most recent balance sheet data prior to the valuation date. These amounts are then restated to market value by estimating the current cost to purchase or replace the asset on the balance sheet. This approach is based on the theory that an investor would not pay more for an asset, company, or business interest than the cost of obtaining (buy vs. build) a substitute asset of similar economic utility (principle of substitution).

The adjusted book value method of the asset approach requires the valuation analyst to examine each tangible and intangible asset and each liability to determine its market value. In accordance with generally accepted accounting principles (GAAP), most assets are reported on the balance sheet at book value, determined by the original purchase price less accumulated depreciation. The value of certain assets such as cash, accounts receivable, and to a lesser extent inventory, may closely approximate book value.

However, the value of other reported assets usually will not approximate book value. The value of assets such as property, plant, and equipment (PP&E) rarely equals book value. Additionally, internally developed intangible assets (as opposed to those purchased individually or as part of an acquisition) may not even be recorded on the books. Therefore, these assets must be restated to market value to correct for the historical nature of GAAP statements. In many cases in which this method is adopted, the valuation professional will have to rely on other professionals. For example, to determine the fair market value of machinery and certain specialized equipment, the business valuation professional may rely on an equipment dealer or auctioneer to assist with their valuation.

Once the asset side of the balance sheet has been restated to market value, liabilities can be subtracted to derive the market value of the equity of the business or business interest being valued. When examining the liability side of the balance sheet, various adjustments may also be required. These adjustments could include the write-down or write-off of accounts payable that are significantly aged where management does not believe the amounts will be paid, or the addition of various contingent liabilities such as tail liabilities relating to certain prior activities that are uninsured, or other contingent claims.

Another method to estimate value under the asset approach is the replacement cost method. Under this method, value is derived by determining the cost to replace the company's assets.

The asset approach is typically used for asset-heavy or capital-intensive companies. The asset approach should not be used for companies with limited hard assets and significant intangible assets, such as service companies or technology companies (in those cases, the income or market approach is usually more appropriate). In many cases, the asset approach provides a safe floor value of a company.

## Income Approach

The income approach is an *intrinsic* valuation approach that values an enterprise based on its own expected future cash flow(s). There are two primary valuation methods associated with this approach:

- Discounted cash flow method (DCF)
- Capitalized cash flow method (CCF).

Under the income approach, the value of a company is determined by a process that aggregates the present value of future expected cash flows adjusted for capital expenditures and increases or decreases in working capital. The future expected cash flows are derived based on the business plan and expectations for the company in the future. The successful application of the income approach requires detailed financial-statement analysis, which is discussed later in this chapter, and a comprehensive understanding of the future outlook for the business.

Both the DCF method and CCF method incorporate risk into the valuation through the use of a discount rate or a capitalization rate.

Discount rates and capitalization rates are measures of the risk inherent in the cash flow of the company being valued and are used to determine the present value of the cash flows or expected future returns. Discount rates and capitalizations rates are discussed in more detail in Chapter 4.

## Market Approach

The market approach is a *relative* valuation approach that assesses a company's value by comparing the company being valued to the current market prices of similar companies or the historical sales prices of similar companies. This approach relies on the use of financial ratios and multipliers. There are two primary methods associated with the market approach:

1. Guideline company method
2. Comparable transaction method

The guideline company method estimates the value of the subject company by developing a peer group of similar companies, using peer group market values to calculate market multiples, and then applying those market multiples to the subject company's representative levels of financial performance.

The comparable transaction method estimates the value of the subject company based on transaction prices for control of comparable companies.

A list of comparable transactions is created and the prices paid in those transactions are used to calculate transaction multiples. These multiples are then applied to the subject company's representative levels of financial performance.

The market approach is discussed in more detail in Chapter 5.

## FUNDAMENTALS

Understanding the terms of art and the application of financial statement analysis are fundamental to any business valuation. Business valuation is as much a language as a technical activity. The language can be precise, assigning particular meanings to terms. Therefore, it is important to rely on recognized terms and definitions in valuation discussions, reports, and testimony. An invaluable resource for such information is the *International Glossary of Business Valuation Terms* adopted by the American Institute of Certified Public Accountants (AICPA), American Society of Appraisers (ASA), National Association of Certified Valuation Analysts (NACVA), International Business Appraisers (IBA), and The Canadian Institute of Chartered Business Valuators (CICBV). The glossary is included for reference in Appendix A.

Certain critical terms such as *market value* and *enterprise value* may be easily confused. The appropriate use of these terms is essential to differentiate between the value of assets available to the equity holders (market value) and the value of assets available to both debt and equity holders (enterprise value).

In addition to the proper application of the valuation language, detailed financial analysis is the underpinning of all meaningful valuation opinions. Without detailed financial statement analysis, the valuation process becomes dogmatic, formulaic, and prone to error. Thorough financial analysis provides a clear understanding of the history of the business being valued and provides insight into the company's future operations. Financial analysis also provides insight into the operations of potential guideline companies and transactions that could be selected for use in the market approach.

Furthermore, financial analysis is critical to understanding the factors affecting the value of assets available to debt holders and equity holders. Financing decisions, collection efficiency, and investment policies, for instance, can all be evaluated through the development of financial ratios. These ratios can be used for comparison to industry norms and potential guideline companies, and they can be used in projecting future cash flows and profitability.

Since understanding the definitions of *market value* and *enterprise value* is critical to communicating the valuation opinion and financial analysis is critical to understanding the subject business, these topics are discussed in more detail in the following sections.

## Market Value versus Enterprise Value

Market value is the value of all assets of a company, operating or not, available to equity holders after debt claims are satisfied. In a public company, the market value or equity value is the value of a company's stock as determined by its stock price times the number of shares of the company outstanding. Other terms for market value include:

Equity value

Market capitalization

Offer value

There are many terms that reflect the enterprise value of a company including:

Company value

Transaction value

Total enterprise value

Total consideration

Aggregate value

Market value of invested capital (MVIC)

Total invested capital (TIC)

Firm value

Enterprise value represents the total value of the operations of a company including both tangible and intangible assets. Enterprise value does not include nonoperating or redundant assets. Although nonoperating and redundant assets are not included in determining the enterprise value of a business, in a bankruptcy setting, creditors have claims on all assets of the debtor whether these assets are utilized in the operation of the business or not.

If a company does not have nonoperating or redundant assets, the enterprise value is equal to the market value of its equity plus the value of its debt. However, as discussed in Chapter 7, most bankruptcy courts recognize that the prices the *market* places on a distressed company's debt and equity securities pre-bankruptcy and during bankruptcy are not relevant when valuing the (soon to be) reorganized company at a contested plan confirmation hearing.

## Financial Statement Analysis

As previously discussed, thorough financial statement analysis is a fundamental and critical component of the valuation process. Historical financial statements provide insight into what has occurred in the past and what may be expected in the future.

However, when dealing with companies coming out of a bankruptcy, or that have been restructured, an examination of company projections in light of new business plans or operating models is critical. For example, the expected future financial performance of a company that closed or sold unprofitable plants in a bankruptcy is, by definition, going to be different from the company's historical performance. Notwithstanding this, valuable information such as relationships between financial metrics can be gleaned from a thorough analysis of historical financial information.

The best indicator of the future is not always the past, particularly when dealing with companies that have been restructured in or out of bankruptcy. In situations in which a company has gone through significant operational or financial change, the historical financial analysis that is so important in a typical valuation assignment may play a less important role. Regardless, strong financial analysis provides insight to the valuation process.

The basic elements of financial statement analysis include:

1. Understanding the source of financial data and underlying accounting policies
2. Trend analysis and common-sized analysis
3. Ratio analysis
4. Comparison of financial statements to industry norms and peers

**Understanding the Source of Financial Data and Underlying Accounting Policies** Financial data used in a valuation may come from a variety of sources: data extractions from accounting systems, internal financial statements, audited financial statements, or tax returns. Each of these data sources provides the valuation practitioner with a different comfort level based on the reliability of the data. Audited financial statements and financial data that are tied to tax returns typically provide the greatest level of reliability.

In addition to the source of the data, the valuation analyst should understand the accounting policies used by the company and how these policies may affect the valuation process. For instance, if the company being valued adopted an inventory valuation method or depreciation method that was significantly different from the policies of other companies in the same industry, the subject company's ratios and other statistics may not provide a reasonable basis for comparison. The selection of policies outside of industry norms may also indicate an attempt by the company to appear more profitable as compared to its peers.

**Trend Analysis and Common-Sized Analysis**   Trend analysis is another important part of financial statement analysis. Trend analysis provides insight into a company's historical and future growth, profitability, and financial requirements. An analysis of trends also identifies seasonality and business cycles, which are important in the preparation of projections. Trend analysis and common-sized analysis go hand in hand. Common-sized analysis converts the dollar values of financial statements into percentages; amounts included in income statement accounts are reflected as a percentage of sales; balance sheet amounts are reflected as a percentage of total assets. These percentages allow for identification of trends and anomalies in the data and the comparison of financial information to potential guideline companies and industry norms.

Exhibit 3.2 is an example of a common-sized income statement that demonstrates the importance of trend analysis and common-sized analysis. If the financial results for only 2007 were examined in isolation, one might conclude that the business shown is a relatively poor performing entity. However, when the trend is examined it is evident that the prior years were much more profitable. This analysis would result in the valuation analyst investigating this decline in revenue and profitability to obtain an understanding of the reasons behind these declines. For instance, the valuation analyst would want to know if these declines were company specific or industry-wide, and if the declines were likely to be temporary or permanent.

In addition to the questions raised by the trend analysis, the common-sized analysis also raises important questions for the valuation analyst. During the period shown in exhibit 3.2, where sales decrease by approximately 7.0 percent per year, selling, general, and administrative (SG&A) expenses increased roughly 2.7 percent per year from just under 41 percent of sales to almost 50 percent of sales. If you relied on the common-size financials alone, you might think that SG&A expenses were increasing; however, if you look back to the actual financial results, it appears that the SG&A have remained fairly constant in real dollars. It is likely that the valuation analyst would want to understand the reason(s) for these increasing relative costs and what, if any, adjustments would have to be made to these expenses for the purposes

**EXHIBIT 3.2** Common-Sized Income Statement

| | Income Statement (Actual) | | | Common-Sized Income Statement | | |
|---|---|---|---|---|---|---|
| | 2005 | 2006 | 2007 | 2005 | 2006 | 2007 |
| Sales | $3,231.1 | $2,989.9 | $2,795.1 | 100.0% | 100.0% | 100.0% |
| Cost of sales (excluding depreciation) | 1,397.1 | 1,303.6 | 1,173.9 | 43.2% | 43.6% | 42.0% |
| Gross profit | 1,834.0 | 1,686.3 | 1,621.2 | 56.8% | 56.4% | 58.0% |
| SG&A expenses | 1,321.2 | 1,356.8 | 1,392.4 | 40.9% | 45.4% | 49.8% |
| EBITDA | 512.8 | 329.5 | 228.8 | 15.9% | 11.0% | 8.2% |
| Depreciation | 105.2 | 112.3 | 127.5 | 3.3% | 3.8% | 4.6% |
| Amortization | 30.3 | 29.2 | 19.5 | 0.9% | 1.0% | 0.7% |
| EBIT (operating income) | 377.3 | 188.0 | 81.8 | 11.7% | 6.3% | 2.9% |
| Interest expense | 44.1 | 58.6 | 43.2 | 1.4% | 2.0% | 1.5% |
| Interest (income) | (4.5) | (7.9) | (3.4) | (0.1%) | (0.3%) | (0.1%) |
| Other non-operating (income)/expense | (4.2) | 0.0 | 0.0 | (0.1%) | 0.0% | 0.0% |
| EBT (pretax income) | 341.9 | 137.3 | 42.0 | 10.6% | 4.6% | 1.5% |
| Income taxes | 126.8 | 56.3 | 16.4 | 3.9% | 1.9% | 0.6% |
| (Income)/loss from joint ventures | (10.1) | (27.1) | (4.5) | (0.3%) | (0.9%) | (0.2%) |
| Minority interest expense/(income) | 0.3 | (0.4) | (0.1) | 0.0% | 0.0% | 0.0% |
| Net income | $224.9 | $108.5 | $30.2 | 7.0% | 3.6% | 1.1% |

of the valuation. In this case, either the company has not cut expenses to match its decline in revenue, or the SG&A expenses are fixed in nature. In either case, this simple analysis provokes further investigation.

Finally, this type of analysis is critical to the development of meaningful projections for the company that will be relied on in the valuation process.

**Ratio Analysis**   Financial ratio analysis also provides a method to analyze historical performance over time and against peers and industry norms. A wide variety of ratios can be used to analyze a company's operational efficiency, profitability, leverage, liquidity, and growth. These ratios, like common-sized and trend analyses, can also identify anomalies in the financial data that require additional research. Ratios are commonly used by lenders in borrowing covenants, so it is important to understand how these ratios are derived. For example, a company that has a covenant based on a certain asset-to-debt ratio may find itself out of covenant if that ratio includes marketable securities and the value of those securities significantly declines. In this case, a borrower may find itself in default of a loan covenant when nothing has changed at the business. In other words there may have been no change in sales, operations, gross margin, and so on, but due to the inclusion of marketable securities as part of the borrowing base a borrower can easily be in default based on external factors.

**Comparison of Financial Statements to Industry Norms and Peers**   The comparison of financial-statement ratios and trends to industry data is helpful because it can also identify areas for further investigation by the valuation analyst. The comparison of a subject business to similar entities or industry norms will provide the valuation analyst with a better understanding of whether anomalies within the subject's business operating results are the result of internal or external factors. For instance, if sales are declining, does this represent a loss of market share by the subject company or a reduction in global demand for the product or service? Furthermore, if the entire industry is impacted, what are future expectations for the industry, and how will the subject company compare to those future expectations?

In addition, the comparison of the subject company to industry data might yield further insight into the financial and operational management of the subject company. For example, if the majority of industry participants have a gross margin in the range of 30 to 35 percent and the subject company has a gross margin of 50 percent, on the face of it a financial statement reader might attribute the excellent relative performance to an experienced management team or sales professionals. A deeper review could reveal a different story. It might indicate that the subject company's revenue recognition policies are out of line with the industry, or that, perhaps, certain cost of goods sold are being accounted for in the SG&A segment of the income statement, resulting in the gross margin being overstated. Furthermore, if in fact the margin is much greater than industry norms, it might foreshadow increased competition because the subject company will soon be faced with additional competition as others are attracted to the specific product or service they sell.

The analysis of peer group financial information is a valuable tool for the valuation analyst. As more fully discussed in Chapter 5, the analysis of peer group financial information is an integral part of the peer group development, which is a necessary component of the comparable guideline company method of the market approach.

**Normalizing Historical Financial Statements**   During the analysis of the subject company's historical financial statements, certain nonrecurring or nonoperating income or expenses may be identified. The process of normalizing financial statements eliminates items that are not part of the company's core operations or are unlikely to occur in the future. Normalized financial statements are used to

- Prepare projections of future sales, costs, cash flows, and capital expenditures used in the income approach.
- Compare the subject company to potential guideline companies and comparable transactions in the market approach.
- Provide a more accurate measure of operational metrics on which multiples may be applied.

Caution must be exercised when normalizing the subject company's metric (such as EBITDA) for use with a multiple derived from the EBITDA of the comparable companies. The failure to make similar adjustments to both sides of the equation will yield misleading results.

**Normalizing Adjustments**   Normalizing adjustments come in as many forms as there are businesses. The requirement for such adjustments may not be apparent from a cursory overview of a company's financials but only through interviews with management or other parties. Typical items requiring a normalizing adjustment include

- Unusual, nonrecurring, and extraordinary items
- Nonoperating items
- Changes in accounting methods

Exhibit 3.3 illustrates an example of normalizing an income statement for nonrecurring items.

**EXHIBIT 3.3**   Normalizing Adjustments to the Income Statement

|  | Reported | Adjustment | | Normalized |
|---|---|---|---|---|
| Revenue | $1,248 | | | $1,248 |
| Cost of goods sold | 773 | | | 773 |
| Gross profit | 475 | | | 475 |
| | | | | |
| SG&A expense | 275 | | | 275 |
| Restructuring charge | 48 | (48) | a. | — |
| EBIT | 152 | | | 200 |
| *% margin* | *12.2%* | | | *16.0%* |
| | | | | |
| Interest expense | 38 | | | 38 |
| Interest (income) | (2) | | | (2) |
| Pretax income | 116 | | | 164 |
| | | | | |
| Income taxes @ 36% | 42 | 17 | b. | 59 |
| Net income | $74 | | | $105 |

Notes: During Q1, the company took a restructuring charge of $48 million ($31 million after-tax).

Non-recurring items
| | |
|---|---|
| Pre-tax amount | 48 a. |
| Less: (After-tax amount) | (31) |
| = Adjustment to taxes | 17 b. |

**Removing the non-recurring item from the normalized income statement causes:**
   Earnings to increase
   Taxes to increase

   In the example shown in Exhibit 3.3, certain restructuring charges have been isolated and identified as nonrecurring. The exhibit shows that by isolating and normalizing these charges, the earnings were actually better than reported. The exhibit also shows the tax effect of the normalization.
   *Unusual, nonrecurring, and extraordinary* items include events or transactions that possess a high degree of abnormality, events or transactions that are not reasonably expected to recur in the foreseeable future, and events or transactions that are distinguished by their unusual nature and by the infrequency of their occurrence.
   Some items considered unusual, nonrecurring, and extraordinary include

- Expenses or losses incurred as a result of a natural disaster or act of war
- One-time write-downs or write-offs of receivables, inventory, equipment leased to others, or intangible assets

- Gain (loss) from exchange or translation of foreign currencies
- Gain (loss) on the disposal of a segment of the company
- Gain (loss) from sale or abandonment of PP&E
- Adjustment of accruals on long-term contracts
- Gain (loss) from restructuring charges

*Non-operating assets* include items such as excess cash and marketable securities in excess of a company's operating requirements; equity investments or earnings in unconsolidated affiliates; and other assets such as condominiums and certain real estate that may be on the books of the company but that are not used by or do not contribute to the business. If an asset is classified as nonoperating, related cash flows (positive or negative) should be identified and normalized so that the resulting cash flows would be appropriate to use for the DCF method.

Valuation analysts often encounter financial statements reflecting a *change in accounting* methodology from one year to the next. Valuation analysts must understand the effect that these changes have on a company's financial statements and determine if a normalization adjustment is necessary. Some common examples of changes in accounting methods are

- Change in inventory accounting method, such as FIFO (first in, first out) to LIFO (last in, first out) or vice versa
- Change in the depreciation method such as changing from straight-line method to accelerated method or vice versa

Additional adjustments to consider when normalizing income statements, particularly income statements of a distressed or private company, include the following:

**Cost of Goods Sold:** In distressed companies, cost of goods sold may increase, lowering margins because of:
  - A lack of discounts from vendors due to decreased purchasing volume or increased credit risk
  - An increase in costs associated with hurried projects due to poor planning or liquidity issues

**Restructuring Charges:** In a turnaround scenario, a company hires financial advisors, lawyers, turnaround managers, valuation analysts, and other advisors. These expenses should be subtracted from a company's financial statements to reflect a lower cost of conducting business during periods of normalcy.

**Excess Compensation:** In a private company, owners may pay non-market salaries, either higher or lower, to family members. Going forward, these salaries should be adjusted to market levels indicative of the actual costs of management.

**Atypical Rental Expense:** Private companies may rent or lease space from a related entity. These rents may need to be adjusted to market rates.

Financial analysis of the subject company, peer-group companies, and comparable transactions (when available) is fundamental to valuation. The breadth of information gained by financial analyses impacts all areas of the valuation and is sometimes the only source for such information. Cash flow projections; selection of peer-group companies; necessity and/or extent of discounts, premiums, and adjustments, for example, are all based on financial analyses and the resulting understanding of the company's operations. Failure to conduct such analyses or to go beyond the numbers to understand their meanings and relationships can lead to an unreasonable valuation conclusion.

## CONCLUSION

The basics of business valuation begin with more questions than answers. What is the purpose of the valuation? What is the standard of value and the appropriate premise of value for this situation? What is being valued, the enterprise, a "control" ownership position in the equity, or a minority equity interest with no control? What is the primary business of the company and what approach (or approaches) is appropriate to use in this situation? How is the business performing financially, operationally, and in comparison to peers and/or the industry? Unless these questions are answered and understood, the approaches and methodologies used to reach a conclusion of value are simply mathematical and theoretical exercises that provide little or no value to the user.

## NOTES

1. See Rev. Rul. 59–60, 1959-1 C B 237.
2. *Hintmann v. Fred Weber, Inc.*, 1998 WL 83052, at *8 (Del. Ch. Feb. 17, 1998) ("[T]his Court recently stated: 'a holding company's ownership of a controlling interest in its subsidiaries is an independent element of value that must be taken into account in determining a fair value for the parent company.' ").

# CHAPTER 4

# Income Approach

The premise of the income approach is that the value of a company is equal to the present value of all future benefits (i.e., cash flows) generated by its assets, discounted at a company's targeted weighted average cost of capital (WACC). It is an *intrinsic* valuation approach that assesses a company's value based on the cash flows inherent to a company and the riskiness of those cash flows. This is distinguished from the *extrinsic* market approach, described more fully in Chapter 5, which relies on the current valuations of other similar companies, or the previous sales prices of similar companies, to determine value.

> *In the simplest sense, the theory surrounding the value of an interest in a business depends on the future benefits that will accrue to the owner of it. The value of the business interest, then, depends upon an estimate of the future benefits and the required rate of return at which those future benefits are discounted back to the valuation date.*
>
> **Valuing a Business**, Pratt, Reilly and Schweihs

> *Value today always equals future cash flow discounted at the opportunity cost of capital.*
>
> **Principles of Corporate Finance**, Richard A. Brealey and Stewart C. Myers

As a general rule, in the case of an ongoing business, bankruptcy courts and valuation treatises agree that valuations should be based on the expectation of future earnings. This principle and the uncertainties inherent in such an approach were forcefully stated in a leading bankruptcy case decided in 1941 by the Supreme Court of the United States, *Consolidated Rock Products Co. v. Du Bois.*

The Supreme Court criticized the methods of valuation used by the lower court, and clearly pointed to the income approach, stating:

> *From this record it is apparent that little, if any, effort was made to value the whole enterprise* by a capitalization of prospective earnings. *The necessity for such an inquiry is emphasized by the poor earnings record of this enterprise in the past. Findings as to the earning capacity of an enterprise are essential to a determination of the feasibility as well as the fairness of a plan of reorganization. Whether or not the earnings may reasonably be expected to meet the interest and dividend requirements of the new securities is a* sine qua non *to a determination of the integrity and practicability of the new capital structure. It is also essential for satisfaction of the absolute priority rule . . . .*
>
> *As Mr. Justice Holmes said in [an earlier case], 'the commercial value of property consists in the expectation of income from it.' Such criterion is the appropriate one here, since we are dealing with the issue of solvency arising in connection with reorganization plans involving productive properties . . . .* The criterion of earning capacity is the essential one if the enterprise is to be freed from the heavy hand of past errors, miscalculations or disaster, *and if the allocation of securities among the various claimants is to be fair and equitable.*
>
> *Since its application requires a prediction as to what will occur in the future,* an estimate, as distinguished from mathematical certitude, is all that can be made. *But that estimate must be based on an informed judgment which embraces all facts relevant to future earning capacity and hence to present worth, including, of course, the nature and condition of the properties, the past earnings record, and all circumstances which indicate whether or not that record is a reliable criterion of future performance. A sum of values based on physical factors and assigned to separate units of the property without regard to the earning capacity of the whole enterprise is plainly inadequate.*
>
> **Consolidated Rock Products Co. v. Du Bois, 312 U.S. 510, 525–526(1941) (emphasis added)**

There are two generally accepted methods to value a company under the income approach: the discounted cash flow (DCF) method and the capitalized cash flow (CFC) method. Because the capitalized cash flow method has limitations, it is seldom used in complex valuation assignments. These limitations are discussed in more detail later in this chapter.

# DISCOUNTED CASH FLOW METHOD

As stated in the preceding section, the premise of the DCF method is that the value of a company is equal to the present value of its expected future cash flows discounted at a suitable discount rate, which is often the company's WACC. Regardless of how the assets are financed, the returns generated by these assets are available to all providers of capital (debt and equity). Therefore, cash flows should be considered free from financing considerations. Free cash flows (FCF) are the cash flows available after a company has paid its operating expenses, but prior to principal and interest payments to lenders, or dividend payments to shareholders. Free cash flows are, therefore, the cash flows available to all providers of capital.

The following are some strengths and weaknesses of the discounted cash flow method:

## Strengths

- Less influenced by *extrinsic factors* (e.g., market volatility or macroeconomic factors) than other valuation approaches
- Flexible, forward-looking method that can incorporate expected changes to a company's operating strategy and key variables (i.e., growth rates, operating margins, required operating working capital, and expected capital expenditures)
- Allows the valuation analyst to consider many variables and assumptions

## Weaknesses

- May be based on financial projections that could be overly optimistic or overly pessimistic, based on the motivations and perspectives of the party seeking the valuation opinion and the expected use of the opinion
- Highly sensitive to assumptions used to derive cash flows, discount rate, and terminal value

Valuation studies should include the preparation of a valuation under the DCF method, or at least the detailed consideration of one. For a valuation analyst to simply omit the DCF method without good reason could be a fatal flaw and could lead to the exclusion of an expert's testimony based on a Daubert challenge, which is further discussed in Chapter 10.

## Building Blocks of the Discounted Cash Flow Method

The DCF method is based on the following key elements:

Free cash flows (FCF): represents cash flows from operations, independent of leverage and nonoperating investments.

Terminal value (TV): represents the estimated value of a company from the end of the discrete projection period into perpetuity.

Weighted average cost of capital (WACC): represents the weighted average cost of all forms of capital used by a company to finance its operations, including debt and equity.

Both components of value, each future year's projected FCF during the discrete projection period and the terminal value, are discounted to their present value using the WACC.

## Free Cash Flows

Free cash flow is the operating income generated by the company's operating assets (those that are used to produce goods or services), adjusted for taxes, noncash expenses (such as depreciation and amortization), operating working capital requirements, and capital expenditures. Free cash flows are determined independent of the capital structure.

Occasionally, valuation analysts will equate earnings before interest, taxes, depreciation, and amortization (EBITDA) with FCF, but EBITDA is merely a proxy for cash flow and does not always accurately estimate FCF. Although EBITDA removes charges for interest, and, therefore, eliminates the effects of capital structure and leverage, it does not take into account taxes that must be paid or capital expenditures that may be needed to maintain or expand the business. FCF should take these items into account. For some businesses, EBITDA is a good starting point for the DCF but it should not be blindly assumed to be the same as FCF.

In terms of taxes, there are certain occasions in which the appropriate cash flow stream to rely on in the DCF method is the pretax cash flow. For example, if the enterprise being valued is a nontaxable entity, such as an S Corporation, some would say that the DCF should be prepared on a pretax basis. This topic is generally beyond the scope of this text, but it is something to be aware of.

**Calculating Free Cash Flows**  Exhibit 4.1 illustrates the most commonly used approach to calculate FCF from a review of financial statements and projections.

The determination of FCF begins with earnings before interest and taxes, also known as EBIT, a measure of accounting earnings, and converts it to FCF, a measure of cash earnings. This is done first by tax-affecting

**EXHIBIT 4.1**  Top-Down Approach Free Cash Flow Calculations

| | Historical Year Ended December 31, | | | Discrete Projection Period—Projected Year Ending December 31, | | | | |
|---|---|---|---|---|---|---|---|---|
| | 2006 | 2007 | 2008 | 2009 | 2010 | 2011 | 2012 | 2013 |
| Earnings before interest and taxes (EBIT) | $377.4 | $348.9 | $345.0 | $234.0 | $228.0 | $279.7 | $345.6 | $432.0 |
| Less: Taxes @ 41.0% | (154.7) | (143.0) | (141.5) | (95.9) | (93.5) | (114.7) | (141.7) | (177.1) |
| Net operating profit after taxes (NOPAT) | 222.7 | 205.9 | 203.5 | 138.1 | 134.5 | 165.0 | 203.9 | 254.9 |
| Plus: Depreciation | | | | 152.5 | 153.8 | 155.1 | 156.7 | 158.8 |
| Plus: Amortization | | | | 11.9 | 9.8 | 9.3 | 8.8 | 6.6 |
| Plus: Change in Operating Working Capital | | | | 41.2 | (0.8) | (14.3) | (14.1) | (15.1) |
| Less: Capital Expenditures | | | | (165.0) | (162.6) | (164.3) | (170.4) | (181.3) |
| Unlevered Free Cash Flow for Discounting | | | | $178.7 | $134.7 | $150.8 | $184.9 | $223.9 |

EBIT at the marginal tax rate resulting in the NOPAT (net operating profit after tax).

After NOPAT is calculated, noncash expenses, such as depreciation and amortization, are added back. In addition, changes in operating working capital (either a source or use of cash) and capital expenditures to maintain or expand plant, property and equipment (a use of cash), or other capital expenditures that result from the normal course of operations are factored in.

FCF analysis also allows management and shareholders to consider important business questions such as how much cash flow can be used for new ventures, capital expenditures, debt reduction, or dividend payments, to mention a few.

**Preparing Cash Flow Projections** The process of projecting FCF requires thorough review of historical data, a comprehensive understanding of the relationship between significant financial-statement variables, in-depth discussions with management, and a clear-eyed assessment of the assumptions underlying the company's projections. In the situation of a Chapter 11 bankruptcy, cash flow projections must be consistent with the contemplated postrestructuring plan taking into account any structural changes, such as the sale of a division, closure of a plant, rejection of leases or executory contracts, or termination of product lines. The assessment of the projections is often the most important aspect to a valuation.

The more information that is known about the company, the industry, and the company's position within the industry, the more realistic and supportable the assumptions made in the projections will be.

Some of the key questions the valuation analyst should answer before developing or relying on projections are listed below:

Industry

- Have there been any recent changes in the industry?
- Is the industry undergoing consolidation?
- Is the industry high growth, slow growth, or mature in nature?
- What is the overall market size of the industry?

Company

- What is the subject company's position within the industry (niche player, volume or quality leader, etc.)?
- What are management's future expectations for the company (gaining/losing market share, etc.) and are these expectations reasonable?
- What issues is the subject company likely to face currently or in the future?

■ Has management provided any guidance regarding internally developed projections?

There are many methods that can be used to develop projections, but the most common approach is to apply the historical relationship between revenues and operating expenses to projected revenue. In its simplest form, there is a direct relationship between each operating-expense line item and revenue. Once this historical relationship is identified, and verified to be applicable in the future, quantified, it can be applied to projected revenues to develop the valuation analyst's cash flow projections.

As noted earlier, with more information and access to management the valuation analyst can develop more reliable projections. For example, with limited information, the valuation analyst may rely on the prior year's revenue growth rate or the average of the previous three years to project the future growth rate. However, with a better understanding of the company and the industry, the valuation analyst may be able to develop more detailed and reliable projections. For example, revenue projections based on the projected size of the overall market and the subject company's expected market share within that market, or detailed revenue projections built up by unit sales and product information, may ultimately be more reliable than simply forecasting revenue based on an average of historical data.

An analysis of each operating expense classification or line item is necessary to determine its nature and relationship to other line items in the cash flow projection. Typically, an operating expense is considered to be fixed or variable to revenue (although expenses may occasionally have relationships to other expenses, such as payroll taxes being related to payroll instead of revenue) and this relationship can oftentimes be identified through an examination of the historical activity. Thus, even if revenues are changing (increasing or decreasing) significantly, a fixed expense would remain constant, whereas a variable expense would fluctuate (increasing or decreasing) based on the change in revenue.

Operating expenses that are fixed in one type of industry may be variable in another type of industry, and vice versa. For example, for most service companies, utilities would typically be fixed. However, in heavy manufacturing, utility expense is oftentimes dependent on production volumes, and thus variable. In addition, rent expense for most businesses is fixed, but in certain industries, such as retail, where a percentage of sales may be charged along with a base rent payment, this expense can be more dependent on sales levels. As a result, it is important for the valuation analyst to understand the particular circumstances of the subject company and the subject's industry.

Further analysis of an operating expense line item may reveal that the expense is neither truly variable nor fixed, but rather semivariable. A semivariable expense is an expense that appears to be fixed over certain revenue or volume levels, but if the revenue or volume level changes significantly enough, the expense will jump to another level. When semivariable expenses are charted against revenue/volume, they often look like stairs with sharp increases at particular points. A simple example of a semivariable expense is a delivery company that leases the trucks it uses. Assuming the company can make 10 deliveries per day per truck, and the company has only one truck, the company's truck leasing expense is fixed, as long as it makes no more than 10 deliveries per day. However, if business increases to more than 10 deliveries per day, the company would have to lease another truck, and the truck leasing expense would double, even if the company was making only 11 deliveries per day. Therefore, in certain instances, a small change in revenue/volume could lead to significant changes in costs. Since semivariable expenses are not always obvious at first glance, the greater the valuation analyst's understanding of the company and the industry, the more likely these instances will be incorporated into the cash flow projections.

Once the valuation analyst has completed the analysis and projections of both revenues and expenses, EBIT can be calculated. As mentioned previously, FCF begins with EBIT and converts it to FCF by tax-affecting EBIT at the marginal tax rate and adding back noncash expenses, which were included either in the cost of sales or in the selling, general, and administrative costs, and adjusting for changes in working capital requirements and capital expenditures.

Working capital is a balance-sheet metric. It is calculated by deducting certain current liabilities (except those mentioned later) from certain current assets. Working capital is comprised of items such as accounts receivable, inventory, prepaid expenses, accounts payable, and accrued liabilities, but excludes nonoperating assets, such as excess cash and financing items (such as short-term debt). Any changes in working capital from period to period should be included in the FCF calculation. An increase in working capital results in a reduction of FCF because funds are being retained by the business and are not available for distribution, and vice versa. Generally, valuation analysts project operating working capital using the following methods:

- Project each operating working capital account, or.
- Project net operating working capital as a percentage of revenue.

For companies that are growing rapidly, the projections and assumptions around working capital requirements have a significant impact on the overall value of a company. For example, companies that are growing rapidly may hold larger inventories to meet anticipated increases in demand and thus have less FCF.

One of the assumptions of the DCF method is that a company is a going concern. As such, capital expenditures (cash flows necessary to maintain and expand property, plant and equipment) and investments in definite-life intangibles (e.g., copyrights, trademarks, customer lists, patents, etc.) are required to maintain or increase a company's competitive position. Because these activities use cash, they reduce the amount of FCF available. If a company frequently engages in asset sales and/or sale leasebacks, proceeds from these transactions are netted against new capital expenditures in the cash-flow model. Valuation analysts generally project capital expenditures based on a percentage of revenue or a detailed review of historic balance sheets to determine the expected annual capital expenditure requirements at certain activity levels. Because many capital expenditures are discretionary in nature, it is helpful to have management's expectations in this area.

In financially distressed situations, constraints in short-term liquidity and interest payments may have resulted in deferred capital expenditures during the previous periods. The discrete projection period should reflect the level of capital expenditures required to maintain the projected level of sales. If sufficient capital expenditures are not included in the calculation to sustain the projected level of cash flow, the ultimate valuation will be unreliable.

**Projection Period**   Typically valuation analysts develop a discrete projection period for a number of years, followed by a simplifying assumption applied to valuing the remaining life of the company into perpetuity, that is, the terminal value (discussed later). The discrete projection period must be long enough so that the company has reached a steady state of operations (i.e., long-term sustainable growth prospects, stable capital structure, or an end to restructuring). Further, for businesses with a definite cycle, the discrete projection period should be considered against that cycle.

The discrete projection period should be long enough for the valuation analyst to be comfortable projecting a long-term perpetuity growth rate. Valuation analysts typically project a discrete period of one to ten years for most companies; however, high-growth or cyclical companies may need a longer time. If the forecast period is too short, it may result in an undervaluation of the company or result in a long-term growth assumption that is too high and overstates the terminal value and the resulting overall opinion.

## Calculating the Terminal Value

The present value of the expected FCF during the discrete projection period represents one portion of the enterprise value. Since the assumption in most valuations is that the subject business is a going concern, a company is expected to generate cash flows beyond the discrete projection period. However, it is impractical to project FCF indefinitely on an annual basis. As a result, valuation analysts make an assumption of the subject company's value at the end of the discrete projection period. This is usually called the *terminal value*.

The sum of the present values of (1) the FCF generated during the discrete projection period plus (2) the present value of the terminal value is the *enterprise value*.

Depending on the specific projections involved, the length of the discrete projection period, the WACC, and other factors, it is possible that the present value of the discrete period cash flows will represent a minority of the overall value of the firm. Such instances are often used to point out the "speculative" nature of a DCF-derived valuation opinion.

There are two typically accepted methods for estimating the terminal value:

1. Perpetuity growth rate method
2. Terminal multiple method

Both methods are discussed in more detail below.

**Growth in Perpetuity Method**   This method assumes a company will operate into perpetuity, with sustainable cash flows and a fixed long-term growth rate, after the discrete projection period. For this method, cash flow in the last projected year is increased by the perpetuity growth rate. The perpetuity growth formula is based on the principle that the terminal value of a company is the value of its cash flows into perpetuity, divided by a capitalization rate [discount rate ($r$) less long-term growth rate ($g$)]. This is essentially the capitalization of the last year's cash flows. The calculated terminal value in this case is then discounted back to the valuation date by the WACC and added to the present value of the cash flows from the discrete projections period.

The formula for perpetuity and a growing perpetuity is as follows:

**Perpetuity Growth Rate Formula**

$$\text{Terminal Value} = \frac{FCF_n \times (1 + g)}{(r - g)}$$

$FCF_n$ = expected free cash flow in last projected year
$(r - g)$ = capitalization rate
$r$ = discount rate
$g$ = expected long-term growth rate

**Terminal Multiple Method**   The terminal multiple method, also known as the *exit multiple method,* calculates the terminal value by calculating the purchase price of the subject company at the end of the discrete projection period. This is achieved by applying a multiple to EBITDA (or another relevant metric) projected for the final year. In the same manner as discussed above, this terminal value is then discounted back to the valuation date and added to the present value of the discrete projection period cash flows.

### Terminal Value Formula

$$\text{Terminal Value} = \text{EBITDA}_n \times \text{Multiple}$$

In some cases where the business is expected to be liquidated at the end of the discrete projection period, a projected liquidation value is assumed to be the terminal value. Although this approach is less common, it may be appropriate for businesses that have a defined life with no expectation of a going concern beyond a certain time period. One such case could be a business that is completely dependent on a license or other form of agreement when there is no chance of renewal beyond the contract term.

Exhibit 4.2 illustrates an example of the DCF method.

## Calculating the WACC

A company's after-tax, weighted average cost of capital is typically the most appropriate discount rate with which to discount estimated FCF and the terminal value. The WACC can be broken down into an equity component (cost of equity financing) and a debt component (cost of debt financing, net of the tax benefit of using debt), based on the respective proportion of each in a company's *target* capital structure.

A key assumption associated with the WACC is that a company manages toward a long-term maintainable target capital structure. The reasoning for this assumption is that, if the current capital structure is not sustainable, it will not be maintained by the company under normal market pressures over the long run. In the case of a Chapter 11 bankruptcy, this is more than just an assumption—it is almost always the case that the company filed bankruptcy because its capital structure was unsustainable (over-leveraged), and the purpose of the plan of reorganization is to de-leverage the company. Therefore, the valuation analyst assumes a *target* or *optimal* capital structure based on an analysis of the comparable companies' capital structures.

The two parts of the WACC (cost of equity and cost of debt) are calculated separately, and their relative impact (or "weighed average") on the

**EXHIBIT 4.2**  Discounted Cash Flow Method

Weighted average cost of capital (WACC) | 12.0%

Discrete Projection Period—Projected Year Ending December 31,

| Year | 2009 | 2010 | 2011 | 2012 | 2013 |
|---|---|---|---|---|---|
| Period (n) | 1 | 2 | 3 | 4 | 5 |
| Free Cash Flow for discounting | $178.7 | $134.7 | $150.8 | $184.9 | $223.9 |
| Divided by: $(1+WACC)^n$ | 1.1200 | 1.2544 | 1.4049 | 1.5735 | 1.7623 |
| Equals: PV of each Free Cash Flow | $159.6 | $107.4 | $107.3 | $117.5 | $127.0 |
| Sum of the PV of Free Cash Flows | [$159.6 + $107.4 + $107.3 + $117.5 + $127.0] = | | | | $618.8 |

**Terminal Value Calculation**

| | | |
|---|---|---|
| PV of Free Cash Flow in last projected year | [PV of Free Cash Flow in 2013] = | $127.0 |
| Long-term growth rate of Free Cash Flow after 2012 | | 3.0% |
| PV of Free Cash Flow in 2013 | [$127.0 × (1 + 3.0%)] = | 130.8 |
| Present Value of Terminal Value | [$130.8/(12.0% − 3.0%)] = | $1,453.3 |

**Enterprise Value and Market Value Calculation**

| Enterprise Value (value of operating assets) | [$618.8 + $1,453.3] = | $2,072.1 |
|---|---|---|

| | | | |
|---|---|---|---|
| Plus: Non-operating Assets | | | |
| Excess cash | | 51.5 | |
| Plus: Equity investments | | 137.8 | |
| Equals: Total non-operating assets | | $189.3 | $189.3 |
| | | | |
| Value of operating & nonoperating assets | | | $2,261.4 |
| Less: Non-equity claims | | | |
| Total debt | | 1,035.0 | |
| Plus: Minority interest | | 5.9 | |
| Equals: Total non-equity claims | | $1,040.9 | ($1,040.9) |

| Market Value | $1,220.5 |
|---|---|

final weighted average cost of capital is the result of the target capital structure as determined by the expert. If, for example, the expert determines that 45% of the capital structure will be funded with debt and 55% of the capital structure will be funded with equity, those percentages are applied to the underlying calculations of the cost of debt and the cost of equity to calculate the WACC. Since the cost of equity is higher than the cost of debt, this ratio can have a significant effect on the WACC. For example, assume that the after-tax cost of debt is calculated to be 6.50% and the cost of equity is calculated to be 9.50%. Within certain ranges, the *lower* the percentage of the debt component the higher the WACC, and therefore, a lower value indication from the DCF method. However, increasing debt past a certain percentage (to the point of over-leverage) dramatically raises the ultimate cost of equity. The impact of a slightly different debt/equity ratio can be seen in the table below.

| | 40/60 Debt/Equity Ratio | 45/55 Debt/Equity Ratio |
|---|---|---|
| a. Cost of Debt (after tax) | 6.50% | 6.50% |
| b. Debt/(Debt + Equity) | 40% | 45% |
| c. (a × b) *Cost of Debt Portion* | 2.60% | 2.93% |
| | | |
| d. Cost of Equity | 12.00% | 12.00% |
| e. Equity/(Debt + Equity) | 60% | 55% |
| f. (d × e) *Cost of Equity Portion* | 7.20% | 6.60% |
| | | |
| c + f = **WACC** | 9.80% | 9.53% |

The mathematical formula to calculate the WACC looks like this:

$$\text{WACC} = K_e \times \frac{E}{EV} + K_d \times (1 - T) \times \frac{D}{EV}$$

$K_e$ = cost of equity financing[1]
$E/EV$ = market value of equity to enterprise value
$K_d$ = cost of debt financing
$D/EV$ = market value of debt to enterprise value
$T$ = marginal tax rate
$(1 - T)$ = interest tax shield

**Cost of Debt ($K_d$)**   The cost of debt represents the required return on debt. The pretax cost of debt is a company's cost to borrow new long-term debt in current market conditions. The cost of debt is calculated as a weighted average for all tranches of debt. Because interest is tax deductible, the true cost of borrowing is the after-tax cost of debt, not the nominal pretax cost.

In certain industries in which off-balance-sheet financing is prevalent (e.g., retailing and airlines), it may be appropriate to include operating leases in debt because they have similar economics to capital leases. Capitalizing operating leases requires adjustments to income to exclude operating lease expense and substitute additional interest expense and depreciation on the capitalized lease asset.

**Cost of Equity ($K_e$)**   The cost of equity represents the opportunity cost of investing in alternative investments with similar risk. Cost of equity is usually determined using the Modified Capital Asset Pricing Model (MCAPM). The cost of equity consists of several components of "risk," all of which are added together to calculate the cost of equity. Any calculation of the cost of equity will include (1) the risk-free rate of return, (2) the equity risk premium (which consists of two elements), (3) the size premium, and (4) the unsystematic risk premium, or the "alpha" premium. In some cases a premium for geographic concentration is appropriate. The mathematical formula is:

$$K_e = r_f + \beta \times \left(r_m - r_f\right) + S_p + \alpha$$

$$
\begin{aligned}
K_e &= \text{cost of common equity financing} \\
r_f &= \text{risk-free rate of return} \\
\beta &= \text{equity beta of the security} \\
r_m &= \text{rate of return in the market} \\
(r_m - r_f) &= \text{market risk premium} \\
S_p &= \text{size premium} \\
\alpha &= \text{alpha premium}
\end{aligned}
$$

In addition to MCAPM, some valuation analysts use the simpler build-up method, particularly for smaller privately held companies. The build-up method builds up a rate of return on equity using the risk-free rate, market risk premium, size premium, and alpha premium (company specific risk factors). Both the MCAPM and the build-up method are similar; the difference is that the build-up method implicitly assumes an equity beta of 1, which is equal to the equity beta of the overall market (see the following section).

**The Risk-Free Rate** *(r$_f$)*   The risk-free rate is the rate of a zero-risk investment with a maturity that generally correlates with the discrete projection period. Generally, a U.S. Treasury security of the appropriate length is used as a proxy. The current yield on a medium to long-term U.S. Treasury bond can be found on the Federal Reserve's web site or services such as Bloomberg.

**Equity Risk Premium** ($\beta \times (r_m - r_f)$)
*Market Risk Premium (r$_m$ − r$_f$)*   The market risk premium (also known as equity risk premium) represents the additional return an investor expects to be compensated for because of the additional risk of investing in an equity market portfolio as compared to a risk-free investment. One source for the market risk premium can be found in Ibbotson Associates *SBBI Valuation Edition Yearbook*. The market risk premium is the risk required to attract investors from risk-free investments to the *overall public equity market* (generally the S&P 500).

*Beta (β)*   Beta measures the volatility of a company's common stock price *relative to* the overall market (captured in this formula as the market risk premium, above). This measures the degree of correlation between the return on a company's common stock price and the market return.

   **Equity beta of 1.0**—expected equity returns equal the expected market returns.

   **Equity beta of 0.0**—expected equity returns are not correlated to expected market returns.

   **Equity beta of −1.0**—expected equity returns are the inverse of expected market returns.

   Even where the historical beta for the subject company (now in bankruptcy) can be calculated from historical returns, the historical beta is likely much higher than will be appropriate for the reorganized company after it exits bankruptcy and operates over a long-term horizon at the target or optimal capital structure contemplated by the DCF method. This is because the historical beta is necessarily calculated from the period when the subject company was under operational or financial stress leading up to a bankruptcy filing.

Thus, the proper method in this situation is to either calculate the historical beta for healthy comparable companies, or use the predicted beta for those companies. The equity betas for the comparable companies can be calculated from historical data or obtained from easily available data sources. Predictive beta calculations for comparable companies can be obtained for a fee from Barra.

By using betas from healthy comparable companies (which, by definition, will be in the same industry as the subject company) to calculate a median or mean for the comparable set, the valuation analyst will have derived an *industry* beta that shows how the subject company's cost of equity, simply because it is in that industry, should vary from the overall market. Other risk adjustments applicable to the subject company's cost of equity, such as the size of the subject company, or other factors, are taken into account in other parts of this calculation.

Just as the choice of comparable companies and comparable transactions can have a big impact on the multiples used in the two Market Approach methodologies, the choice of comparable companies used to compute beta can have a big impact on this component of WACC.

Betas for the comparable companies that make up the relevant set of comparable companies (and therefore, the relevant industry) are available from several statistical services, including OneSource, Value Line, Bloomberg, and Barra.

The equity beta obtained from comparable companies is adjusted for differences in financial leverage between the comparable companies and the subject company. The beta is "unlevered" and then "relevered."

The relevered beta and the market risk premium are multiplied to obtain the equity risk premium component of the cost of equity calculation.

**Size Premium/Discount**   The size premium/discount reflects the additional premium or risk associated with an equity investment in a company of a particular size. This "size" (or "small size") premium is derived from historical differences in returns between small companies and large companies. The cost of equity for thinly capitalized companies would be underestimated if the S&P 500 is used as a basis for determining the market risk premium and beta in MCAPM.

The size premium/discount data can be found in Ibbotson Associates *SBBI Valuation Edition Yearbook* and *Duff & Phelps' Risk Premium Report*. The *SBBI Valuation Yearbook* "slices" the data into deciles (with an added breakdown of the 10th decile) and in three more granular groupings of the decile information (mid-cap companies, low-cap, companies and micro-cap). The 2009 Ibbotson *SBBI Valuation Yearbook's* alternative ways of looking at the data are as follows:

| | Market Capitalization of Smallest Company (in millions) | Market Capitalization of Largest Company (in millions) | Size Premium (Return in Excess of CAPM) (%) |
|---|---|---|---|
| 1-Largest | 18,627,540 | 465,651,938 | −0.36 |
| 2 | 7,434,806 | 18,503,467 | 0.62 |
| 3 | 4,229,323 | 7,360,271 | 0.74 |
| 4 | 2,785,698 | 4,225,152 | 0.97 |
| 5 | 1,849,950 | 2,785,538 | 1.54 |
| 6 | 1,198,013 | 1,848,961 | 1.63 |
| 7 | 753,676 | 1,197,133 | 1.62 |
| 8 | 453,398 | 753,448 | 2.35 |
| 9 | 218,743 | 453,254 | 2.71 |
| 10-Smallest | 1,575 | 218,533 | 5.81 |

| | | | |
|---|---|---|---|
| 10a | 136,599 | 218,533 | 4.11 |
| 10b | 1,575 | 136,500 | 9.53 |

| | | | |
|---|---|---|---|
| Mid-Cap, 3-5 | $1,849,950 | $7,360,271 | 0.94 |
| Low-Cap, 6-8 | 453,398 | 1,848,961 | 1.74 |
| Micro-Cap, 9-10 | 1,575 | 453,254 | 3.74 |

The choice of mid-cap, low-cap, or micro-cap "slices" versus decile slices can have a significant effect on the size premium used. For instance, if the estimated market capitalization of the subject company was $450,000,000, the micro-cap size premium is 3.74%, but the size premium for the 9th decile is 2.71%.

It should also be noted that the calculation of the size premium component of the cost of equity can be an iterative process. This is because the applicable size premium is determined by the subject company's equity value. Under the DCF method the target debt for the subject company is deducted from the total enterprise value to derive the equity value. Any change to the total enterprise value of the company (which is impacted by the WACC) results in a corresponding change in the target debt amount and a corresponding change in the equity value, which *could* change the applicable decile or mid, low, or micro-cap grouping. If the applicable grouping changes, that changes the size premium component of the WACC, which changes total enterprise value. Where estimates of equity value are close to the edge of a decile/mid, low, or micro-cap range, the valuator should remember to be mindful of the possible need to make an iterative calculation. Finally, if all of the comparable companies whose betas were used to calculate the industry beta are in the same market capitalization decile or grouping as the subject company (perhaps an unlikely case), it may be worth considering whether it would be "double counting" to include a size premium component in the cost of equity.

**Unsystematic Risk or "Alpha" Premium ($\alpha$)**   The alpha premium ($\alpha$) (often referred to as the *unsystematic risk premium*) is a subjective premium for other risk factors unique to the subject company (as compared to industry risks) that is included in the cost of equity portion of the WACC. The alpha premium is an estimate of the added return needed to compensate investors for taking the idiosyncratic risks associated with investing in the subject company, and which are not attributable to overall market returns, industry risk, or size risk. In general, the following criteria, among others, may result in an alpha premium ($\alpha$): lack of diversification, lack of depth of management, key supplier dependence, key customer risk, and key person dependence.

Courts have cast a critical eye on this component of WACC. As one example, consider the following comments of the Delaware Chancery court, in an "appraisal" case:

> [The expert] added a 3% "company specific risk premium" to the WACC. An investment specific premium may be appropriate to account for risks not captured in the equity risk premium and the small size premium. Unlike those two premia, which are commonly determined by reference to the published results of empirical research, a company specific risk premium "remains largely a matter of the analyst's judgment, without a commonly accepted set of empirical support evidence." Thus, the factors relied upon in assessing an investment specific premium should be carefully explained to the Court. As with all aspects of a party's valuation for purposes of [Delaware's appraisal statute], the proponent of a company specific premium bears the burden of convincing the Court of the premium's appropriateness.

>  *[The expert's] support for the extra premium was limited to
>  two differing, conclusory statements. [The] Valuation Report
>  merely states that this extra premium was necessary to reflect "the
>  risk we believe was inherent in management's projections." At
>  trial, [the expert's] argument in support of the company specific
>  premium changed entirely, and he stated that this was necessary
>  because [the subject company] was "much more geographically
>  constrained than was the case in the public companies that we
>  looked at . . . ." [He] did not explain, however, exactly how either
>  of his proposed reasons for adding the extra premium translated
>  into greater risk. Moreover, if a company specific risk premium is
>  to be added at all, it is to be added in as a cost of equity, to be given
>  its appropriate weight in a company's capital structure and aver-
>  aged with the cost of debt; it is not appropriate to tack the full
>  premium onto the WACC. I find that Respondent has failed to
>  carry its burden of proving the appropriateness of adding a 3%
>  company specific risk premium.*
>
>  *Hintmann v. Fred Weber, Inc.*, 1998 WL 83052 at *5
>  (Del. Ch. Feb. 17, 1998) (unpublished decision)

The calculation of WACC is somewhat rigid. An appraiser with experience in valuing a variety of companies should test the result of this calculation against their past experience. That comparison may suggest that the
appraiser reconsider the validity of one or more of the inputs into the
WACC calculation.

**Application of the WACC—the Midpoint Convention**   Because cash flows are
usually generated throughout the course of a year, rather than at the end
of a year, each period's cash flows during the discrete projection period
are discounted back from the midyear to the present to allow non-
seasonal companies to estimate steady cash flows throughout the year.
This assumes that cash flows take place at the midpoint of each year
(i.e., cash flows in year 1 are discounted half a year, cash flows in year 2
are discounted one-and-a-half years, etc.). For certain industries characterized by seasonality (e.g., retail), an end-of-year discounting convention
may be more appropriate.

## CAPITALIZED CASH FLOW METHOD

The capitalized cash flow (CCF) method is an abbreviated version of the
discounted cash flow (DCF) method. This method uses a single-period

model to estimate value from capitalizing normalized cash flows (based on historical performance and future expectations). The method assumes that FCF grows at a constant rate into perpetuity.

The CCF calculation corresponds to the terminal value of the DCF method. Other terms used to describe the CCF method are capitalization of historical earnings method and direct capitalization method.

No matter the name, the general formula is the same as described in the following formula.

**Capitalized Cash Flow Formula**

$$PV = FCF1/(r-g)$$

$PV$ = present value
$FCF1$ = expected free cash flow in the next 12-month period
$(r-g)$ = capitalization rate
$r$ = discount rate
$g$ = expected long-term growth rate

An implicit assumption in the CCF method is that the expected cash flows grow into perpetuity at a constant rate and the capitalization rate is also constant, meaning that the cash flow represents a steady state. This method assumes that a company will be operated into perpetuity and will grow at a long-term growth rate $(g)$ with normalized net operating profit after taxes (NOPAT). If cash flows are expected to change because of operating profitability or changes in the business plan, then the CCF method is not practical, and the DCF method should be considered. Additionally, in financially distressed situations, a debtor may have operating losses in the trailing 12-month or forward-looking 12-month period, or even in the foreseeable future, making the CCF method less useful.

The distinction between a discount rate and a capitalization rate is important: a discount rate is a rate of return used to discount projected cash flows to a present value, whereas a capitalization rate is a rate used to capitalize a single period cash flow that represents a steady state with constant growth into perpetuity.

Practically speaking, this methodology is seldom used in complex valuation assignments.

## CONCLUSION

The underlying premise of the income approach is that the value of a company or business interest is equal to the present value of all future cash flows generated by its assets, discounted at a company's weighted average cost of capital (WACC). Free cash flow (FCF) represents cash flows from operations, independent of leverage and nonoperating investments. Because it is not practical to compute cash flows forever, this is broken into two components of value: (1) the FCF for a discrete number of years (the period it takes for the company to reach steady-state growth, for example) and (2) the terminal value as of the end of that discrete period. Both components are discounted to their present value using the WACC.

The most commonly accepted methods under the income approach are the DCF method and the CCF method. Because the DCF is based on projected FCF, caution should be exercised in developing credible forecasts. In the situation of Chapter 11 bankruptcy, cash-flow projections should be consistent with the proposed plan of reorganization.

The income approach is generally considered the best approach for determining the intrinsic value of a company, because it is based on cash flows inherent to a company and the riskiness of those cash flows.

# NOTE

1. If the equity component will include preferred stock, the formula is as follows:

$$\text{WACC} = K_e \times \frac{E}{EV} + K_d \times (1 - T) \times \frac{D}{EV} + K_p \times \frac{P}{EV}$$

$K_e$ = cost of common equity financing
$E/EV$ = market value of common equity to enterprise value
$K_d$ = cost of debt financing
$D/EV$ = market value of debt to enterprise value
$T$ = marginal tax rate
$(1-T)$ = interest tax shield
$K_p$ = cost of preferred equity financing
$P/EV$ = market value of preferred equity to enterprise value

# CHAPTER 5

# Market Approach

The premise of the market approach is that the value of a company can be determined by comparing the subject company to the values assigned by the current market for similar companies or the prices paid in the past for similar companies. It is a *relative* valuation approach that assesses a company's value by calculating multiples of the trading value of similar companies or the price paid in transactions for similar companies and applies those multiples to the corresponding financial metric of the subject company, to derive its value.

The term *trading* or transaction multiple associated with this approach is a financial ratio of value to an operating or financial metric, such as revenue, EBITDA, EBIT, or net income.

There are two generally accepted core methods to value a company under the market approach: the guideline company method, and the comparable transaction method.

## GUIDELINE COMPANY METHOD

The premise of the guideline company method is that the equity of companies with similar operational and financial characteristics should trade in the public markets at similar market multiples.

This method estimates the value of a company by analyzing the common stock prices of comparable publicly traded companies and applies the results of that analysis to the financial information of the company being valued.

Once a peer group is identified, market multiples are derived from their financial metrics and those multiples are then applied to the subject company's selected financial metrics to establish a relative value. For example, to calculate the enterprise value of a company, the *enterprise value to EBITDA ratio* of the peer group would be applied to the EBITDA of the subject company.

Because privately held companies do not trade in the public stock markets, there is limited financial information readily available to assess their value on a regular basis. For this reason, this method relies on publicly traded companies, not privately held ones.

The following are some strengths and weaknesses of the guideline company method:

## Strengths

- It is based on common stock prices, which are readily observable in the public stock markets and reflective of the assessment of large numbers of buyers and sellers. Common stock prices are generally considered the leading valuation indicator, assuming efficient markets.
- It provides an objective indication of value that relies on the public markets, and the value placed on comparable companies by the public markets, to weigh industry trends, growth prospects, risk factors, profitability expectations, and anticipated future performance.

## Weaknesses

- It may be difficult to develop a comparable peer group that resembles the subject company due to size constraints, breadth of product line, geography, and so on.
- It assumes that common stock prices correctly reflect the value of individual stocks. If the markets in a particular sector are inefficient, the common stock prices may be substantially over- or undervalued.
- It focuses on market conditions, industry trends, and growth prospects as of the valuation date and may not take into account longer-term issues.
- Company-specific issues may limit the comparability and the usefulness of the valuation data.

While some courts have criticized use of the guideline company method, it is still a regularly used methodology.

An analysis of comparable publicly traded companies involves three broad steps:

1. Identifying a potential peer group
2. Calculating selected market multiples
3. Selecting and applying the market multiples to the corresponding financial metric of the subject company.

## Step 1: Identifying a Potential Peer Group

The guideline company method is a comparison-based, relative valuation method. Therefore, the process begins with a thorough analysis of the subject company's operational and financial characteristics, in order to identify potentially comparable publicly traded companies (a potential peer group).

The following illustrates examples of operational and financial characteristics to consider in identifying a potential peer group:

### Operational Characteristics

- Industry
- Lines of business (products/services)
- Competitive set
- Target market, customer base
- Distribution channels
- Competitive position (leader, follower)
- Diversity (geographic, product mix)
- Seasonality/cyclicality

### Financial Characteristics

- Size (market value, revenues)
- Profitability/margins
- Growth prospects
- Capital structure (leverage)
- Cost structure
- Liquidity constraints
- Financial condition
- Shareholder base

The characteristics listed may appear objective; however, the process of including or excluding a specific company in the peer group can be very subjective. The ideal comparable publicly traded company would be a pure play (i.e., a company that operates only in one line of business) whose business line resembles that of the subject company. In many cases, a pure play will not exist; in such an event, it is important to select companies that are as analogous as possible to the subject company.

Potential comparable publicly traded companies can be identified using sources such as the following:

- Industry classification systems such as North American Industry Classification System (NAICS) and Standard Industrial Classification (SIC) codes

- Press releases and industry and trade journals
- Public filings, including Form 10-K (competition section), fairness opinions (found in merger proxy statements or Form S-4), proxy statements, IPO prospectus
- Company, industry, or sector research reports, including equity research reports, Standard & Poor's Industry Surveys, Value Line Industry Reports, Bloomberg, and so forth

After a potential peer group has been identified, the financials of each company within the group are normalized as discussed in Chapter 3. These normalized financials are used to calculate market multiples.

## Step 2: Calculating Market Multiples

After selecting a potential peer group, market values are calculated for each company within the group, which in turn are used to calculate enterprise values. Then the enterprise and market values are used to calculate industry-relevant market multiples for each company within this group. The market value and enterprise value formulas are as follows:

$$\text{Market Value} = \text{Stock Price} \times \text{Shares Outstanding}$$
$$\text{Enterprise Value} = \text{Market Value} + \text{Total Debt} - \text{Excess Cash}$$

(assuming no preferred stock, minority interest or equity investments)

Once market and enterprise values are calculated for each of the companies, multiples can be calculated. Multiples can be classified in one of two categories: enterprise value multiples and market value multiples. Enterprise value multiples apply to all debt and equity holders and are based on financial statement metrics prior to deducting interest expense, preferred dividends, equity investments, and minority interest expense. Common enterprise value multiples include:

- Enterprise Value/EBITDA
- Enterprise Value/EBIT
- Enterprise Value/Revenue

Market value multiples apply exclusively to equity holders, and not to other forms of capital holders. These are based on financial statement metrics after deducting interest expense, preferred dividends, equity investments, and minority interest expense. A common market value multiple is:

$$\text{Market Value}/\text{Net Income}$$

In financially distressed situations, enterprise value multiples are generally more applicable than market value multiples. Since enterprise value multiples are calculated prior to interest payments, they are not impacted by capital structure, and, therefore, they facilitate a better comparison across companies with varying degrees of leverage. Each of these enterprise and market multiples are discussed in additional detail in the following section.

**Enterprise Value/EBITDA Multiple**   Earnings before interest, taxes, depreciation, and amortization (EBITDA) is an indicator of a company's operating performance. It eliminates the effect of financing and accounting decisions, capital expenditures (fixed assets), and associated noncash (depreciation and amortization) expenses, providing a comparison of profitability between companies and industries utilizing varying accounting methodologies.

Although EBITDA is a popular measure of a company's financial performance, it is a non-GAAP term. As previously discussed, EBITDA is not always an appropriate metric proxy for cashflow in capital-intensive industries because it does not consider a company's relatively high level of required capital investment.

EBITDA does, however, exclude a company's interest expense, facilitating an apples-to-apples comparison between companies and industries with varying degrees of financial leverage. Additionally, it excludes the effect of taxes, which may fluctuate depending on a company's accounting methodology. Because EBITDA is calculated prior to interest payments, it represents funds available to both debt and equity holders, and, therefore, it is considered a reasonable metric for enterprise value calculations.

**Enterprise Value/EBIT Multiple**   EBIT (earnings before interest and taxes) is also an indicator of a company's operating performance. EBIT eliminates the effect of financing decisions but includes the effects of accounting decisions.

Because EBIT includes depreciation and amortization expenses (resulting from capital investments and acquisitions), it is more relevant than EBITDA for capital-intensive industries.

Financing decisions determine a company's capital structure and influence a company's interest expense. The interest expense affects taxable income and a company's tax expense, which together determine its net income. EBIT separates operating activities from financing activities. For example, companies with similar operating characteristics may be financed differently. Because EBIT is calculated before interest payments, it is available to all capital holders, both debt and equity holders, and, therefore, it is considered a metric for enterprise value.

**Enterprise Value/Revenue Multiple**   Revenue multiples are also used in some cases to determine value. For certain industries and unprofitable or distressed companies, where there are low or negative cash flows, it may be useful to rely on these multiples.

One of the limitations of a revenue multiple is that a distressed company may generate high levels of revenue but have little or no profitability, implying a high value despite this lack of corresponding profitability.

**Market Value/Net Income Multiple**   Since the net income of a company is calculated after payments to debt holders, it is the residual amount available to equity holders. The price-to-earnings ratio is generally equal to the net income multiple, as follows:

$$\frac{\text{Market Value}}{\text{Net Income}} \div \frac{\text{Shares Outstanding}}{\text{Shares Outstanding}} = \frac{\text{Price per Share}}{\text{Earnings per Share}} = \text{PE ratio}$$

This multiple does not neutralize accounting decisions or debt/equity capitalization decisions as previously discussed. Another common market multiple is market value to revenue.

**Rules of Thumb**   In certain industries, rules of thumb may provide guidance about the indication of value based on multiples of a particular benchmark. Exhibit 5.1 illustrates examples of industry benchmarks.

Although most rules of thumbs are developed from actual valuations and may be helpful, they are a rough starting point and should not be relied on exclusively, nor should they replace other valuation methods that are applicable to the business being valued.

**Latest Twelve Months**   In most cases, the valuation date does not fall conveniently on a date that a company reports its financial results for the full

**EXHIBIT 5.1**   Examples of Industry Benchmarks

| Industry | Metric |
| --- | --- |
| Nursing Homes | Number Of Beds |
| Natural resources | Quantity of reserves |
| Telecommunications | Assets or subscriber base |
| Cable television | Subscribers |
| Financial institutions | Book value |
| Internet web site | Page views or number of subscribers |

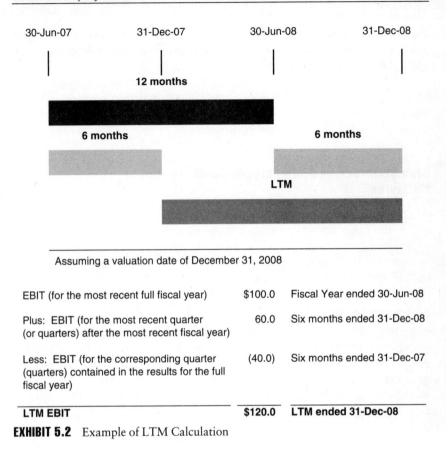

| 30-Jun-07 | 31-Dec-07 | 30-Jun-08 | 31-Dec-08 |
|---|---|---|---|

**12 months**

**6 months**      **6 months**

**LTM**

Assuming a valuation date of December 31, 2008

| EBIT (for the most recent full fiscal year) | $100.0 | Fiscal Year ended 30-Jun-08 |
|---|---|---|
| Plus:  EBIT (for the most recent quarter (or quarters) after the most recent fiscal year) | 60.0 | Six months ended 31-Dec-08 |
| Less:  EBIT (for the corresponding quarter (quarters) contained in the results for the full fiscal year) | (40.0) | Six months ended 31-Dec-07 |
| **LTM EBIT** | **$120.0** | **LTM ended 31-Dec-08** |

**EXHIBIT 5.2**   Example of LTM Calculation

fiscal year. In order to compare companies over a similar historical time period, valuation analysts sometimes use latest-twelve-months (LTM) or trailing-twelve-months (TTM) figures prior to the valuation date.

In the example shown in Exhibit 5.2, the valuation date is December 31, 2008. If the valuation analyst simply used the latest fiscal year EBIT of $100 for the fiscal year ending June 30, 2008 as opposed to LTM EBIT of $120 as the basis of the valuation, the results would be very different. The use of LTM allows a comparison between peer companies with varying fiscal year ends, and it takes seasonality into consideration.

In this example, LTM is calculated by starting with the reported financial results from the most recent fiscal year (in this case, FYE June 30, 2008), adding the reported financial results from the most recent quarter (or quarters, as applicable—in this example, Q1 and Q2 of FYE June 30,

2009), and then subtracting financial results of the same quarter (or quarters) included in the results for the prior full fiscal year (in this example, Q1 and Q2 of FYE June 30, 2008).

Although theoretically correct, the LTM calculation can be time consuming and complex. In some cases, the LTM calculation may not enhance the quality of the valuation if the company's financial results have not varied significantly over the period in question.

## Step 3: Selecting and Applying the Market Multiples

After the market multiples are calculated for each company within the group, the valuation analyst must analyze each peer group multiple and then apply the selected multiples to the subject company. As part of this analysis, outliers that trade at a significant premium or discount to the group may be excluded when selecting multiples to apply to the subject company.

**Analyzing Multiples**   Analyzing multiples of the peer group companies is a subjective process, since multiples generally trade at a premium or discount to one another based on a number of factors, including size, risk, and growth prospects. To understand why a company trades at a premium or a discount to its peers, the peer group should be compared and analyzed across all representative levels of financial performance. This may be facilitated by preparing a performance analysis as shown in Exhibit 5.3. Some companies may trade more in line than others, making them more relevant to the analysis.

Generally, a higher multiple indicates a higher value attributed to future earnings (as measured by EDITDA, EBIT, or net income); in other words, the higher the multiple, the more investors are willing to pay (or were willing to pay) for a company. All things being equal, high-growth companies typically have higher multiples, whereas lower multiples are usually attributed to mature, slow growth, or negative growth companies.

Factors that influence whether a company trades at a premium or a discount to the peer group include:

Size: Companies with higher market share or sector dominance generally trade at a higher multiple to companies with lower market share or sector dominance. Companies that are significantly larger or smaller relative to the subject company may not be comparable because larger companies generally have greater economies of scale (cost savings), which provide higher operating margins and profitability (EBITDA, EBIT, net income).

**Growth:** Companies with higher growth prospects generally trade at a premium to companies with lower growth prospects. High growth prospects generally occur in new industries or from the development of new products or services.

**Operating Performance:** Companies with greater operating performance or margins generally trade at a premium to companies with lower operating performance or margins because they reflect efficient use of capital.

**Financial Risk:** Companies with lower financial risk (leverage) generally trade at a premium to companies with higher financial risk. Higher debt levels increase the risk to equity holders because of the pressures of higher interest payments and covenant restrictions.

Exhibit 5.3 illustrates an example of a performance analysis used to analyze guideline companies.

Exhibit 5.4 shows that as of the valuation date selected, publicly traded companies within the newspaper and media industry traded within a broad range, 4.5–7.8 times LTM EBITDA. There were, however, two major outliers: McClatchy and Gannett. McClatchy was trading at 4.5 times, had low estimated EPS growth of 5.0 percent, and as a pure-play publisher was heavily exposed to the deteriorating fundamentals of the newspaper industry. Gannett was trading at 4.7 times, also had low estimated EPS growth of 3.3 percent, and lacked any near-term catalysts. Although both newspapers had the strongest margins in the peer group (see Exhibit 5.3), they still traded at a discount to peers because weak growth was a major obstacle facing the industry. Excluding these two comparables, the peer group traded within a narrower range, 7.3–7.8 times LTM EBITDA.

Instead of excluding certain companies in the peer group, the valuation analyst may decide to develop a weighted multiple. Figure 5.5 illustrates an example of a weighted multiple calculation. In this example, the valuation analyst applied various weightings to each multiple based on an analysis of each of the peer group companies.

These weightings are based on the valuation analyst's careful analysis of the peer group and each company's similarity to the subject company.

Pearson, Washington Post, New York Times, and Media General were all trading in line with one another. The New York Times margins were the lowest among its peers: its estimated EPS growth was only 5.6 percent, and the stock was trading at approximately 31.3 percent off from its 52-week high (see Exhibit 5.3). However, its stock had been fairly resilient, compared to its peer group, because it had one of the strongest franchises in the industry and owned digital media assets with upside potential.

**EXHIBIT 5.3** Guideline Company Method: Performance Analysis

*($ in millions)*

| Company | (1) LTM Ended | (2) % Off 52-Week High | LTM Margins | | | (6) Debt/Book Capital | (7) Total Debt/ EBITDA | (8) LTM EBITDA/ Int Exp |
| --- | --- | --- | --- | --- | --- | --- | --- | --- |
| | | | (3) EBITDA | (4) EBIT | (5) Net Inc. | | | |
| Pearson PLC | 12/31/07 | 26.8% | 21.1% | 13.2% | 7.5% | 29.3% | 1.8× | 5.9× |
| Gannett Company, Inc. | 03/30/08 | 50.3% | 27.6% | 23.8% | 14.2% | 30.5% | 2.0× | 8.6× |
| The Washington Post Company | 03/30/08 | 24.5% | 17.2% | 11.3% | 6.8% | 11.9% | 0.6× | 29.6× |
| The New York Times Company | 03/30/08 | 31.3% | 14.7% | 10.3% | 5.6% | 53.4% | 2.4× | 10.9× |
| The McClatchey Company | 03/30/08 | 68.6% | 24.9% | 18.1% | 6.7% | 83.3% | 3.8× | 2.9× |
| Media General, Inc. | 03/31/08 | 60.2% | 17.4% | 9.0% | 1.9% | 48.0% | 5.3× | 2.8× |
| High | | | 27.6% | 23.8% | 14.2% | 83.3% | 5.3× | 29.6× |
| Mean | | | 20.5% | 14.3% | 7.1% | 42.7% | 2.7× | 10.1× |
| Median | | | 19.3% | 12.3% | 6.8% | 39.3% | 2.2× | 7.3× |
| Low | | | 14.7% | 9.0% | 1.9% | 11.9% | 0.6× | 2.8× |
| **Subject Company** | | | 17.4% | 12.2% | 7.0% | 18.7% | 1.7× | 6.6× |

(1) LTM Ending = Year ended + Latest Period − (Latest Period − 1 Year).
(2) Percent off 52-week high = (1 − stock price)/52 high.
(3) LTM EBITDA margin = LTM EBITDA/LTM Revenue.
(4) LTM EBIT margin = LTM EBIT/LTM Revenue.
(5) LTM Net Income margin = LTM Net Income/LTM Revenue.
(6) Total Debt/Book Capital. Book Capital = Market Value + Book Value of Debt + Preferred stock + Minority Interest.

70

**EXHIBIT 5.4**  Guideline Company Method

*($ in millions, except per share data)*

| Company | (1) Stock Price | (2) Shares Outstanding | (3) Market Value | (4) Net Debt | (5) Enterprise Value | Enterprise Value | | | (10) Estimated EPS Growth | (11) PEG Ratio | (12) Dividend Yield |
|---|---|---|---|---|---|---|---|---|---|---|---|
| | | | | | | (7) LTM Revenue | (8) LTM EBITDA | (9) LTM EBIT | | | |
| Pearson PLC | $13.02 | 796,267 | $10,367 | $2,184 | $12,551 | 1.55× | 7.3× | 11.7× | 9.0% | 1.4× | 4.7% |
| Gannett Company, Inc. | 29.75 | 228,686 | 6,803 | 2,758 | 9,561 | 1.31× | 4.7× | 5.5× | 3.3% | 2.4× | 5.4% |
| The Washington Post | 668.50 | 9,540 | 6,377 | (681) | 5,696 | 1.34× | 7.8× | 11.8× | 10.0% | 2.0× | 1.3% |
| The New York Times Company | 18.47 | 143,777 | 2,656 | 809 | 3,465 | 1.10× | 7.5× | 10.7× | 5.6% | 3.7× | 5.0% |
| The McClatchey Company | 9.28 | 82,318 | 764 | 1,662 | 2,426 | 1.11× | 4.5× | 6.1× | 5.0% | 2.1× | 7.8% |
| Media General, Inc. | 15.10 | 22,862 | 345 | 802 | 1,147 | 1.31× | 7.5× | 14.6× | 16.0% | 1.0× | 6.1% |
| High | | | | | | 1.55× | 7.8× | 14.6× | 16.0% | 3.7× | 7.8% |
| Mean | | | | | | 1.29× | 6.6× | 10.1× | 8.2% | 2.1× | 5.1% |
| Median | | | | | | 1.31× | 7.4× | 11.2× | 7.3% | 2.1× | 5.2% |
| Low | | | | | | 1.10× | 4.5× | 5.5× | 3.3% | 1.0× | 1.3% |
| Subject Company's Results | | | | | | $643.9 | $112.2 | $78.6 | | | |
| Times: Selected Multiple | | | | | | 1.30× | 7.5× | 11.0× | | | |
| Equals: Indicated Enterprise Value | | | | | | $837.1 | $841.5 | $864.6 | | | |
| Weighting | | | | | | 20.0% | 50.0% | 30.0% | | | |
| Concluded Indicated Enterprise Value | | | | | | | | $847.6 | | | |

(1) Stock Price: represents the closing stock price as of the valuation date.

*(Continued)*

**EXHIBIT 5.4** (Continued)

(2) Shares Outstanding represent diluted shares outstanding. However, basic shares outstanding may be used as a simplifing assumption.

(3) Market Value = Stock Price × Shares Outstanding.

(4) Net Debt represents the market value of short-term debt (incl. current portion of long-term debt) + long-term debt + convertible debt + capitalized leases + preferred stock − excess cash.

(5) Enterprise Value = Market Value + Net Debt.

(7) Enterprise Value/LTM Revenue: represents last reported 12-month revenue calculated using SEC filings prior to the valuation date.

(8) Enterprise Value/LTM EBITDA: represents normalized last reported 12-month EBITDA calculated using SEC filings prior to the valuation date.

(9) Enterprise Value/LTM EBIT: represents normalized last 12-month EBIT calculated using SEC filings prior to the valuation date.

(10) Estimated EPS growth: represents estimates for 5-year EPS (earnings per share) CAGR (compound annual growth rate).

(11) PEG Ratio = (Price/FY1 earnings)/(Estimated EPS Growth × 100).

(12) Dividend yield = (last quarterly dividend × 4)/Stock Price.

**EXHIBIT 5.5** Example of Weighted Multiple Calculations

| Target Company Market Multiples | 4.5× | 4.7× | 7.3× | 7.5× | 7.5× | 7.8× |
|---|---|---|---|---|---|---|
| Weighting | 0.0% | 0.0% | 25.0% | 20.0% | 25.0% | 30.0% |
| **Concluded Market Multiple 7.5×** | | | | | | |

Based on the understanding of how each company within the peer group traded, the valuation analyst can compare the subject company to its peers. In this example, the subject's profitability (EBITDA and EBIT margins) and growth prospects are in line with its peers; however, its risk profile (debt/book capital, debt/EBITDA, and EBITDA/interest expense) is on the lower end of its peers. A further analysis shows the subject's profitability, risk profile, and growth prospects are most comparable to The Washington Post Company. Based on an understanding of the subject company and industry-relevant multiples, the valuation analyst subjectively concluded and weighed the market multiples as follows: 1.30 times LTM revenue multiple weighed at 20 percent, 7.5 times LTM EBITDA multiple weighed at 50 percent, and an 11.0 times LTM EBIT multiple weighed at 30 percent. The concluded indicated enterprise value for the subject company is $847.6 million, as illustrated in Exhibit 5.6.

## COMPARABLE TRANSACTION METHOD

The comparable transaction method is similar to the guideline company method in that multiples are used to determine the value of a company. However, the comparable transaction method uses transaction prices paid for comparable companies, instead of common stock prices, to calculate multiples (transaction multiples). Once a set of comparable transactions is identified, transaction multiples are applied to the same financial metrics of the subject company to establish a relative value.

**EXHIBIT 5.6** Concluded Indicated Enterprise Value

| ($ in millions) | | | |
|---|---|---|---|
| Subject Company's Results | $643.9 | $112.2 | $78.6 |
| Times: Selected Multiple | 1.30× | 7.5× | 11.0× |
| Equals: Indicated Enterprise Value | $837.1 | $841.5 | $864.6 |
| Weighting | 20.0% | 50.0% | 30.0% |
| **Concluded Indicated Enterprise Value** | | | **$847.6** |

The premise of the comparable transaction method is that companies within the same industry should sell in a *change-of-control* transaction (but not in a liquidation scenario) for similar relative values, as measured by a multiple of financial performance.

As with the guideline company method, it is important to note that data on transactions involving privately held companies and subsidiaries is limited, so the transaction list is generally derived from disclosed data on transactions involving publicly traded companies, although in some instances privately held companies may be used depending on the level of disclosure.

The following are some strengths and weaknesses of the comparable transaction method:

### Strengths

- It is easy to apply.
- It provides an objective comparison of companies acquired or sold within the subject company's industry.

### Weakness

- Developing a transaction list for companies that resemble the subject company can be challenging.
- If the markets are viewed as inefficient, the transactions may be substantially over- or undervalued.
- If significant synergies exist and the analyst is not aware of them, the selected multiple will be too high.
- Periods of low merger and acquisition activity may cause available comparable transaction data to be outdated, reducing their usefulness.
- Depending on the level of disclosure, it may be difficult to locate data on transactions.

Outdated transaction data may not be useful if there have been significant changes to the market. As one court observed:

> *The Court noted that using comparable transactions that occurred more than four years previous were "not useful in this matter since the experts agreed that the market had changed considerably since 2000."*
>
> ### *In re Exide Technologies*, 303 B.R. 48, 63 (D. Del. 2003)

The same three general steps used in the guideline company method are used in the analysis of transaction comparables. In place of common stock prices, prices paid in actual merger and acquisition transactions of similar companies are used.

An analysis of transactions involves three broad steps:

1. Identifying potential comparable transactions
2. Calculating transaction multiples
3. Selecting and applying transaction multiples to the subject company

## Step 1: Identifying Comparable Transactions

The comparable transaction method is a comparison-based, relative valuation method. Therefore, determining the subject company's value begins with identifying a group of comparable transactions (a transaction list) for the purchase of companies with similar operating and financial characteristics. As with comparable publicly traded companies, the process of identifying a transaction list can be subjective.

In addition to characteristics listed under the guideline company method, there are some other items to consider:

**Operational Characteristics**

- Economic conditions
- Industry-wide events (consolidation wave)
- Nature (hostile/contested/friendly transaction, single/multiple bidders)
- Buyer (strategic/financial)

**Financial Characteristics**

- Transaction size
- Consideration (cash, stock, combination)
- Profitability/margins

Similar to the guideline company method, the characteristics just listed may appear objective; however, the process of including or excluding a particular transaction in a comparable transaction list can be a very subjective process. Although exact transactions of similar companies may not exist, it is important to select transactions that are as analogous as possible to the subject company.

Potential comparable transactions can be identified using sources such as the following:

- Transaction search by industry or by NAICS (North American Industry Classification System) or SIC (Standard Industrial Classification) using a database such as Thomson Financial, Capital IQ, Dealogic, Mergerstat, Pratt Stats, or BizComps
- Newsletters and merger-and-acquisition journals

After a transaction list has been identified, the financials of each company within the transaction list are normalized as described in Chapter 3. These normalized financials are used to calculate transaction multiples.

## Step 2: Calculating Transaction Multiples

After selecting a transaction list, the ultimate transaction value for each comparable transaction is calculated by adding the net debt to the offer value or price received for the stock of the company. Then the transaction values are used to calculate industry-relevant transaction multiples for each transaction.

These transaction multiples are then analyzed and applied to the subject company to derive an indicated value as demonstrated in Exhibit 5.8.

## Step 3: Selecting and Applying Transaction Multiples

After the transaction multiples are calculated for each transaction within the transaction list, the valuation analyst must analyze each transaction multiple and then apply the selected multiples to the subject company. As part of this analysis, outliers that sold for significantly more or less than the group may be excluded when selecting multiples to apply to the subject company. Pricing differences may be caused by the control premium, the type of transaction, and the timing of the transaction.

**Analyzing Multiples**    Factors that influence whether a company receives a high or low price include:

Control Premium: A control premium is the premium an acquirer pays in excess of the market price in order to gain control of the target company. This premium may incorporate potential synergies (cost savings and revenue enhancements) that the acquirer expects to realize. It is the control premium that usually causes transaction multiples to be higher than the trading multiples derived from comparable publicly traded companies.

**Transaction Type:** Companies acquired in a merger of equals transaction and acquisitions involving a minority stake in another company generally are purchased at lower premiums.

**Timing:** Current economic and market conditions may vary drastically when comparing precedent transactions that occurred at different times. All other things being equal, the more recent the transaction the more comparable the transaction.

Using the calculated transaction multiples, the valuation analyst weighs the different indicated values derived from the various multiples to determine a single indicated value for the comparable transaction method.

Exhibit 5.7 illustrates an example of a margins and premiums paid analysis under the comparable transaction method.

Exhibit 5.8 shows that in the last three years, five selected transactions were announced and completed within the newspaper and media industry. These transactions were selected because they were acquisitions in which the target was similar to the subject company, which was a well-recognized publishing franchise, focused on newspapers. The transaction list shows that transaction values of the acquired companies fell within a broad range, 9.5–23.7 times LTM EBITDA. Although the transactions included were comparable on a strategic basis, the prices paid do not reflect the deteriorating operating conditions of the industry as of the valuation date and are likely too high. In addition, as Exhibit 5.8 illustrates, the premiums paid varied greatly.

Based on an understanding of how each company within the transaction group was acquired, the valuation analyst can compare the subject company to the transaction list. In this example, the subject's profitability (EBITDA, EBIT, net income margins) is below the profitability of the acquired companies in the transaction list, indicating that the subject company may be valued at a discount to the industry average. Using an understanding of the subject company and industry-relevant transaction multiples, the valuation analyst may either weight each of the various multiples to develop a weighted multiple calculation similar to Exhibit 5.5 or use professional judgment to develop the transaction multiple. In Exhibit 5.7, the valuation analyst subjectively concluded and weighed the transaction market multiples as follows: 1.40 times LTM revenue multiple weighed at 20.0 percent, and 8.0 times LTM EBITDA multiple weighed 80.0 percent. The concluded indicated transaction value for the subject company is $898.4 million, a 6.0 percent premium to the guideline company method.

**EXHIBIT 5.7**  Comparable Transaction Method: Margins and Premiums Paid Analysis

*($ in millions)*

| | (1) | (2) | (3) | (4) | (5) | (6) |
|---|---|---|---|---|---|---|
| | LTM Margins | | | | Premiums Paid | |
| Target/Acquirer | EBITDA | EBIT | Net Income | 1 Day Prior | 1 Week Prior | 1 Month Prior |
| Reuters Group PLC/The Thomson Corporation | 15.4% | 10.9% | 10.2% | 43.2% | 48.1% | 46.0% |
| Dow Jones & Company/News Corporation | 14.3% | 9.0% | 4.9% | 65.2% | 64.0% | 74.1% |
| Tribune Company/Sam Zell/ESOP | 23.5% | 19.2% | 9.3% | 5.9% | 9.3% | 13.1% |
| Knight-Ridder, Inc./McClatchy Co. | 20.8% | 17.5% | 9.3% | 3.5% | 7.8% | 5.8% |
| Pulitzer Inc./Lee Enterprises Inc. | 24.3% | 19.8% | 10.3% | 1.7% | (2.5%) | (1.3%) |
| High | 24.3% | 19.8% | 10.3% | 65.2% | 64.0% | 74.1% |
| Mean | 19.7% | 15.3% | 8.8% | 23.9% | 25.3% | 27.5% |
| Median | 20.8% | 17.5% | 9.3% | 5.9% | 9.3% | 13.1% |
| Low | 14.3% | 9.0% | 4.9% | 1.7% | (2.5%) | (1.3%) |
| **Subject Company's Results** | 17.4% | 12.2% | 7.0% | | | |

(1) LTM EBITDA margin = LTM EBITDA/LTM Revenue.
(2) LTM EBIT margin = LTM EBIT/LTM Revenue.
(3) LTM Net Income margin = LTM Net Income/LTM Revenue.
(4) Represents the percentage over the Offer Price and Target's Stock Price one day prior to Announcement Date.
(5) Represents the percentage over the Offer Price and Target's Stock Price one week prior to Announcement Date.
(6) Represents the percentage over the Offer Price and Target's Stock Price one month prior to Announcement Date.

**EXHIBIT 5.8**  Comparable Transaction Method

*($ in millions, except per-share data)*

| | (1) | (2) | (3) | (4) | (5) | (6) | (7) | (8) | (9) | | (10) | (11) | (12) |
|---|---|---|---|---|---|---|---|---|---|---|---|---|---|
| | | | | | | | | Pre-Synergies | | | | | Transaction Value/ |
| | | | | | | | | Transaction Value/ | | LTM | | Synergies | |
| Target/ Acquiror | Deal Announced | Offer Price | Shares Outstanding | Option Proceeds | Offer Value | Net Debt | Tranaction Value | LTM Revenue | LTM EBITDA | EBITDA Margin | Announced Synergies | as % of Revenues | Adjusted EBITDA |
| Reuters Group PLC/The Thomson Corporation | 05/04/07 | $14.00 | 1,319,932 | ($427.4) | $18,051.6 | $586.5 | $18,638.1 | 3.66× | 23.7× | 15.4% | $500.0 | 9.8% | 14.5× |
| Dow Jones & Company/News Corporation | 05/01/07 | 60.00 | 92,143 | (421.6) | 5,107.0 | 409.4 | 5,516.4 | 2.96× | 20.7× | 14.3% | 50.0 | 2.7% | 17.5× |
| Tribune Company/Sam Zell/ESOP | 04/02/07 | 34.00 | 248,801 | (134.9) | 8,324.3 | 4,774.1 | 13,098.4 | 2.40× | 10.2× | 23.5% | NA | NA | NA |
| Knight-Ridder, Inc./McClatchy Co. | 03/12/06 | 67.20 | 74,466 | (435.1) | 4,569.0 | 1,475.9 | 6,044.9 | 1.97× | 9.5× | 20.8% | 60.0 | 2.0% | 8.7× |
| Pulitzer Inc./Lee Enterprises Inc. | 01/30/05 | 64.00 | 24,338 | (113.1) | 1,444.5 | 16.0 | 1,460.5 | 3.29× | 13.5× | 24.3% | 7.0 | 1.6% | 12.7× |
| | | | | | | | High | 3.66× | 23.7× | 24.3% | | 9.8% | 17.5× |
| | | | | | | | Mean | 2.86× | 15.5× | 19.7% | | 4.0% | 13.4× |
| | | | | | | | Median | 2.96× | 13.5× | 20.8% | | 2.4% | 13.6× |
| | | | | | | | Low | 1.97× | 9.5× | 14.3% | | 1.6% | 8.7× |

(Continued)

# EXHIBIT 5.8  (Continued)

*($ in millions, except per-share data)*

| Target/ Acquiror | (1) Deal Announced | (2) Offer Price | (3) Shares Outstanding | (4) Option Proceeds | (5) Offer Value | (6) Net Debt | (7) Tranaction Value | (8) Pre-Synergies Transaction Value/ LTM Revenue | (9) LTM EBITDA | LTM EBITDA Margin | (10) Announced Synergies | (11) Synergies as % of Revenues | (12) Transaction Value/ Adjusted EBITDA |
|---|---|---|---|---|---|---|---|---|---|---|---|---|---|
| **Subject Company's Results** | | | | | | | | $643.9 | $112.2 | | | | |
| Times: Selected Multiple | | | | | | | | 1.40× | 8.0× | | | | |
| Equals: Indicated Enterprise Value | | | | | | | | $901.5 | $897.6 | | | | |
| Weighting | | | | | | | | 20.0% | 80.0% | | | | |
| **Concluded Indicated Enterprise Value** | | | | | | | | $898.4 | | | | | |

(1) Deal Announced: Date transaction was publicly announced.

(2) Offer Price: represents the price paid per share for the equity of the Target.

(3) Shares outstanding = basic shares outstanding + "in-the-money" options + shares from "in-the-money" convertible securities. However, basic shares outstanding may be used as a simplifing assumption.

(4) Option proceeds.

(5) Offer Value = (Total Shares Outstanding × Offer Price Share) − Option Proceeds. However, offer price × shares outstanding may be used as a simplifing assumption. Also called Market Value.

(6) Net Debt = Market value of Target's short-term debt (including current portion of long-term debt) + long-term debt + convertible debt + capitalized leases + preferred stock − excess cash.

(7) Transaction Value = Offer Value + Net Debt. Also called Enterprise Value.

(8) Transaction Value/LTM Revenue.

(9) Transaction Value/LTM EBITDA.

(10) Announced Synergies: Synergies expected to be realized from the transaction.

(11) Synergies as a % of Target Revenues.

(12) Adjusted EBITDA = Target's LTM EBITDA + announced annual synergies.

## CONCLUSION

The market approach includes the guideline company method and the comparable transaction method. These methods are similar in that multiples are derived from public market trading values or publicly disclosed sales prices, and are applied to the corresponding financial metrics of the subject company to determine its value. The difference between the two methods is that the comparable transaction method uses transaction prices paid for comparable companies to calculate transaction multiples, which could include a premium for synergies and other strategic benefits, whereas the guideline company method uses common stock prices to calculate trading multiples (which shows the value of a minority, tradable interest, without consideration of the value of control).

# CHAPTER 6

# United States Bankruptcy Code

## INTRODUCTION TO THE STRUCTURE OF THE BANKRUPTCY CODE

Valuation professionals who provide valuations in connection with a bankruptcy case need to have a good background in bankruptcy law. This chapter is designed to introduce and explain key concepts of bankruptcy law that are frequently relevant to valuation practice. To be sure, the following discussion is simplified, and some nuances are ignored, in an effort to communicate the key principles. When the expert is hired to give an opinion in a bankruptcy case, it is critical that the expert take enough time to understand the full context of his or her work and the legal principles applicable to it.

The United States Bankruptcy Code is organized into chapters, but most people are generally aware of and focus on only Chapter 7 (liquidations) and Chapter 11 (reorganizations). There are quite a few more, and Chapters 1, 3, and 5 contain provisions that are generally applicable to the other chapters.

Chapter 1 of the Bankruptcy Code contains general provisions, including definitions; a section that describes the powers (and certain limitations) of the bankruptcy court (§ 105); and the rules governing which entities can or cannot file for bankruptcy (§ 109).

Chapter 3 of the Bankruptcy Code covers various aspects of case administration, including how a voluntary bankruptcy case (§ 301) and an involuntary bankruptcy case (§ 303) are commenced; and requiring the debtor to attend a meeting of creditors (§ 341). Chapter 3 also contains the following key provisions that implicate valuations and are discussed later: § 361, regarding adequate protection; § 362, regarding the automatic stay and the basis for relief from the automatic stay; and § 363, governing a debtor's use, sale, or lease of property. Rules governing a debtor's ability to borrow money are found at § 364.

Chapter 5 of the Bankruptcy Code, entitled "Creditors, the Debtor, and the Estate," contains a wide variety of provisions relating to the filing (§ 501) and allowance (§ 502) of prepetition claims and postpetition administrative expenses (§ 503). It also includes the "avoiding powers," that is, the ability of the trustee or debtor in possession to avoid (and recover damages for) preferential transfers (§ 547) and fraudulent transfers (§ 548).

Chapter 7 of the Bankruptcy Code, discussed briefly later, contains the provisions applicable only to a liquidation of a debtor under Chapter 7.

Chapter 11 of the Bankruptcy Code, discussed in more detail below, contains the provisions applicable only to a reorganization (or attempted reorganization) of a debtor under Chapter 11. Chapter 11 is the principal vehicle for reorganizing commercial entities such as corporations, limited liability companies, and partnerships. Although individuals are eligible to file Chapter 11 cases, the most common use of Chapter 11 is by companies in operational or financial distress who need the protections of Chapter 11 so that they can restructure their debt obligations and have a chance to fix operational issues.

Chapter 9 of the Bankruptcy Code is applicable only to bankruptcy filings by insolvent political subdivisions of a state. Chapter 12 applies only to family farmers and family fisherman with regular income. Chapter 13 applies only to individuals with regular income who meet certain debt limits. Chapter 15 contains rules applicable to cross-border cases. Chapters 9, 12, 13, and 15 of the Bankruptcy Code will not be discussed further in this book.

## COMMENCEMENT OF A BANKRUPTCY CASE AND FILING OF SCHEDULES

A voluntary bankruptcy case is commenced by the filing with the bankruptcy court of a petition. Among other things, the petition indicates whether the company filing the petition (the debtor) is filing under Chapter 7 or Chapter 11 (or one of the other chapters already mentioned). After the bankruptcy petition has been filed, the company that filed for bankruptcy is typically referred to as the *debtor* and, unless a trustee is appointed by the court to take over the business, the *debtor in possession*. Shortly following the bankruptcy filing, the debtor is required to file its schedules of assets and debts and its statement of financial affairs (sometimes referred to as the *SOFA*). Information contained in the schedules and SOFA can be of significant use to any expert in connection with valuation testimony.

## CHAPTER 7 OF THE BANKRUPTCY CODE

A "person" (which includes individuals, partnerships, and corporations (which in turn includes limited liability corporations, or LLCs) but does not include a "governmental unit") who "resides or has a domicile, a place of business, or property in the United States" may be a debtor under Chapter 7, only if such "person" is not a railroad, a domestic or foreign insurance company, bank, savings and loan association, or other similar organization. Upon the filing of a Chapter 7 case, the Office of the United States Trustee appoints an initial trustee, who will continue to serve as trustee unless a different trustee is chosen by the creditors. The trustee collects and sells the debtor's assets. Secured creditors that are owed more money than their collateral is worth usually get the right to foreclose by seeking relief from the automatic stay (which, if not terminated, would prevent a foreclosure). The trustee investigates and asserts claims to recover preferences and fraudulent conveyances. After the liquidation process is complete, the trustee distributes the funds collected, net of the fees and costs, to creditors in accordance with the priorities set forth in the Bankruptcy Code.

## CHAPTER 11 OF THE BANKRUPTCY CODE

### Overview

Only a "person" that can be a debtor under Chapter 7 (but not stockbrokers or commodity brokers), a railroad, an uninsured state member bank, or certain corporations that operate certain multilateral clearing organizations, may be debtors under Chapter 11 of the Bankruptcy Code. More simply stated, most commercial ventures are eligible to file for reorganization under Chapter 11 of the Bankruptcy Code.

Chapter 11 is designed to preserve the debtor's going-concern value while it reorganizes its debts. There is no requirement that the entity be insolvent in order to seek voluntary relief under Chapter 11 of the Bankruptcy Code. Ordinarily, the debtor remains in possession of its property (as the "debtor in possession") and operates its business while it formulates a plan of reorganization (or liquidation). Under certain circumstances, a trustee may be appointed to take over management and operation of the debtor's business, and a Chapter 11 case can be converted to a Chapter 7 case. A debtor in possession has all of the important powers of a trustee, such as avoiding powers, discussed later. Usually, when the Bankruptcy Code uses the word *trustee* it also refers to the debtor in possession. The bankruptcy judge can also dismiss a Chapter 11 case.

The ultimate goal of a Chapter 11 case is the confirmation of a Chapter 11 plan (described later). If confirmed, the plan is a binding contract (with the binding force of a final judgment of the bankruptcy court) among the debtor, its creditors, and equity holders. The confirmed plan (and in larger cases, together with ancillary agreements such as the credit agreements put in place in connection with the exit financing) functions as a "super" credit agreement, which, among other things, restructures a company's debts.

An increasingly common path taken in Chapter 11 cases is the sale of all, or substantially all, of the debtor's assets by the use of Section 363 of the Bankruptcy Code (a § 363 sale). A § 363 sale is typically used in situations in which the company does not have sufficient liquidity to continue to absorb losses over the time period necessary to confirm a plan. After a § 363 sale, the case is sometimes converted to a Chapter 7 case, and the trustee collects any preferences or fraudulent transfers, or those claims (together with miscellaneous assets that were not part of the § 363 sale), are transferred to a liquidating trust for prosecution (or later sale) for the benefit of the creditors.

## The Debtor in Possession

The debtor generally remains in possession of its assets and continues to manage the business. The debtor is now referred to as a debtor in possession (DIP) by the Bankruptcy Code (but colloquially is usually still referred to as the "debtor") unless a trustee is appointed and takes over control and management of the debtor's property. The board of directors of the debtor acts as a fiduciary and is responsible for maximizing the value of "the estate" (all of the assets of the debtor). Directors of a debtor continue to owe a duty of loyalty, care, and good faith to the corporation and its shareholders, but when a corporation becomes insolvent, under the laws of most states, the directors owe those duties to creditors, too. Although it is beyond the scope of this book, in such a case, creditors (and not just shareholders) have standing to assert breach of fiduciary duty claims on the company's behalf.

## Use, Sale, or Lease of Property

While in bankruptcy, the debtor has the power to operate the business, sell property or businesses, file lawsuits, employ professionals, collect debt, and so forth. The debtor may engage in transactions in the ordinary course of business without court approval. Advance notice to creditors, and sometimes a court hearing and court approval, is required for transactions outside the ordinary course of business. Any use, sale, or lease of property outside ordinary course by a Chapter 11 debtor requires notice to creditors. Upon a creditor's filing of a proper objection and request for a hearing, the court will determine whether to permit a proposed sale or transaction. Sales of all or substantially all assets prior to confirmation of a plan are usually allowed, although some courts have restrictive views on such a transaction; in particular transactions that are "creeping plans of reorganization" will usually not be approved. These "363 sales" have been an increasingly popular tool because the assets are quickly sold to the highest bidder and some of the costs of a long, drawn-out reorganization case are avoided.

## Use of Cash Collateral

The debtor must obtain court approval (or secured creditor consent) to use cash collateral (cash or cash equivalents in which a party has a secured interest). Absent consent, the court can authorize the use of the cash collateral only if the debtor persuades the court it can provide adequate protection to the secured creditor. The existence of an equity cushion can constitute adequate protection. If a secured creditor is willing to work with the debtor while the debtor attempts to reorganize, the secured creditor often will agree to DIP financing, rather than merely consent to the debtor's use of cash collateral.

## Automatic Stay and Relief from the Automatic Stay

One of the fundamental protections of the Bankruptcy Code is the automatic stay. The filing of a bankruptcy petition (including a Chapter 7 or Chapter 11 case), *operates as a stay*, applicable to all entities, of (among other things)

1. The commencement or continuation of a judicial, administrative, or other action against the debtor that was or could have been commenced before the commencement of the bankruptcy case, or to recover a claim against the debtor that arose before the commencement of the bankruptcy case
2. The enforcement, against the debtor or against property of the estate, of a judgment obtained before the commencement of the bankruptcy case
3. Any act to obtain possession of property of the estate or of property from the estate or to exercise control over property of the estate
4. Any act to create, perfect, or enforce any lien against property of the estate
5. Any act to create, perfect, or enforce against property of the debtor any lien to the extent that such lien secures a claim that arose before the commencement of the bankruptcy case

6. Any act to collect, assess, or recover a claim against the debtor that arose before the commencement of the bankruptcy case
7. The setoff of any debt owing to the debtor that arose before the commencement of the bankruptcy case against any claim against the debtor

Of particular interest to a debtor and its creditors is the simple fact that the automatic stay stops the usual collection efforts (demand letters, lawsuits, and foreclosure proceedings). There are numerous exceptions to the scope of the automatic stay, but where there is no applicable exception, as a general rule, the court is supposed to give a creditor relief from the stay (by terminating, modifying, or conditioning the stay) either (1) for cause, which is defined to include the lack of adequate protection of an interest in property; or (2) with respect to a stay of an act against property if (a) the debtor does not have an equity in such property and (b) such property is not necessary to an effective reorganization. Under either prong, a valuation is or may be needed.

## Adequate Protection for a Secured Creditor

When a secured creditor is entitled to adequate protection, such adequate protection may be provided by

1. Requiring the trustee (which term, when used in the Bankruptcy Code, includes the debtor in possession) to make cash payments to such entity, to the extent that the automatic stay, the use, sale, or lease of the property, or any grant of a lien to secure a loan, results in a decrease in the value of such creditor's interest in such property
2. Providing to such creditor an additional or replacement lien to the extent that such stay, use, sale, lease, or grant results in a decrease in the value of such entity's interest in such property
3. Granting such other relief as will result in the realization by such creditor of the "indubitable equivalent" of such creditor's interest in such property

Concepts of value, and decrease in value, are key to any negotiation or court fight over adequate protection.

## DIP Financing

A debtor's ability to borrow is altered in Chapter 11. Without any court authorization, a debtor can incur ordinary course of business trade debt that will be allowed as an administrative expense in the bankruptcy case. Administrative expenses (postbankruptcy obligations) are generally paid as they come due in the ordinary course of business during the pendency of the case (assuming the debtor has sufficient operating funds).

Unsecured debt that is incurred outside the ordinary course of business must be authorized by the court. If the debtor is unable to obtain unsecured credit (which is typically the case), the court may authorize debt secured by the debtor's unencumbered property, or secured by a junior lien on encumbered property, or by an administrative priority claim, which is given a priority over all other administrative expenses.

The court can authorize the obtaining of credit secured by a senior or equal lien on encumbered property of the estate only if (1) the debtor is unable to obtain credit otherwise and (2) there is adequate protection of the interest of the holder of the lien on the property on which such senior or equal lien is proposed to be granted. This is usually referred to as *DIP financing*. In addition to the usual covenants and conditions found in a credit agreement, a DIP lender typically requires a series of extra covenants and conditions to financing that will be utilized to maintain leverage and control over the case. For example, the DIP lender will usually establish tight time deadlines to require the debtor to move the process along and to allow the lender to foreclose if a plan or sale has not been achieved within a specified period of time.

## Official Committee of Unsecured Creditors

In most bankruptcy cases, a creditors' committee is appointed. The office of the U.S. Trustee (an arm of the Department of Justice) will appoint (usually) the seven largest unsecured creditors eligible and willing to serve. The creditors' committee may (among other things) (1) consult with the debtor in possession concerning the administration of the case; (2) investigate the acts, conduct, assets, liabilities, and financial condition of the debtor, the operation of the debtor's business and the desirability of the continuance of such business, and any other matter relevant to the case or to the formulation of a plan; (3) participate in the formulation of a plan, and advise those represented by such committee of such committee's determinations as to any plan formulated; and (4) request the appointment of a trustee or examiner.

## Trustee

Although the general rule is that a debtor remains in possession, the court is supposed to order the appointment of a trustee (1) for cause (which is defined to include fraud, dishonesty, incompetence, or gross mismanagement of the affairs of the debtor by current management, either before or after the commencement of the case); or (2) if such appointment is in the interests of creditors, any equity security holders, and other interests of the estate, without regard to the number of holders of securities of the debtor or the amount of assets or liabilities of the debtor.

## Examiner

If a trustee has not been appointed, the bankruptcy court may order the appointment of an examiner for the purpose of investigating the debtor and the debtor's affairs as may be appropriate, including an investigation of any allegations of fraud, dishonesty, incompetence, misconduct, mismanagement, or irregularity in the management of the debtor by current or former management.

## Plan of Reorganization—Exclusivity

A debtor has an exclusive period to file a plan of reorganization—120 days after the bankruptcy filing—and then to seek acceptances of that plan—within 60 days. Those exclusive periods are of significant negotiating benefit to the debtor because they require the various constituencies to negotiate with and through the debtor with respect to a particular plan or other course of action. The exclusive period may be extended by the court for cause, and the courts will usually grant extensions, at least for the first few months of the case. However, exclusivity is limited to an extension for 18 months to file a plan and 20 months to seek acceptance of the claim. The bankruptcy court may terminate exclusivity for cause. The appointment of Chapter 11 trustee automatically terminates exclusivity.

## Plan of Reorganization—Contents

A plan of reorganization *must* (among other things):

1. Designate classes of claims.
2. Specify any class of claims or interests that is not impaired under the plan.
3. Specify the treatment of any class of claims or interests that is impaired under the plan.
4. Provide the same treatment for each claim or interest of a particular class, unless the holder of a particular claim or interest agrees to a less favorable treatment of such particular claim or interest.
5. Provide adequate means for the plan's implementation, such as:
   a. Retention by the debtor of all or any part of the property of the estate
   b. Transfer of all or any part of the property of the estate to one or more entities, whether organized before or after the confirmation of such plan

    c. Merger or consolidation of the debtor with one or more persons

    d. Sale of all or any part of the property of the estate, either subject to or free of any lien, or the distribution of all or any part of the property of the estate among those having an interest in such property of the estate

    e. Satisfaction or modification of any lien

    f. Cancellation or modification of any indenture or similar instrument

    g. Curing or waiving of any default

    h. Extension of a maturity date or a change in an interest rate or other term of outstanding securities

    i. Amendment of the debtor's charter

    j. Issuance of securities

A plan of reorganization *may*:

1. Impair or leave unimpaired any class of claims, secured or unsecured, or of interests.
2. Provide for the assumption, rejection, or assignment of any executory contract or unexpired lease of the debtor not previously rejected under such section.
3. Provide for:
   a. The settlement or adjustment of any claim or interest belonging to the debtor or to the estate or
   b. The retention and enforcement by the debtor, by the trustee, or by a representative of the estate appointed for such purpose, of any such claim or interest
4. Provide for the sale of all or substantially all of the property of the estate, and the distribution of the proceeds of such sale among holders of claims or interests.
5. Modify the rights of holders of secured claims, other than a claim secured only by a security interest in real property that is the debtor's principal residence, or of holders of unsecured claims, or leave unaffected the rights of holders of any class of claims.
6. Include any other appropriate provision not inconsistent with the applicable provisions of the Bankruptcy Code.

## Disclosure Statement

An acceptance or rejection of a plan may not be solicited after the commencement of the bankruptcy case unless, at the time of or before such solicitation, a summary of the plan and a court-approved disclosure statement is transmitted. The Bankruptcy Code provides that the bankruptcy court can approve a disclosure statement without a valuation of the debtor or an appraisal of the debtor's assets. However, if the plan wipes out old equity or a class of creditors, it is typical for the disclosure statement to include a liquidation analysis of the debtor.

The disclosure statement is much like a prospectus. The disclosure statement is intended to provide creditors and parties in interest with adequate information to make an informed judgment on the plan. *Adequate information* means information of a kind, and in sufficient detail, as far as is reasonably practicable in light of the nature and history of the debtor and the condition of the debtor's books and records, including a discussion of the potential material federal tax consequences of the plan, that would enable such a hypothetical investor to make an informed judgment about the plan. In a small business case, the court may determine that the plan itself provides adequate information and that a separate disclosure statement is not necessary.

## Acceptance of Plan by Creditors

A class of claims has accepted a plan of reorganization if such plan has been accepted by creditors that hold at least *two-thirds in amount* and *more than one-half in number* of the allowed claims of such class *that have actually voted* to accept or reject such plan, not including any acceptance or rejection that was not in good faith, or was not solicited or procured in good faith.

In order to confirm a plan, if *any* class of claims is *impaired, at least one class of claims that is impaired under the plan must accept the plan* (determined without including any acceptance of the plan by any insider).

It doesn't take much to impair a class of claims or interests, though some cases have rejected artificial impairment. A class of claims or interests is impaired under a plan unless, with respect to each claim or interest of such class, the plan

1. Leaves unaltered the legal, equitable, and contractual rights to which such claim or interest entitles the holder of such claim or interest or
2. Notwithstanding any contractual provision or applicable law that entitles the holder of such claim or interest to demand or receive accelerated payment of such claim or interest after the occurrence of a default
   a. Cures any such default that occurred before or after the commencement of the case other than certain ipso facto defaults (e.g., the filing of a bankruptcy case)
   b. Reinstates the maturity of such claim or interest as such maturity existed before such default

    c. Compensates the holder of such claim or interest for any damages incurred as a result of any reasonable reliance by such holder on such contractual provision or such applicable law

    d. If such claim or such interest arises from any failure to perform a nonmonetary obligation, other than a default arising from failure to operate certain nonresidential real property leases, compensates the holder of such claim or such interest (other than the debtor or an insider) for any actual pecuniary loss incurred by such holder as a result of such failure

    e. Does not otherwise alter the legal, equitable, or contractual rights to which such claim or interest entitles the holder of such claim or interest

## Confirmation of Plan

The bankruptcy court will hold a hearing on the confirmation of the plan and any party in interest can object to the confirmation of the plan. The Bankruptcy Code sets out many specific requirements that must be met before the court can confirm a plan, including the following:

1. The plan complies with the applicable provisions of the Bankruptcy Code;
2. The proponent (typically, the debtor is the proponent of the plan, but as noted earlier, once exclusivity has lapsed, a party other than the debtor may propose a plan) of the plan complies with the applicable provisions of the Bankruptcy Code; and
3. The plan has been proposed in good faith and not by any means forbidden by law;
4. Confirmation of the plan is not likely to be followed by the liquidation, or the need for further financial reorganization, of the debtor, unless such liquidation or reorganization is proposed by the plan.

    **Best Interests of Creditors Test.** There are several specific requirements to confirmation that implicate valuation matters. The first is known as the "best interest of creditors" test (even though it applies to equity interests, too), which essentially means that for *any* creditor in an impaired class that votes "no," the plan must provide at least as good a result as that creditor would get *under a Chapter 7 liquidation*. Specifically, the test states:

> *With respect to each impaired class of claims or interests, (A) each holder of a claim or interest of such class (i) has accepted the plan; or (ii) will receive or retain under the plan on account of such claim*

*or interest property of a value, as of the effective date of the plan, that is not less than the amount that such holder would so receive or retain if the debtor were liquidated under chapter 7 of this title on such date.*

**Cram Down.** Another requirement for confirmation of a plan is that, with respect to each class of claims (or interests), (1) such class has accepted the plan, or (2) such class is not impaired under the plan. If all the requirements for confirmation of a plan are met except for this one, the plan can still be confirmed *if* the plan does not discriminate unfairly, and is *fair and equitable* with respect to each class of claims or interests that is impaired under, and has not accepted, the plan. This is known as *cram down* and is discussed in detail in chapter 7.

## Effect of Confirmation

The plan of reorganization will be binding on all creditors and parties in interest regardless of whether those creditors accept the plan. The general effect of the bankruptcy plan is to discharge prebankruptcy indebtedness.

## AVOIDING POWERS UNDER THE BANKRUPTCY CODE—PREFERENCES

The power to avoid preferences helps to ensure the equality of distribution to creditors. For example, one creditor might be more aggressive in its prebankruptcy collection efforts than another. If the debtor can't pay everyone, the aggressive creditor will benefit to the detriment of the less aggressive creditor. Preference law tries to equalize the relative recoveries by bringing the payments back into the bankruptcy estate to be redistributed pro rata to all creditors. As stated by the Supreme Court:

> *[Preferences] facilitate the prime bankruptcy policy of equality of distribution among creditors of the debtor. Any creditor that received a greater payment than others of his class is required to disgorge so that all may share equally. The operation of the preference section to deter "the race of diligence" of creditors to dismember the debtor before bankruptcy furthers the second goal of the preference section—that of equality of distribution.*[1]

The Bankruptcy Code sets out the requirements the debtor must establish to avoid a preference and recover the amount transferred. In general, a preference is a transfer (typically a payment by check or wire transfer) by the debtor to a creditor, on account of an antecedent debt (typically trade debt), made while the debtor was insolvent and within 90 days before the date the bankruptcy case was filed (one year in the case of a transfer to an insider), that enables the creditor to receive more than it would have received if the transfer had not been made and the creditor received payment in a Chapter 7 case.

From a valuation standpoint, the key question is whether the debtor was insolvent at the time of the transfer. During the 90-day reachback period, insolvency is presumed (but can be rebutted), but for transfers that occur in the 90-day to one-year period, the trustee has to prove insolvency.

## AVOIDING POWERS UNDER THE BANKRUPTCY CODE—FRAUDULENT TRANSFERS

There are two principal types of fraudulent transfers that can be recovered for the benefit of creditors: (1) transfers made by a debtor with the actual intent to hinder, delay, or defraud creditors (sometimes referred to in this book as an *actual intent* case), and (2) transfers made by a debtor that are constructively fraudulent with reference to creditors. In the simplest example, a transfer by a debtor is constructively fraudulent if the debtor (1) made the transfer without receiving a reasonably equivalent value in exchange for the transfer and (2) was insolvent at that time.

When a transfer is attacked as constructively fraudulent, the need for at least one valuation is obvious: in order to win the case, the trustee must prove *that the debtor was insolvent* at the time of transfer. This issue—insolvency of the debtor—is equally important in an actual intent case, because when the jury or fact finder answers the question about whether the debtor made the transfer with actual intent, the jury is entitled to consider (among other circumstantial evidence) whether the debtor was insolvent when the transfer was made.

## VALUATION PRINCIPLES FROM THE BANKRUPTCY COURTS

Bankruptcy courts are obviously confronted with valuation questions at many times in a bankruptcy case. As noted earlier, § 506 of the Bankruptcy Code provides that "value shall be determined in light of the purpose of the valuation and of the proposed disposition or use of such property, and in conjunction with any hearing on such disposition or use or on a plan affecting such creditor's interest." Sometimes the language of the Bankruptcy

Code provides more guidance for the expert and the court. For example, the Bankruptcy Code defines the term *insolvent*. In the case of an entity such as a corporation, *insolvent* means the "financial condition such that the sum of such entity's debts is greater than all of such entity's property, at a fair valuation. . . . " (The full definition includes some additional details that are not relevant here.) But the Bankruptcy Code doesn't give any particular guidance about what "at a fair valuation" means, or how an expert should go about the process of reaching an opinion of a fair valuation.

The bankruptcy courts are forced to deal with these underlying issues on a case-by-case basis. As this book shows, different methods and approaches to valuations have been used, and sometimes those approaches are unique to the legal context before the court. In later chapters, this book will give examples of how courts have defined the task of the expert or have discarded the opinions of experts who have not approached the valuation issues in the appropriate (at least to the judge) manner.

As a general rule, however, in the case of an ongoing business, bankruptcy courts and valuation treatises agree: valuations are based on the expectation of future earnings. This principle—and the uncertainties inherent in such an approach—was forcefully stated in a leading bankruptcy case decided in 1941 by the Supreme Court of the United States, *Consolidated Rock Products Co. v. Du Bois*.[2] This case was previously referred to in Chapter 4.

## CONCLUSION

Valuations are at the heart of many aspects of a bankruptcy case, including:

- Use of collateral (including cash collateral)
- Granting of priority liens in one creditor's collateral to secure a DIP loan from another lender
- Relief from the automatic stay
- Sales of assets
- Recovery of preferences
- Recovery of fraudulent transfers
- Confirmation of a plan—best interest of creditor's test
- Confirmation of a plan—cram down

## NOTES

1. *Union Bank V. Wolas*, 502 U.S. 151, 161 (emphasis added) (quoting H.R. Rep. No. 95-595, at 177-78 (1977), reprinted in 1978 U.S.C.C.A.N. 5963, 6137-38).
2. 312 U.S. 510 (1941).

# CHAPTER 7

# Valuations in Bankruptcy as of the Date of the Hearing

## INTRODUCTION

In many circumstances, the valuation question before the bankruptcy court is, "What is the valuation of the asset now?" The question can arise immediately after the bankruptcy case is filed when, for instance, a secured creditor asks the bankruptcy court to lift the automatic stay so the creditor can foreclose. The debtor's request to sell its assets in a § 363 sale can spark the need for a valuation, particularly when the auction process is less than robust. The question can also arise at the end of the reorganization process, when the debtor seeks to confirm a plan of reorganization. While the Bankruptcy Code uses the word *value* over a hundred times and sometimes uses the phrase *replacement value*, it does not tell the bankruptcy courts how to determine value. As the Fifth Circuit noted in *Sutton v. Bank One, Texas, N.A. (In re Sutton)*, "Congress did not dictate a particular appraisal method." 904 F.2d 327, 330 (5th Cir. 1990). As noted earlier, § 506 of the Bankruptcy Code provides that "value shall be determined in light of the purpose of the valuation and of the proposed disposition or use of such property, and in conjunction with any hearing on such disposition or use or on a plan affecting such creditor's interest."[1] This gives the bankruptcy court and the parties the ability to match the valuation question to the context of the issue before the court.

With one exception, this chapter is limited to valuations *as of (or close to) the date of the hearing*, as compared to valuations at some point *in the past* (which is the context for avoidance actions, discussed in the next chapter). Valuations as of the date of the hearing are never complicated by hindsight or subsequent events, an issue of considerable controversy.

Matters that arise in a bankruptcy case in which valuations are important include:

- Motions for relief from the automatic stay or for adequate protection
- Sales of property under § 363
- Approval of loans to the debtor in possession (DIP financing)
- Approval of a disclosure statement
- Confirmation of a plan

Each of these is discussed in the following sections.

## RELIEF FROM THE AUTOMATIC STAY AND ADEQUATE PROTECTION

The typical secured creditor is restrained from foreclosing on its collateral by the automatic stay. During the case, the secured creditor is entitled to adequate protection of its interest (see Chapter 6). In addition, the Bankruptcy Code provides a way for the typical secured creditor to get relief from the automatic stay. Specifically, § 362(d)(1) and (2) of the Bankruptcy Code provide as follows:

> On request of a party in interest and after notice and a hearing, the court shall grant relief from the [automatic] stay . . . , such as by terminating, annulling, modifying, or conditioning such stay—
> (1) for cause, including the lack of adequate protection of an interest in property of such party in interest;
> (2) with respect to a stay of an act against property . . . , if—
> (A) the debtor does not have an equity in such property; and
> (B) such property is not necessary to an effective reorganization . . .
>
> 11 U.S.C. § 362(d)(1) and (2)

A secured creditor's request for relief from the automatic stay under subsection (2) obviously requires a valuation of the property, but subsection (1) often does, as well.

During the real-estate downturn of 1989–1994, the bankruptcy courts were inundated with filings by companies that owned a single apartment complex or an office building and that had little or no realistic hope of confirming a plan of reorganization. Congress, concerned about abuse of the Bankruptcy Code, passed a special rule applicable to a single-asset real-estate case. It provides as follows:

*On request of a party in interest and after notice and a hearing, the court shall grant relief from the [automatic] stay . . . , such as by terminating, annulling, modifying, or conditioning such stay— . . .*

  *(3) with respect to a stay of an act against single asset real estate . . . , by a creditor whose claim is secured by an interest in such real estate, unless, not later than the date that is 90 days after the entry of the order for relief (or such later date as the court may determine for cause by order entered within that 90-day period) or 30 days after the court determines that the debtor is subject to this paragraph, whichever is later —*

    *(A) the debtor has filed a plan of reorganization that has a reasonable possibility of being confirmed within a reasonable time; or*

    *(B) the debtor has commenced monthly payments that—*

      *(i) may, in the debtor's sole discretion . . . be made from rents or other income generated before, on, or after the date of the commencement of the case by or from the property to each creditor whose claim is secured by such real estate . . . ; and*

      *(ii) are in an amount equal to interest at the then applicable nondefault contract rate of interest on the value of the creditor's interest in the real estate. . . .*

                                        11 U.S.C. § 362(d)(3)

This special section also can require valuation testimony.

A motion for relief from the automatic stay will typically contain an allegation of lack of equity in the property as of the date of the filing of the motion. The hearing on a motion to lift the automatic stay is supposed to be held relatively shortly after it has been filed.[2] The valuation date will be the date the motion was filed, and because the hearing held by the bankruptcy court will be shortly thereafter, the valuation date will be very close in time to the opinion date.[3] However, in those cases in which the secured creditor seeks to lift the automatic stay because the asset is declining in value (which can mean that there is a lack of adequate protection), the value must be determined at least two times, in order to show a decline over time.

The need for more than one valuation can also arise when the secured creditor seeks to lift the stay but loses (either because the court finds that the secured creditor is adequately protected by an equity cushion[4] or, if there is no equity cushion, that the value is not declining). It should be noted that deciding whether a debtor has equity in property is based on all of the liens secured by the property, not only the amount of the lien of the moving party.[5] Months later, if things have not gone well for the debtor (and, therefore, for the secured creditor) the secured creditor may come to court again and seek to have the automatic stay lifted, and also seek recovery of a super-priority claim under § 507(b) due to a failure of the supposed adequate protection, because the value has fallen since the first hearing.[6]

The issues of when and what value to apply for purposes of adequate protection and stay relief are both appropriately focused on the value to be realized at liquidation, because that is the value the creditor is trying to protect. For example, in *Chrysler Credit Corp. v. Ruggiere* (*In re George Ruggiere Chrysler-Plymouth, Inc.*)[7], the court held that value for purposes of adequate protection was determined to be the wholesale value because that was the "amount which the creditor would receive by its customary or commercially reasonable means of disposition."[8]

## § 363 SALES

When a company is in financial distress but hasn't filed bankruptcy, one solution is a sale of the business (structured as an asset sale), which allows the seller to pay its debts to the extent of the proceeds of the sale. Such a sale can allow the owners of the company to recover going-concern values in many instances, which benefits them as well as those employees who are able to continue employment with the new owner.

When the proceeds of a sale will not be sufficient to pay all debts in full (other than those assumed by the buyer), the parties may conclude that the best way to implement the sale is through a bankruptcy filing and the use of the § 363 sales process. In other situations, creditor pressure requires a bankruptcy filing before a sale can be put together and closed.

A sale of assets by a debtor in possession, other than in the ordinary course of business, can be accomplished pursuant to the authority contained in § 363 of the Bankruptcy Code. Section 363(b)(1) provides (in pertinent part), that the "trustee, after notice and a hearing, may . . . sell . . ., other than in the ordinary course of business, property of the estate. . . ." Another key provision is § 363(f), which provides (in pertinent part) that the "trustee may sell property . . . free and clear of any interest in such property of an entity other than the estate, only if . . . (3) such interest is a lien and the price at which such property is to be sold is greater than the aggregate value of all liens on such property." In addition, § 363(m) provides protection to a good faith buyer, even if the bankruptcy court's order authorizing the sale is reversed on appeal. It provides that the "reversal or modification on appeal of an authorization under [§ 363] of a sale . . . of property does not affect the validity of a sale . . . to an entity that purchased . . . such property in good faith, whether or not such entity knew of the pendency of the appeal, unless such authorization and such sale or lease were stayed pending appeal."[9]

These sections of § 363 have been interpreted broadly (for the most part) to allow debtors in possession to sell all, or substantially all, of their assets on an expedited (and sometimes on an emergency) basis and give buyers sweeping protections from the creditors of the debtor in possession. This section introduces the valuation analyst to how § 363 works in practice in the context of such a sale, and highlights some (but by no means all) of the issues that are often confronted by the parties to such a sale.

## Sale of All or Substantially All Assets

Courts have recognized that Section 363(b) may be used to sell all or substantially all of a debtor's principal assets.[10] In part, this is because the paramount goal for any proposed sale of property of a bankruptcy estate is to maximize the proceeds received by the estate, and in some cases, a prompt (or even urgent) sale may be the best way to maximize value.[11] A proposed use, sale, or lease of property of the estate may be approved under the Bankruptcy Code § 363(b) if it is supported by sound business justification.[12] Courts have made it clear that a debtor's showing of a sound business justification need not be unduly exhaustive but, rather, a debtor is "simply required to justify the proposed disposition with sound business reasons."[13] Whether there are sufficient business reasons to justify a transaction depends on the facts and circumstances of each case.[14]

Despite this flexibility, a debtor cannot circumvent the requirements of confirming a plan under Chapter 11 of the Bankruptcy Code by, in effect, proposing a *sub rosa* plan in connection with a sale under § 363. (*Sub rosa* means secret, confidential, or private.) In the leading case of *Pension Benefit Guaranty Corp. v. Braniff Airways, Inc. (In re Braniff Airways, Inc.)*,[15] the Fifth Circuit Court of Appeals refused to approve a § 363 sale because the sale included a requirement that (1) a portion of the purchase price be paid to a particular creditor constituency, (2) creditors were required to vote a portion of their deficiency claim in favor of a future plan of reorganization, and (3) broad releases were to be given as part of the transaction. The Fifth Circuit characterized these provisions as a *sub rosa* plan and refused to approve it. The court expressly held that "[t]he debtor and the Bankruptcy Court should not be able to short circuit the requirements of Chapter 11 for confirmation of a reorganization plan by establishing the terms of the plan *sub rosa* in connection with a sale of assets."[16]

## Stalking-Horse Agreements

Any sale under the protection of the bankruptcy court is one that is subject to better bids. A stalking-horse bidder is a buyer that has agreed to buy assets knowing that the agreement is subject to a higher and better bid at an auction. Because the effort put into the sales process may be all for naught if another bidder wins the auction, a stalking-horse bidder will want (and will often obtain) both a breakup fee and reimbursement of expenses, and sometimes even other protections in such a case.[17] Some of the fastest moving sales are those that involve a stalking-horse bidder.

Of course, a debtor in bankruptcy can hold an auction of its assets even when there is no stalking horse. Sometimes efforts to find a buyer pre- and postpetition are unsuccessful, and the debtor determines to proceed with an auction without a stalking-horse bidder. In the auction procedures, the debtor can provide the ability to enter into a stalking-horse agreement during the sales process for the purposes of establishing a minimum bid and a foundation for further bids. The auction procedures (and the order approving them) could preapprove a specific breakup fee (for example, a breakup fee of no more than 3 percent of the cash consideration of such offer, payable only if (1) the stalking-horse bidder reaffirms its offer at the commencement of the auction and (2) an alternative transaction is closed for the same assets, and only from the proceeds of such alternative transaction). In an auction without a stalking-horse bidder, the auction procedures should include a reservation of rights to the debtor to (1) withdraw from the sale any assets at any time prior to or during the auction and to make subsequent attempts to market the same; and (2) reject all bids if, in the debtor's reasonable judgment, no bid is a fair and adequate offer.

## Key Provisions of the Asset Purchase Agreement

The debtor and the stalking-horse bidder will enter into an asset purchase agreement (APA). (The debtor's secured lender and the creditors' committee will have a say—if not a veto—in any material aspect of the § 363 sale process). An APA used for a § 363 will usually contain provisions that would not be seen in an out-of-court asset purchase agreement. In particular, the APA will (or may):

- Make the APA subject to an auction procedures order, the court hearing to approve the sale, and the order approving the sale.
- Specify that avoidance claims are excluded assets and are not being sold.
- Include cure amounts as part of the purchase price.
- Provide that real property will be conveyed by trustee's deed, limited warranty deed, or quit-claim deed.

- Have a breakup fee, expense reimbursement, or other stalking-horse protections.
- Provide that it will terminate upon the closing of a transaction with a third-party overbidder from the auction.
- Provide that the transaction is an "As Is, Where Is, and With All Faults Transaction."
- Have a very limited "operation of the business until closing" provision.
- Provide that representations and warranties will not survive the closing.

## Auction Procedures

A bankruptcy court sale is a multistep process, and to put that process in place, the debtor will file a motion for an order approving the stalking-horse bid (subject to higher and better offers), the auction procedures, and an order authorizing the sale at the conclusion of the auction. The auction procedures (among other things):

- Will address the obligation of potential bidders to enter into a confidentiality agreement and provide information about their financial qualifications.
- May limit participation at the auction to qualified bidders.
- Will set a deadline for bids.
- Will set out minimum requirements for bids (such as being in an amount of at least the required overbid; providing a marked-up and signed version of the stalking-horse bidder's APA; providing an earnest money deposit; and providing written confirmation that the offer is irrevocable and will remain open (1) until the closing of the sale, if the bidder is the winning bidder, and (2) otherwise, until a certain period following the entry of the sale order).
- Set the time and place for the auction.
- Describe any procedures applicable to the auction (such as the secured creditor's right to credit bid, amount of the initial overbid, minimum bidding increments, and the process for determining and announcing the winning bid and next highest bid).
- Set the date and time of the sales hearing and the deadline for objections to any relief sought in the sales motion.
- Set the date and time of the closing.
- Describe the consequences if the winning bidder fails to close, including proceeding to close with the next highest bidder.
- Include a reservation of rights of the debtor to (1) impose, at or prior to the auction, additional terms and conditions on the sale of the assets; and (2) extend the deadlines set forth in the auction procedures,

adjourn the auction at the auction, and/or adjourn the sale hearing in open court without further notice.

## Executory Contracts and Cure Amounts

When a business is purchased using an asset purchase agreement, contracts or leases essential to continued operations must be assigned, too. In bankruptcy, many contracts and leases (executory contracts) can be assigned, even if the debtor is in default, if defaults are cured and adequate assurance of future performance is provided, all as provided in § 365 of the Bankruptcy Code. The sale process should provide that bidders must identify with particularity each executory contract that must be assumed by the debtor and assigned to the bidder as a condition to closing. Before the sale hearing, the debtor should (1) notify each nondebtor entity that is a party to a contract that has been designated by a bidder, or the debtor reasonably expects will be designated by a bidder, as an executory contract to be assigned (a) of the potential assumption of such contract and its assignment to the winning bidder at the auction, and (b) of the proposed cure amount, if any, under such contract; and (2) file a schedule of such executory agreements with the bankruptcy court. The procedures order should require any nondebtor party to an executory contract who objects to assumption and assignment to the winning bidder to file and serve a written objection before the sale hearing, setting forth in reasonable detail the basis of its objection and identifying any defaults under such agreement (including any monetary defaults).

## Free and Clear Sales

Many court decisions support the power of the bankruptcy court to sell assets free and clear of creditor's liens (including undersecured creditors) (sometimes referred to as *lien stripping*) and potential creditor claims (such as successor liability).[18] Any overbreadth in the relief requested or granted has usually been considered immune from any attack on appeal by virtue of § 363(m)—in the absence of a stay pending appeal, the appeal is (usually) dismissed as moot.[19] Even so, some courts have gotten queasy about the breadth of relief sought in connection with § 363 sales, especially if it is buried in the boilerplate. In some courts, local rules or guidelines address these concerns.

## The Role of the Valuation Professional in § 363 Sales

Clearly, a § 363 sale can be the central event in a bankruptcy case. A valuation professional's first involvement may be to help the debtor to estimate value before a § 363 sale is attempted. In other words, the valuation professional's first role may be to help determine what the company can expect to get for the business it hopes to sell. In some cases, the valuation professional may be qualified to have a broader role and can provide advice about marketing the asset or business.

At the hearing to approve the sale, the debtor will ordinarily need to offer evidence that will show that a fair price was obtained. Where there is only one bidder, evidence about the sales and marketing efforts will be important, as well as evidence from the valuation professional that demonstrates that the value obtained is within a reasonable range. Where at least two bidders come to the auction, and where a robust bidding war occurs, an expert's opinion of value may be of less importance in obtaining court approval of the sale.[20]

## USE OF CASH COLLATERAL

Use of cash collateral depends on establishing adequate protection for the use, which, in many circumstances, is dependent on a value determination that an equity cushion exists.[21] In the unusual situation in which a request is made for a priming lien under Section 365(d)(1), the increase in value of the collateral resulting from the expenditure of funds must be found to exceed the amount of the new priming loan, and even then, the law prefers that additional collateral also be provided.[22]

## DISCLOSURE STATEMENT

The Bankruptcy Code provides that the bankruptcy court can approve a disclosure statement without a valuation of the debtor or an appraisal of the debtor's assets.[23] However, if the plan wipes out old equity or a class of creditors, it is typical for the disclosure statement to include a liquidation analysis of the debtor that demonstrates that such claims or interests are out of the money in the opinion of the proponent of the plan. The issue of enterprise valuation in the context of plan confirmation is discussed in further detail in the sections that follow.

## PLAN CONFIRMATION—FEASIBILITY

Valuation can also be important in the context of considering feasibility of a plan where enterprise value impacts the establishment of interest rates as part of the measurement of market underwriting and, thereby, impacts the ability of the reorganized debtor to service its debt and amortize or pay it off by refinancing at maturity. For example, in a simple real estate setting, determining the value of the collateral is essential to establishing basic underwriting. The higher the value, the lower the loan-to-value ratio. The lower the loan-to-value ratio, the lower the risk and therefore the lower the interest rate to support the loan. The lower the interest rate to support the loan, the lower the debt service and the easier to pay it. The easier to pay debt service, the more likely the Court will be able to find that the plan is feasible.

## PLAN CONFIRMATION—BEST-INTERESTS-OF-CREDITORS TEST

The *best-interests-of-creditors test* means that for any creditor in an impaired class that votes "no," the plan must provide at least as good a result as the creditor would get under a Chapter 7 liquidation. Specifically, the test states:

> With respect to each impaired class of claims or interests, (A) each holder of a claim or interest of such class (i) has accepted the plan; or (ii) will receive or retain under the plan on account of such claim or interest property of a value, as of the effective date of the plan, that is not less than the amount that such holder would so receive or retain if the debtor were liquidated under chapter 7 of this title on such date.
>
> 11 U.S.C. § 1129(a)(7)

If a party opposes a plan on this basis (a rare event but a very strong objection when validly made), a valuation would be required.

## PLAN CONFIRMATION—CRAM DOWN

### Examples of Cram Down Plans

If all the requirements for confirmation of a plan are met except for the requirement that each class of claims (or interests) has accepted the plan (or is not impaired under the plan), the plan can still be confirmed if the plan does not discriminate unfairly, and is *fair and equitable* with respect to each class of claims or interests that is impaired under, and has not accepted, the plan. This method of confirming a plan of reorganization is known as cram down.

A typical example of a cram down plan would be one in which the creditors convert their debt to equity and wipe out the old equity owners of the company. Another variation would be one in which the senior creditors convert some of their debt to equity and wipe out both the subordinated debt and the old equity owners.

**What Is Required to Confirm a Plan using Cram Down: The Fair and Equitable Test**

When an equity committee challenges a plan as not meeting the fair and equitable test of § 1129(b), some courts have characterized the challenge as a comparison between the value of the reorganized debtor and the amount of outstanding claims against the debtor.[25] Other courts have held that § 1129(b)'s "fair and equitable" requirement means that senior classes cannot receive more than the value of their claims,[26] because "[a] corollary of the absolute priority rule [contained in § 1129(b)] is that a senior class cannot receive more than full compensation for its claims."[27]

In one recent case the equity committee stated the issue this way: "the Trustee's Plan violates the absolute priority rule and is not fair and equitable because it gives the Noteholders more than the amount of their claims by . . . issuing them all of the stock of Reorganized [debtor]."[28] The "Noteholders receive all the equity in Reorganized [debtor], which is worth much more than the Noteholders' claims. Therefore, the Equity Committee argues that it is not fair and equitable under section 1129(b)."[29] In another case where the equity committee challenged the debtors' plan on the grounds that § 1129(b)(2) was violated the court stated that, "in order to confirm the plan, the Debtors . . . had to establish that their plan . . . does not deprive the equity of any recovery to which it is entitled."[30]

**A Valuation Is Required to Satisfy the Fair and Equitable Test**

Whenever there is a cram down fight at confirmation, a valuation is required: "A valuation of the debtor's business is, by virtue of the statutory language, almost a prerequisite to a determination that a plan satisfies the fair and equitable test of § 1129(b)."[31]

**The Enterprise Value Is to Be Determined as of the Effective Date after Confirmation**

In a cram down fight the court must determine the debtor's enterprise value "as a reorganized entity" as of the date of confirmation.[32] Valuation for confirmation of a plan is prospective—at least by a small time period—because it requires the valuation to be "as of the effective date of the plan"[33] and most plans become effective shortly after the order confirming the plan is entered.[34]

### Value Should Be Determined Using Generally Accepted Business Valuation Approaches Based on the Reorganized Debtor's Earning Capacity

Such valuations are usually based on traditional business valuation approaches. Courts have observed that a debtor's "value, credit-worthiness, and attractiveness as an investment" should be objectively assessed as of the prospective effective date of a plan, and the debtor's earning capacity should not take into account the "taint" of bankruptcy.[35] Further, a debtor's earning capacity should "adequately account for the benefits to debtor [the] of chapter 11."[36] However, risks that would depress the value of an ex-bankrupt entity "may be an appropriate factor where a debtor's business will suffer the public relations disadvantages of bankruptcy or where the debtor is overburdened with debt incurred in satisfaction of claims." [37]

As noted, the determination of the present value of the reorganized entity must be grounded upon its earning capacity as a reorganized entity.[38] The reorganized debtor's earning capacity should be based on projections prepared in a reasonable manner, using supportable assumptions and logically consistent computations.[39]

### Current Market Prices of a Bankrupt Company's Stock, Bonds or Bank Debt Are Not Relevant of Value when Applying the Fair and Equitable Test

In some cases parties have urged the bankruptcy court to take the current stock prices or trading prices for the debtor's bank debt or subordinated debt as the "value" of the debtor set by the market. Courts usually reject such an approach, and should, given the mandate of the *Consolidated Rock* decision, quoted earlier. As one court recently stated:

> *The court must, first, however address at greater length the misperception that Mirant Group's value is properly set by the market place. . . . The market is not the proper measure for the value of Mirant Group for the purpose of satisfying claims. The Corp. Committee even suggested during argument that the market value of publicly traded debt of Mirant today is an accurate reflection of the extent of value of Mirant Group. If Mirant debt trades at less than face value, the Corp. Committee argues, this indicates the market considers the value of Mirant Group to be inadequate to make holders of Mirant debt whole. But, even assuming that the market is a proper gauge of the value of an entity in chapter 11, use of preconfirmation prices of debt cannot be an accurate measure.*

*The market price of Mirant debt preconfirmation must logically be based not only on the capital structure proposed in the Plan. It also would have to take into account the risk the Plan would not be confirmed.*

*Delays in the confirmation schedule, uncertainties as to postpetition, preconfirmation interest rates (on both Mirant and MAG debt) and the possibility of a change in treatment through compromise or valuation would have to be considered when buying Mirant debt preconfirmation.*[40]

### Whether Creditors Are Being Paid More than 100% of Their Claims Should Take into Consideration Interest on Those Claims

The enterprise value so calculated is compared to the debt owed by the company, including interest. In *In re Mirant*, the bankruptcy court for the Northern District of Texas stated that "equity is entitled to a return only after satisfaction of claims against debtors, including interest (calculated for these purposes at contract, non-default rates)."[41]

### Whether Creditors Are Being Paid More than 100% of Their Claims Can Take into Consideration Any Control Premium Applicable to the Equity They Receive under the Plan.

Control exists when a person or group can, among other things: (1) appoint or change management; (2) appoint or change board members; (3) determine management compensation; (4) set operational/strategic strategy; (5) compel the registration of the company's equity; (6) negotiate and/or consummate mergers or asset sales; and/or (7) block any of the above actions.[42]

It is universally accepted that the ability to exercise control has value, and when control exists, the value of control (sometimes referred to as a control premium) can be taken into consideration in determining a company's enterprise value.[43] When determining value in the context of a cram down, bankruptcy courts have taken the value of control into account, and in reaching a determination of value, have included a control premium in a comparable companies analysis.[44]

Where a single creditor or a group of creditors receive, or can obtain by the number of shares that they will receive under the plan, control, the value of control should be taken into account in applying the fair and equitable test. As noted above, the fair and equitable test means that a senior class cannot receive more than full compensation for its claims. Making that determination requires consideration of the economic value received by creditors under the plan, and that requires that the value of control be considered (as compared to the value of a minority, tradable interest).

In *Assocs. Commercial Corp. v. Rash*, 520 U.S. 953 (1997), the Supreme Court also made clear that the valuation standard must be based on the economic benefit of the property being valued under the plan. *Id.* at 963. In *Rash* the property was a truck that the debtor retained under the plan. The debtor wanted to pay the creditor the value the creditor could obtain in a *foreclosure* value if it got the truck back, but the creditor wanted to be paid the value of the truck to the debtor, since the debtor would retain the truck under the plan (*replacement* value). The Supreme Court ruled that the appropriate standard of value was replacement value, since that standard of value reflected the *actual economics* of the plan, rather than a hypothetical foreclosure value (since no foreclosure was occurring). It is just as important to determine the correct standard of value when applying the fair and equitable test of Section 1129(b)(1) of the Bankruptcy Code. In a cram down dispute, whether creditors are getting more than full payment should also require consideration of the "economic benefit" given to them under the plan. If they get control, the value of that control should be considered, as control has a measurable economic benefit.

Where control exists the proper way to compute its value must be considered. The two market approach methods are fundamentally different in this regard. The comparable companies approach gives an indication of value for the trading prices of the subject company's stock, which, by definition, does not include the value of control. The comparable transactions approach includes the value of control, since the observation of value is in the context of a buyer purchasing all the equity of the seller. In fact, the "average" value of control is determined by comparing the sales price of companies that are sold to the trading prices of those companies at various times (1 trading day, 10 trading days, etc.) before the transaction was announced. This research can allow the expert to adjust the minority trading value given by the comparable companies approach to a value that includes a control premium. The indication of value given by the DCF approach can include the value of control if transaction multiples (used in the comparable transaction approach) are used to calculate the terminal value.

Where control exists and its value should be taken into account, should all of the approaches used by the expert be ones that include (or are adjusted to include) the value of control? Logic certainly suggests so—why use an approach that values the wrong thing, and average the value given by that approach with another approach that values the right thing? The Supreme Court's decision in *Rash* is authority for the proposition that averaging "apples and oranges" is wrong, and all methods used should use the same standard of value. In *Rash*, the Supreme Court reviewed the decisions of some lower courts that had avoided choosing between foreclosure value and replacement value by averaging the two values. The Supreme Court rejected such an approach, stating:

> *Nor are we persuaded that the split-the-difference approach adopted by the Seventh Circuit provides the appropriate solution. Whatever the attractiveness of a standard that picks the midpoint between foreclosure and replacement values, there is no warrant for it in the Code. Section 506(a) calls for the value the property possesses in light of the "disposition or use" in fact "proposed," not the various dispositions or uses that might have been proposed.*
>
> *Id.* at 964–65 (internal citations omitted).

## CONCLUSION

In summary, valuations in bankruptcy cases occur at many different times for many different purposes. It is essential to know the context of the proposed valuation, in order to be able to offer a valuation that is responsive to the needs of the court.

## NOTES

1. 11 U.S.C. § 506(a)(1).
2. 11 U.S.C. § 362(e) ("Thirty days after a request under subsection (d) of this section for relief from the stay of any act against property of the estate under subsection (a) of this section, such stay is terminated with respect to the party in interest making such request, unless the court, after notice and a hearing, orders such stay continued in effect pending the conclusion of, or as a result of, a final hearing and determination under subsection (d) of this section. A hearing under this subsection may be a preliminary hearing, or may be consolidated with the final hearing under subsection (d) of this section. The court shall order such stay continued in effect pending the conclusion of the final hearing under subsection (d) of this section if there is a reasonable likelihood that the party opposing relief from such stay will prevail at the conclusion of such final hearing. If the hearing under this subsection is a preliminary hearing, then such final hearing shall be concluded not later than thirty days after the conclusion of such preliminary hearing, unless the 30-day period is extended with the consent of the parties in interest or for a specific time which the court finds is required by compelling circumstances.").

3. *In re Cason*, 190 B.R. 917, 929-31 (Bankr. N.D.Ala. 1995) ("[f]or adequate protection purposes, the initial valuation should be measured at the time of the motion for relief or motion for adequate protection."); *Baybank-Middlesex v. Ralar Distribs., Inc. (In re Ralar Distribs., Inc.)*, 182 B.R. 81, 86 (D. Mass. 1995), *aff'd*, 69 F.3d 1200 (1st Cir. 1995); *In re Continental Airlines, Inc.*, 146 B.R. 536, 539 (Bankr. D. Del. 1992); *In re Wilson*, 70 B. R. 46, 48 (Bankr. N.D. Ind. 1987); *c.f. In re Addison Properties Ltd. Partnership*, 185 B.R. 766 (Bankr. N.D. Ill. 1995); *In re Fulcher*, 15 B.R. 446, 448 (Bankr. D. Kan. 1981). *Philadelphia Consumer Discount Co. v. Commercial Credit Bus. Loans, Inc.*, 37 B.R. 946, 950 (E.D. Pa. 1984) (value as of date of commencement of case); *In re Datair Systems Corp.*, 42 B.R. 241 (Bankr. N.D. Ill. 1984) (same).

4. *In re WRB West Assocs. Joint Venture*, 106 B.R. 215 (Bankr. D. Mont. 1989) (adequate protection in the form of a 40 percent equity cushion is sufficient so as to authorize the debtor's use of cash collateral); but see *Sharon Steel Corp. v. Citibank, N.A. (In re Sharon Steel Corp.)*, 159 B.R. 165 (Bankr. W.D. Pa. 1993) ($40.9 million equity cushion not sufficient protection for use of bank's cash collateral where continuation of debtor's business would likely rapidly deplete value of assets).

5. *Stewart v. Gurley*, 745 F.2d 1194, 1196 (9th Cir. 1984). The court reasoned as follows:

   *The statute does not refer to the debtor's equity as against the only plaintiff-lienholder seeking to lift the stay or persons holding liens senior to that of the plaintiff-lienholder. The minority view improperly focuses upon the interests of junior lienholders as opposed to the interests of the debtor or senior lienholder. As the bankruptcy court in* La Jolla Mortgage Fund v. Rancho El Cajon Associates, 18 B.R. 283, 290 *(Bankr. S.D. Cal. 1982) observed, Chapter 11 reorganization should benefit the debtor's interests and not exclusively those of junior lienholders. Id. (citing* In re Saint Peter's School, 16 B.R. at 408). . . . *Refusing to grant relief from the automatic stay under those circumstances would only promote the junior lienholders' interests over those of the senior lienholder. See* In re Faires, 34 B.R. at 552. *Should the junior lienholders want to protect their interests, they may bid at the foreclosure sale just as if the bankruptcy proceedings had not intervened.*

   *Accord Nantucket Investors II v. California Federal Bank (In re Indian Palms Assocs.), 61 F.3d 197, 208 (3d Cir. 1995).*

6. *Bonapfel v. Nalley Motor Trucks (In re Carpet Ctr. Leasing Co.)*, 991 F.2d 682 (11th Cir. 1993), *In re Continental Airlines*, 91 F.3d 553 (3rd Cir. 1996), *In re Continental Airlines*, 154 B.R. 176 (Bankr. D. Del. 1993), and *In re Continental Airlines*, 146 B.R. 536, 539-40 (Bankr. D. Del. 1992).

7. 727 F.2d 1017 (11th Cir. 1984).

8. *Id.* at 1020. See also *Lane Indus., Inc. v. Abramson (In re Pennyrich Int'l, Inc.)*, 473 F.2d 417 (5th Cir. 1973) (you should value the collateral "by

applying the norm that a prudent businessman would employ to dispose of an asset").

9. 11 U.S.C. § 363(m). A proposed auction involving an open bidding process after appropriate marketing should permit a winning bidder to benefit from the good faith status contemplated by § 363(m). *See, e.g., Polaroid Corp. v. Wind Down Assoc., LLC (In re Polaroid Corp.),* 01-10864-PJW, 2004 WL 2223301, at *2 (D. Del. Sept. 30, 2004) (affirming the bankruptcy court's decision that the buyer was a good-faith purchaser based on the fact that the Debtors' assets had been effectively shopped before the petition was filed, a rigorous auction process was undertaken in which nothing was withheld from the market and all bidders had the opportunity to buy the business, and based on the rigorous efforts of the various constituencies, including the Committee of Unsecured Creditors, to maximize their returns.); *In re Abbotts Dairies of Pa.,* 788 F.2d 143 (3d Cir. 1986); *In re Snyder,* 74 B.R. 872 (Bankr. E.D Pa. 1987). The issue of good faith in connection with the sale outside the ordinary course of business focuses principally on the element of special treatment of the debtor's insiders in the sales transactions and related transactions. *See In re Summit Global Logisitics,* No. 08–11566, 2008 WL 819934, at *9; *In re Medical Software Solutions,* 286 B.R. 431, 445-46 (Bankr. D. Utah 2002); *In re Indus. Valley Refrigeration & Air Conditioning Supplies, Inc.,* 77 B.R. 15 (Bankr. E.D. Pa. 1987); *In re Crutcher Resources Corp.,* 72 B.R. 628 (Bankr. N.D. Tex. 1987) (a sale to insiders requires careful review; "blatant attempt to place pressure on the Court only serves to raise additional suspicions concerning the 'cozy' relationship between the parent and the Lenders and to suggest that this case is being orchestrated not for the benefit of unsecured creditors . . . , but rather for the benefit of the Lenders and the principals of the parent corporation;" no evidence on value of assets being sold other than the self serving statements of the purchasers (who were insiders).

10. For example, in *In re WFDR, Inc.,* 10 B.R. 109 (Bankr. N.D. Ga. 1981), the court authorized the sale of the Chapter 11 debtor's principal assets, the real and personal property comprising a radio station, pursuant to a court-supervised bidding process, commenced upon the debtor's Chapter 11 application to sell. The sale took place prior to the acceptance of a Chapter 11 plan and the court expressly held that Section 363(b) authorizes such a sale outside the ordinary course of business. 10 B.R. at 110. *See also Fla. Dep't of Revenue v. Piccadilly Cafeterias, Inc.,* 128 S. Ct. 2326, 2331 n. 2 (2008) (stating that "Chapter 11 bankruptcy proceedings ordinarily culminate in the confirmation of a reorganization plan. But in some cases, as here, a debtor sells all or substantially all its assets under § 363(b)(1) before seeking or receiving plan confirmation."); In *re All Am.,* 40 B.R. 104 (Bankr. N.D. Ga. 1984) (recognizing authority under Section 363(b) to sell all of the debtor's assets prior to the confirmation of a plan of reorganization). *See Fin. Assocs. v. Loeffler (In re Equity Funding Corp. of Am.),* 492 F.2d 793 (9th Cir.), *cert. denied,* 419 U.S. 964 (1974)). (Section 363(b) sale is authorized when the debtor's estate will be impaired unless the assets are sold quickly).

11. *See,* for example, *Fin. Assocs. v. Loeffler (In re Equity Funding Corp. of Am.),* 492 F.2d 793 (9th Cir.), cert. denied, 419 U.S. 964 (1974)). (Section 363(b) sale

is authorized when the debtor's estate will be impaired unless the assets are sold quickly); *Four B. Corp. v. Food Barn Stores, Inc. (In re Food Barn Stores, Inc.)*, 107 F.3d 558, 564-65 (8th Cir. 1997) (in bankruptcy rules, "a primary objective of the Code [is] to enhance the value of the estate at hand"); *Integrated Resources*, 147 B.R. at 659 (" 'It is a well-established principle of bankruptcy law that the objective of bankruptcy rules and the [Debtor's] duty with respect to such sales is to obtain the highest price or greatest overall benefit possible for the estate.") (quoting *Cello Bag Co. v. Champion Int'l Corp (In re Atlanta Packaging Products, Inc.)*, 99 B.R. 124, 130 (Bankr. N.D. Ga. 1988)).

12. *See In re Country Manor of Kenton, Inc.*, 172 B.R. 217 (Bankr. N.D. Ohio 1994) (proposed sale of nursing home license and beds free and clear did not meet sound business purpose test where the property was not advertised or placed on the real estate market and the proposed sale price appeared to be below market value); Comm. of Equity Sec. Holders v. Lionel Corp. (In re Lionel Corp.), 722 F.2d 1063, 1070 (2d Cir. 1983). *See also Golf 25, Inc. v. Eggman*, 07-MC-15-DRH, 2007 WL 781916, at *3 (S.D. Ill. Mar. 14, 2007) (holding that although Section 363(b)(1) allows a debtor to sell substantially all its assets, it must first satisfy the Third Circuit's "sound business test."); *In re Summit Global Logisitics*, No. 08-11566, 2008 WL 819934, at *9 (Bankr. D.N.J. Mar. 26, 2008) (citing Second Circuit authority for the "sound business justification" test).

13. *In re Baldwin United Corp.*, 43 B.R. 888, 906 (Bankr. S.D. Ohio 1984).

14. *Lionel*, 722 F.2d at 1071.

15. 700 F.2d 935 (5th Cir. 1983).

16. *Id.* at 940.

17. Many courts have approved break-up fees and/or expense reimbursements for the stalking-horse bidder, but some courts are only comfortable with one or the other, but not both. *See*, for example, *Reagan v. Wetzel (In re Reagan)*, 403 B.R. 614, 619 n.3 (B.A.P. 8th Cir. Mar. 30, 2009) (stating that "[i]n the event that the stalking horse bidder is outbid, courts often approve break-up fees '[t]o compensate the stalking horse for the 'cost' of showing its hand before the auction, conducting due diligence and otherwise facilitating the creation of a market.'"); *In re Nashville Senior Living Ctr.*, No. 08-07254, 2008 WL 5062366, at *2 (Bankr. M.D. Tenn. Oct. 22, 2008) (stating that "[e]xcept in extremely large transactions, break-up fees ranging from one to two percent of the purchase price have been authorized by some courts."); *The Official Comm. of Subordinated Bondholders v. Integrated Res., Inc. (In re Integrated Resources, Inc.)*, 147 B.R. at 650, 659(S.D.B.N.Y. 1992) (break-up fees are "important tools to encourage bidding and to maximize the value of the debtor's assets"); *In re Crowthers McCall Pattern, Inc.*, 166 B.R. 908, 913 (Bankr. S.D.N.Y. 1990) (decision to enter into agreement including break-up fee amply justified by need to prevent prospective bidder from withdrawing from transaction); *In re HHL Financial Services, Inc.*, No. 97-398 (SLR) (D. Del. March 31, 1997) (approving 5.5 to 5.9 percent break-up fees); *In re Am. White Cross, Inc.*, No. 96-1109 (PJW) (Bankr. D. Del. March 31, 1997) (approving up to 5.8 percent break-up fee plus up to $450,000 in expense reimbursement);

*In re Mid-American Waste Sys., Inc.*, No. 97-0104 (PJW) (Bankr. D. Del. Jan. 21, 1997) (3 percent break-up fee plus up to $1 million in expense reimbursement approved); *In re Simmons Upholstered Furniture, Inc.*, Case No. 94-635 (HSB) (Bankr. D. Del. Aug. 10, 1995) (approving 4.64 percent break-up fee and up to $650,000 in expense reimbursement).

While not a valuation issue, it should be noted that collusive bidding is prohibited by the Bankruptcy Code. Section 363(n) provides that:

*The trustee may avoid a sale under this section if the sale price was controlled by an agreement among potential bidders at such sale, or may recover from a party to such agreement any amount by which the value of the property sold exceeds the price at which such sale was consummated, and may recover any costs, attorneys' fees, or expenses incurred in avoiding such sale or recovering such amount. In addition to any recovery under the preceding sentence, the court may grant judgment for punitive damages in favor of the estate and against any such party that entered into such an agreement in willful disregard of this subsection.*

18. *See*, for example, *In re Beker Indus. Corp.*, 63 B.R. 474, 476-77 (Bankr. S.D. N.Y. 1986) (lien stripping); *c.f. Clear Channel Outdoor, Inc. v. Knupfer (In re PW, LLC)*, 391 B.R. 25 (B.A.P. 9th Cir. 2008) discussed in the next footnote. *In re Collins*, 180 B.R. 447, 450-51 (Bankr. E.D. Va. 1995) (lien stripping); *In re Leckie Smokeless Coal Co.*, 99 F.3d 573, 582 (4th Cir. 1996) (holding that coal mine operators could sell their assets free and clear of successor liability that would otherwise attach under federal statute); *In re Medical Software Solutions*, 286 B.R. at 446 (stating that "the court has the power to order the assets of a seller to be transferred free and clear of all claims, including successor liability claims.").

19. *See*, for example, *In re The Charter Co.*, 829 F.2d 1054, 1056 (11th Cir. 1987) (holding that the purchaser of debtor's assets could not retrospectively question validity of sale or seek partial refund of purchase price; rather, any appeal from bankruptcy court order authorizing sale was rendered moot by parties' failure to obtain stay pending appeal); *In re Trism, Inc.*, 328 F.3d 1003, 1007 (8th Cir. 2003). The protection provided by § 363(m) and "mootness" has recently been called into question by *Clear Channel Outdoor, Inc. v. Knupfer (In re PW, LLC)*, 391 B.R. 25 (B.A.P. 9th Cir. 2008), an opinion that some courts may find persuasive. In *Clear Channel*, an appeal of the *sale* of real estate under § 363 was moot, but an appeal of the lien stripping—a part of the sale that the buyer considered essential to the sale—was *not moot*, and was reversed and remanded.

20. *In re Planned Sys., Inc.*, 82 B.R. 919 (Bankr. S.D. Ohio 1988) (where no evidence of value of property presented, court cannot conclude that private sale of property is in the best interest of the estate, and orders public sale); *In re Country Manor of Kenton, Inc.*, 172 B.R. 217 (Bankr. N.D. Ohio 1994) (proposed sale of nursing home license and beds free and clear did not meet sound business purpose test where the property was not advertised or placed on the real estate

market and the proposed sale price appeared to be below market value); *In re Crutcher Resources Corp.*, 72 B.R. 632 (Bankr. N.D. Tex. 1987) (a sale to insiders requires careful review; "blatant attempt to place pressure on the Court only serves to raise additional suspicions concerning the 'cozy' relationship between the parent and the Lenders and to suggest that this case is being orchestrated not for the benefit of unsecured creditors . . ., but rather for the benefit of the Lenders and the principals of the parent corporation"; no evidence on value of assets being sold other than the self serving statements of the purchasers (who were insiders); no evidence of business justification from the standpoint of the parent; notice not sufficient; approval of sale denied).

21. *In re WRB West Assocs. Joint Venture*, 106 B.R. 215 (Bankr. D. Mont. 1989) (adequate protection in the form of a 40 percent equity cushion is sufficient so as to authorize the debtor's use of cash collateral); *Sharon Steel Corp. v. Citibank, N.A. (In re Sharon Steel Corp.)*, 159 B.R. 165 (Bankr. W.D. Pa. 1993) ($40.9 million equity cushion not sufficient protection for use of bank's cash collateral where continuation of debtor's business would likely rapidly deplete value of assets).

22. *In re Swedeland Development Group, Inc.*, 16 F.3d 552, 566 (3d. Cir. 1994).

23. 11 U.S.C. § 1125(b).

24. 312 U.S. 510, 61 S.Ct. 675, 85 L.Ed. 982 (1941).

25. *See, In re Coram Healthcare Corp.*, 315 B.R. 321, 337 (Bankr. D. Del. 2004). Note that this characterization is not entirely accurate. A court is actually attempting to determine whether the value received by a creditor exceeds the value of that creditor's claims; as such, in the case when non-homogeneous securities (such both common stock and warrants) are distributed to various creditors, courts have entertained valuations of specific values of the securities to be received by the creditors. *See*, for example, *In re Allegheny Int'l, Inc.*, 118 B.R. 282, 304-305 (Bankr. W.D. Pa. 1990).

26. *See*, for example, *In re MCorp Fin., Inc.*, 137 B.R. 219, 235 (Bankr. S.D. Tex. 1992). *In re Exide Techs.*, 303 B.R. 48, 61 (Bankr. D. Del. 2003); *Genesis Health Ventures*, 266 B.R 591, 612. (Bankr. D. Del. 2001).

27. *In re MCorp Fin., Inc.*, 137 B.R. 219, 235 (Bankr. S.D. Tex. 1992) ("[i]f former stockholders' interests are eliminated, a valuation is required to make sure that the senior classes of claims are not being provided for more than in full"), *In re Genesis Health Ventures*, 266 B.R 591, 612. (Bankr. D. Del. 2001) (citing *In re MCorp Financial, Inc.*).

28. *In re Coram Healthcare Corp.*, 315 B.R. 321, 329 (Bankr. D. Del. 2004).

29. *Id.*

30. *In re Oneida Ltd.*, 351 B.R. 79, 87 (Bankr. S.D.N.Y. 2006).

31. *In re Johns-Manville Corp.*, 68 B.R. 618, 636 (Bankr. S.D.N.Y. 1986); see also *Consolidated Rock Products Co. v. Du Bois*, 312 U.S. 510 (1941).

32. *In re Bush Indus.*, 315 B.R. 292, 299 (Bankr. W.D.N.Y. 2004).

33. The statutory language "at least the allowed amount of such claim, of a value, as of the effective date of the plan, of at least the value of such holder's interest in the estate's interest in such property" has been interpreted to require the

valuation to be as of the effective date, and the calculation of the interest factor to be measured from the effective date.

34. *Dewsnup v. Timm*, 502 U.S. 410, 417-18, (1992) ("[a]ny increase over the judicially determined valuation during bankruptcy rightly accrues to the benefit of the [secured] creditor, not to the benefit of the debtor and not to the benefit of other unsecured creditors. . . ."); *In re T-H New Orleans, Ltd Partnership*, 116 F.3d 790 (5th Cir. 1997) ("A flexible approach recognizes the fact that a creditor's allowed claim, which is being reduced over time, may become entitled to accrue postpetition interest, and that under the plain language of § 506(b) there is nothing limiting that right. A flexible approach also recognizes that any increase over the judicially determined valuation during bankruptcy rightly accrues to the benefit of the creditor, and not to the debtor. Moreover, as the bankruptcy court in re Addison Properties noted, the single valuation approach generally balances the bankruptcy process in favor of the debtor. Because of the equitable nature of bankruptcy in seeking a balance between debtors and creditors (debtor's right to a fresh start versus the creditor's right to the value of its claim), we reject the single valuation approach under the particular facts of this case.") (citations omitted); *In re Broomall Printing Corp.*, 131 B.R. 32, 34-35 (Bankr. D. Md. 1991) ("[i]n the confirmation context, the value of the collateral is determined as of the effective date of the plan so the payments will assure the secured creditor the then present value of its collateral"); *In re Seip*, 116 B.R. 709, 712 (Bankr. D. Neb. 1990) ("for purposes of confirmation, the collateral securing a creditor's claim should be valued at a date in close proximity to the confirmation date"); *In re Landing Assocs., Ltd.*, 122 B.R. 288, 293 (Bankr. W.D. Tex. 1990) (the Bankruptcy Court reasoned that the provisions of Sections 506(a), 1129(b)(2)(A)(i), and 1129(a)(7) should be read together leading to "[t]he inescapable conclusion from the foregoing statutory provisions is that a secured creditor's interest in the estate's interest in property may well *grow* during the pendency of a case, augmenting the secured creditor's secured claim. The *entire* secured claim must be properly treated pursuant to Section 1129 or the plan cannot be confirmed. The allowed secured claim to which Section 1129 refers must mean the claim allowed *as of confirmation*."); *In re Hemisphere Int'l Ctr., Inc.*, 59 B.R. 289 (Bankr. S.D. Fla. 1986) (recognizing that a creditor that is undersecured at the beginning of the case may nevertheless be entitled to Section 506 interest if the value of the collateral increases during the bankruptcy case so as to render that creditor oversecured).

35. *In re Exide Techs.*, 303 B.R. at 66 (stating that "[t]he 'taint' of bankruptcy will cause the market to undervalue the securities and future earning capacity of the Debtor.")

36. *In re Mirant Corp.*, 334 B.R. 800, 833, 834 (Bankr. N.D. Tex. 2005) (stating "indeed, the mere fact that any expert would fail to appreciate the benefit to Debtors not only of resolving expensive litigation on which Debtors' cash flow is contingent, but of the claims process and the savings through contract rejection and other special powers afforded by the Code, demonstrates that the market does not fully accord Mirant Group the value enhancement achieved in the course of these cases.")

37. *Id.* at 835 (stating that in the case of Mirant "neither of these conditions exists . . . . Merchant energy companies [(such as Mirant)] sell into a marketplace in which either they are parties to contracts or they are effectively anonymous participants in an exchange [, and] as to a debt-heavy balance sheet, the result in some reorganization cases, the Plan proposes conversion of substantial debt to equity. Mirant's ratio of debt to capitalization is expected to be about 0.62. The company's capital structure is impressive enough that seven potential lenders initially competed to provide exit financing, and, although the Plan requires only $750 million in exit financing, Debtors have a commitment for up to $ 2.35 billion.")

38. *Consolidated Rock Products Co. v. Du Bois*, 312 U.S. 510, 526, 61 S.Ct. 675, 685, 85 L.Ed. 982 (1941)(concluding that earning capacity is the measure of value and that "[t]he criterion of earning capacity is the essential one if the enterprise is to be freed from the heavy hand of past errors, miscalculations or disaster, and if the allocation of securities among the various claimants is to be fair and equitable."); *In re Bush Indus.*, 315 B.R. 292, 299 (Bankr. W.D.N.Y. 2004).

39. *In re Mirant Corp.*, 334 B.R. 800, 825 (Bankr. N.D. Tex. 2005) (Ordering all parties to use the assumptions in the debtor's business plan for competing valuations because such assumptions were a "fair, reasonable projection of future operations of Mirant Group" and were "prepared in a reasonable manner, using supportable assumptions and logically consistent computations.") *See also, Iridium IP LLC v. Motorola, Inc. (In re Iridium Operating LLC)*, 373 B.R. 283, 351 (Bankr. S.D.N.Y. 2007) (stating that "where alternative projections 'are no better supported by the evidence than are those in the Business Plan,' the projections in management's business plan should be used in the DCF . . ." (citing *In re Mirant Corp.*, 334 B.R. at 825)).

40. *In re Mirant Corp.*, 334 B.R. at 832-33 (footnotes omitted). The *Mirant* decision cited to several other cases that reached the same conclusion:

> *In re Penn Cent. Transp. Co.*, 596 F.2d 1102, 1115 (3d Cir. 1979) (recognizing that, in some instances:, evidence of market value should be ignored because the market can be expected irrationally to undervalue the securities of a once-distressed company emerging from a lengthy reorganization); *In re New York, New Haven & Hartford R.R. Co.*, 4 B.R. 758, 792 (D. Conn. 1980) The stigma of bankruptcy alone is a factor that will seriously depress the market value of a company's securities; *In re Missouri Pac. R. Co.*, 39 F. Supp. 436, 446 (E.D. Mo. 1941) (Debtors have been in the process of reorganization for eight years, which fact alone would necessarily result in a serious depression in the market value of its securities.).

> *Id.* at 822 n.71 *See also In re Exide Technologies*: the bankruptcy court explained that "numerous adjustments" to an expert's opinion to "bring value calculations in line with current market value" is "not appropriate when seeking to value securities of a reorganized debtor since the 'taint' of bankruptcy will cause the market to undervalue the securities and future earning capacity of the Debtor." 303 B.R. at 65.

41. *In re Mirant Corp.*, 334 B.R. 800, 831 n.10 (Bankr. N.D. Tex. 2005) (citing Code § 1129(b)(2)(B); *Liberty Nat'l Enters. v. Ambanc La Mesa Ltd. P'ship (In re Ambanc La Mesa Ltd. P'ship)*, 115 F.3d 650, 654 (9th Cir. 1997) (Chapter 11 plan, which provided for equity to retain interest in debtor, violated the absolute priority rule because it did not provide for payment of interest on objecting creditor's unsecured claim); *Everett v. Perez (In re Perez)*, 30 F.3d 1209, 1214-15 (9th Cir. 1994) (same)).

42. Shannon P. Pratt, *Valuing a Business*, p. 385 (5th Ed. 2007).

43. *See, e.g., City Nat'l Bank v. Am. Commonwealth Fin. Corp.*, 801 F.2d 714, 715 n.1 (4th Cir. 1986) (" '[T]he value of a controlling position in a corporation is worth more on a per share basis than a non-controlling interest.' This enhanced value is termed a control premium." (citation omitted) (quoting *Alna Capital Assocs. V. Wagner*, 758 F.2d 562, 566 (11th Cir. 1985)); *Borruso v. Commc'ns Telesystems Int'l*, 753 A.2d 451, 458 (Del. Ch. 1999); Shannon P. Pratt, *Valuing a Business* (5th Ed. 2007); Dr. Israel Shaked et al., *Liquidity and Control: Valuation Discounts/Premiums and the Bankrupt Firm*, 26 Am. Bankr. Inst. J. 54, 55 (2008).

44. In *In re Nellson Nutraceutical*, the Bankruptcy Court for the District of Delaware concluded that the debtor's enterprise value included a premium associated with the value of "control." No. 06-10072, 2007 WL 201134, at *36 (Bankr. D. Del. Jan. 18, 2007) ("Mr. Braun was the only expert that employed a 'control premium' in connection with his Comparable Companies analysis . . . his conclusion will not be disturbed.") (emphasis added). The Bankruptcy Court for the Middle District of Tennessee approved a similar approach in *In re American Homepatient, Inc.*, 298 B.R. 152, 154-55 (Bankr. M.D. Tenn. 2003).[43] *See also Asarco LLC. v. Americas Mining Corp.*, 396 B.R. 278, 348, 354 (S.D. Tex. 2008) ("The Court finds that a control premium should be added to the market multiples valuation.") (emphasis added).

# CHAPTER 8

# Valuations in Bankruptcy at a Time in the Past—Avoidance Actions

## OVERVIEW

From a valuation standpoint, preference litigation and fraudulent transfer litigation have two important things in common. First, a key issue is whether the debtor was insolvent at the time of the transfer. Second, the valuation opinions delivered at trial always relate to the valuation of a business's assets and debts (and thus, solvency or not) at a time in the past.

This chapter first explains in more detail the key principles of (1) a preference claim under bankruptcy law and (2) a fraudulent transfer claim under bankruptcy law or state law, insofar as the issues in those cases are particularly relevant to the valuation professional. This chapter then sets out the applicable definitions of insolvency, and examines the approaches taken by courts when grappling with valuation concepts and legal standards applicable to a determination of insolvency. Finally, because valuations in preference and fraudulent transfer cases are always at a time in the past, this chapter discusses the different approaches taken by courts regarding the use of hindsight in valuations or solvency determinations.

## AVOIDANCE ACTIONS—PREFERENCES

### *Preference* Defined

The ability of a trustee in bankruptcy to recover preferences is one aspect of the Bankruptcy Code's effort to provide equality of distribution of the debtor's assets to the creditors that have valid claims against the debtor (subject, of course, to the prior payment of secured claims and claims that are given priority pursuant to the Bankruptcy Code). A creditor that manages to obtain payment of its claim by the debtor shortly before a bankruptcy filing might get paid in full when other unsecured creditors, who made their demand later, or whose lawsuits moved a little slower, might get only pennies on the dollar from the bankruptcy case. Preference law attempts to rectify that situation, at least in part.

Section 547 of the Bankruptcy Code provides (in pertinent part) that the trustee may avoid any transfer of an interest of the debtor in property

1. *to or for the benefit of a creditor;*
2. *for or on account of an antecedent debt owed by the debtor before such transfer was made;*
3. *made while the debtor was insolvent;*
4. made
   (A) *on or within 90 days before the date of the filing of the petition; or*
   (B) *between ninety days and one year before the date of the filing of the petition, if such creditor at the time of such transfer was an insider; and*
5. *that enables such creditor to receive more than such creditor would receive if—*
   (A) *the case were a case under chapter 7 of [the Bankruptcy Code];*
   (B) *the transfer had not been made; and*
   (C) *such creditor received payment of such debt to the extent provided by the provisions of [the Bankruptcy Code].*[1]

## Valuation Can Be Central to a Preference Case

Clearly, the issue of whether a debtor was solvent is critical to a preference case. In many cases, however, there is little or no debate regarding the debtor's insolvency at the time of the challenged transfer. Most importantly, for the purposes of the preference section of the Bankruptcy Code, the debtor is *presumed to have been insolvent* on and during the 90 days immediately preceding the date of the filing of the bankruptcy case.[2] Although the defendant may rebut this presumption, it can do so only by producing affirmative evidence that the debtor was solvent during the preference period. This can be an expensive proposition, and in the usual case (particularly if the challenged transfer is relatively small) a defendant is not likely to spend a great deal of money in the hopes of proving that a company that filed bankruptcy was in fact solvent in the three months leading up to the bankruptcy filing. Accordingly, most noninsider preference cases are defended based on one or more of the statutory defenses to a trustee's right to recover a transfer as preferential. These defenses include, for example, that the transfer was a contemporaneous exchange for new value,[3] or was a payment "in the ordinary course."[4]

Where insolvency is contested, the applicable standards (the definition of insolvency, and the court's approaches to insolvency determinations) are essentially the same when the issues arise in the context of fraudulent transfer litigation.

## AVOIDANCE ACTIONS—FRAUDULENT TRANSFERS

### There Are Two Principal Kinds of Fraudulent Transfer Claims

Although it may be human nature for a debtor, faced with overwhelming debts, to transfer his or her assets to family or friends in the hopes of keeping some property from the debt collectors, such transfers have been condemned by the law since ancient times.[5]

Today, there are two principal types of prepetition transfers that can be recovered for the benefit of creditors as fraudulent transfers. The first type is a transfer made by a debtor with the *actual intent* to hinder, delay, or defraud creditors (actual fraudulent intent). The law also allows the recovery of transfers that are called *constructively fraudulent* transfers. In the simplest example, a transfer by a debtor is constructively fraudulent if (1) the debtor made the transfer without receiving a reasonably equivalent value in exchange for the transfer, and (2) the debtor was insolvent at that time. In such a case, the trustee does not have to prove that the debtor made the transfer with actual fraudulent intent. (A debtor can also enter into a fraudulent obligation, but the more common cases involve transfers of assets. In the interest of readability, no further specific reference to fraudulent obligations will be included, and any reference to the governing statutes will omit references to fraudulent obligations).

Valuations are at the heart of any litigation brought to recover fraudulent transfers. When a transfer is attacked as constructively fraudulent, the need for at least one valuation is obvious: In order to win the case, the trustee must prove *that the debtor was insolvent* at the time of transfer. This issue—insolvency of the debtor—is equally important in an actual fraudulent intent case, because when the judge answers the question of whether the debtor made the transfer with actual fraudulent intent, the judge is entitled to consider (among other circumstantial evidence) whether the debtor was insolvent when the transfer was made.

In some fraudulent transfer cases, more valuations are needed. For instance, if the property transferred was anything other than cash, then that property must be valued, because if the trustee wins the case, the trustee will be entitled to a judgment *for the value of the asset* at the time of the transfer (subject to adjustment as the law may allow).[6] When a transfer is attacked as constructively fraudulent, both the property transferred and the property received may need to be valued, so the jury can determine whether the two have reasonably equivalent value.

The applicable valuation standards (the definition of *insolvency,* and the court's approaches to insolvency determinations) for a fraudulent transfer case are essentially the same when solvency is at issue in preference litigation. However, at least in part because the reach-back period for fraudulent transfers is longer than for preference cases, it is more common to need valuations in fraudulent transfer cases compared to preference cases.

## Sources of Fraudulent Transfer Law

When no bankruptcy has been filed, a creditor can bring a fraudulent transfer case under state law. When a bankruptcy has been filed, the trustee (but not individual creditors) can bring a lawsuit to recover a fraudulent transfer under the provisions of bankruptcy law (§ 548) *or* state law.[7] Although there are differences between federal bankruptcy law and state laws regarding fraudulent transfers, most of the big-picture issues are the same. This is true because nearly every state has enacted (typically with only minor variations) the Uniform Fraudulent Transfer Act (usually referred to as UFTA), and UFTA was based on the sections of the Bankruptcy Code that deal with fraudulent transfers.[8] There is one key difference between § 548 of the Bankruptcy Code and UFTA—the reach-back period. Under § 548(a) of the Bankruptcy Code, the trustee can attack transfers that occurred up to two years before the filing of the petition,[9] but under the provisions of the Bankruptcy Code that allow the trustee to use state fraudulent transfer law for the benefit of creditors, the trustee can use UFTA's longer (usually four-year) reach-back period.[10]

### *Actual Fraudulent Intent* Transfers Defined

Section 548 of the Bankruptcy Code defines an actual fraudulent intent case as follows:

> *The trustee may avoid any transfer . . . incurred by the debtor, that was made . . . on or within 2 years before the date of the filing of the petition, if the debtor voluntarily or involuntarily—*

*made such transfer . . . with actual intent to hinder, delay, or
defraud any entity to which the debtor was or became, on or after
the date that such transfer was made . . . , indebted. . . .*

11 U.S.C. § 548(a)(1)(A). References to a special rule relating to
employment contracts and the general reference to fraudulent
obligations have been omitted for simplicity's sake.

Section 4 of UFTA defines an actual fraudulent intent case as follows:

*(a) A transfer made . . . by a debtor is fraudulent as to a creditor,
whether the creditor's claim arose before or after the transfer was
made . . . , if the debtor made the transfer . . . :*
   *(1) with actual intent to hinder, delay, or defraud any creditor
of the debtor. . . .*

UFTA § 4. References to fraudulent
obligations have been omitted.

## Solvency Issues in Actual Fraudulent Intent Cases

As noted earlier, even though nothing about insolvency is mentioned in the
definition of an actual fraudulent intent transfer, whether the debtor was
insolvent at the time of the transfer is critically important. This is because
the drafters of the laws allowing the recovery of fraudulent transfers realized that proving actual fraudulent intent can be very difficult. In the usual
case, the defendant will never admit to having the actual intent to hinder,
delay, or defraud creditors, and accordingly, the plaintiff will have to prove
its case using circumstantial evidence. Years of experience have allowed
courts to characterize some recurring examples of circumstantial evidence
as badges of fraud. When one or more badges of fraud are present, they can
support a judgment that a transfer was made with actual fraudulent intent,
even when there is no direct evidence of such intent. Cases decided under
§ 548 of the Bankruptcy Code take into account the same badges of fraud
that UFTA actually lists in the statute. In this regard, § 4(b) of UFTA provides that:

*in determining actual intent [to hinder, delay, or defraud], consid-
eration may be given, among other factors, to whether:*

1. *The transfer . . . was to an insider*
2. *The debtor retained possession or control of the property
   transferred after the transfer*
3. *The transfer . . . was disclosed or concealed*

4. *Before the transfer was made . . . , the debtor had been sued or threatened with suit*
5. *The transfer was of substantially all the debtor's assets*
6. *The debtor absconded*
7. *The debtor removed or concealed assets*
8. *The value of the consideration received by the debtor was reasonably equivalent to the value of the asset transferred . . .*
9. *The debtor was insolvent or became insolvent shortly after the transfer was made . . .*
10. *The transfer occurred shortly before or shortly after a substantial debt was incurred; and*
11. *The debtor transferred the essential assets of the business to a lienor who transferred the assets to an insider of the debtor.*[11]

As can be seen, § 4(b)(9) of UFTA, and cases decided under the Bankruptcy Code, put the issue of solvency front and center in any actual fraudulent intent case.

In a case in which the debtor had been sued (or threatened with suit) before the transfer was made (a badge of fraud under § 4(b)(4) of UFTA and cases decided under the Bankruptcy Code), the very existence of that lawsuit (or threat of same) can greatly complicate the determination of insolvency. In the usual case, the debtor will have denied the allegations of the lawsuit, and, therefore, the claim is a disputed claim. Similarly, if the debtor signed a large guaranty before the transfer, that guaranty can be relevant in two ways. First, the guaranty would be (at least before it was called upon) a contingent claim. As such, whether it was a substantial debt (and could be a badge of fraud) would depend on a valuation of that contingent claim. In addition, if the contingent guarantee was, in fact, substantial, it could impact the solvency/insolvency calculation as well.

The valuation impact of disputed and contingent claims is discussed later in this chapter. We also discuss later in this chapter the valuation of a disputed or contingent claim that is resolved (so that it is no longer disputed or contingent) *after* the time of the transfer but before the time of the trial of the case.

### Constructively Fraudulent Transfer Defined

Section 548(a) of the Bankruptcy Code defines a constructively fraudulent transfer as follows:

> *The trustee may avoid any transfer . . . of an interest of the debtor in property . . . , that was made . . . on or within 2 years before the date of the filing of the petition, if the debtor voluntarily or involuntarily— . . .*

*(B) (i) received less than a reasonably equivalent value in exchange for such transfer . . . ; and*

*(ii) (I) was insolvent on the date that such transfer was made . . . , or became insolvent as a result of such transfer . . . ; (II) was engaged in business or a transaction, or was about to engage in business or a transaction, for which any property remaining with the debtor was an unreasonably small capital; [or] (III) intended to incur, or believed that the debtor would incur, debts that would be beyond the debtor's ability to pay as such debts matured. . . .*

**11 U.S.C. § 548(a)(1)(B). References to a special rule relating to employment contracts and references to fraudulent obligations have been omitted for simplicity's sake.**

UFTA contains the same concept, but with slight variations depending on who can bring the claim (a creditor at the time of the transfer vs. a creditor who became a creditor after the transfer). Section 4(a)(2) of UFTA provides:

*(a) A transfer made . . . by a debtor is fraudulent as to a creditor, whether the creditor's claim arose before or after the transfer was made . . . , if the debtor made the transfer . . . : . . . (2) without receiving a reasonably equivalent value in exchange for the transfer . . . , and the debtor:*

*(i) was engaged or was about to engage in a business or a transaction for which the remaining assets of the debtor were unreasonably small in relation to the business or transaction; or*

*(ii) intended to incur, or believed or reasonably should have believed that he [or she] would incur, debts beyond his [or her] ability to pay as they became due.*

**UFTA § 4(a)(2). References to fraudulent obligations have been omitted.**

Section 5(a) of UFTA provides:

*A transfer made . . . by a debtor is fraudulent as to a creditor whose claim arose before the transfer was made . . . if the debtor made the transfer . . . without receiving a reasonably equivalent value in exchange for the transfer . . . and the debtor was insolvent at that time or the debtor became insolvent as a result of the transfer. . . .*

**UFTA § 5(a). References to fraudulent obligations have been omitted.**

The issue of solvency or not is at the center of a constructively fraudulent transfer, but in addition, the case of unreasonably small capital can be at issue. The existence of disputed or contingent claims at the time of the transfer can complicate the solvency analysis, as discussed later in this chapter.

## THE APPLICABLE LEGAL TESTS FOR INSOLVENCY

The law gives some guidance regarding the test for insolvency. The Bankruptcy Code generally defines *insolvent* to mean "an entity's 'financial condition such that the sum of such entity's debts is greater than all of such entity's property, at a fair valuation.'"[12] This is often referred to as the balance-sheet test of insolvency, even though, as will be seen, values found on the balance sheet prepared by a company's accountants (book values) will have little or nothing to do with a fair valuation of such assets.

This definition of *insolvent* applies in both a preference case and a fraudulent transfer case brought under § 548 of the Bankruptcy Code. In a fraudulent transfer case brought under state law, UFTA has a general definition of *insolvency* that is almost identical, as follows: "A debtor is insolvent if the sum of the debtor's debts is greater than all of the debtor's assets, at a fair valuation."[13] In both cases, there are special rules for partnerships, and some assets are excluded from these calculations.[14]

### In Some Cases, Insolvency Is Presumed

*Preferences.* For the purposes of the preference section of the Bankruptcy Code, the debtor is presumed to have been insolvent on and during the 90 days immediately preceding the date of the filing of the bankruptcy case. The defendant may rebut this presumption by producing affirmative evidence that the debtor was solvent during the preference period. If the transferee rebuts the presumption of insolvency, the trustee must prove insolvency.[15] The "trustee must satisfy its burden of proof of insolvency by a preponderance of the evidence."[16]

When a transfer is made to an insider beyond the 90-day period, but within one year of bankruptcy, there is no statutory presumption of insolvency. In such a case, the trustee must present independent proof sufficient to sustain the trustee's "burden of proving insolvency by a preponderance of evidence."[17]

*Fraudulent Transfers.* In a fraudulent transfer case brought under UFTA, UFTA provides that a "debtor who is generally not paying his debts as they become due is presumed to be insolvent."[18] Even if such a state of facts exists, the presumption can be rebutted by a valuation that applies

UFTA's balance-sheet test of insolvency. Under that test, an entity can be solvent even if it is unable to pay its debts as they come due. There is no similar presumption when a fraudulent transfer case is brought under § 548 of the Bankruptcy Code; the trustee will need a valuation that applies the balance-sheet test given by the Bankruptcy Code's definition of insolvency.

The importance of either of these presumptions, when applicable, and the concomitant shifting of the insolvency burden from plaintiff to defendant, cannot be overstated. Without the benefit of a presumption, the plaintiff must offer proof of insolvency by direct evidence on the date of the challenged transfer.

## INSOLVENCY TEST: VALUATION OF DEBTS

It would be easy for a valuation expert to think that the debt side of the insolvency determination is simple, but even in the typical case, the phrase "the sum of . . . debts" presents an immediate difficulty—the debtor's balance sheet can be examined *only as the starting point* to make this calculation. The debts that *are listed* are easily (and are already) summed.[19] But, from the accounting standpoint, of course, the liability side of a balance sheet (even when prepared correctly) doesn't contain all the debts of a company. For example, neither contingent nor disputed claims will be listed on a balance sheet, although they should be discussed in the footnotes if significant. Intercompany liabilities may not be found on the financial statements of affiliated companies, which becomes particularly important when some but not all of the affiliated companies are debtors in bankruptcy.

### Debts Are Defined Expansively

From a legal standpoint, both the Bankruptcy Code and UFTA define *debt* quite expansively. *Debt* means "liability on a claim," and *claim* means "a right to payment, whether or not the right is reduced to judgment, liquidated, unliquidated, fixed, contingent, matured, unmatured, disputed, undisputed, legal, equitable, secured, or unsecured."[20] Accordingly, the expert will need to work with counsel to be sure that *all* the debtor's debts, even those that need not be shown on the accounting balance sheet, are taken into account as part of the balance-sheet calculation of insolvency.

### Valuation of Liquidated, Contingent, and Disputed Debts

Depending on the type of debt (or claim), making a determination of its fair valuation can be complicated. A *liquidated* claim is different from a *contingent* claim, and a contingent claim is different from a *disputed* claim, and those differences have a large impact on the fair valuation of those claims as part of an insolvency determination. Contingent and disputed liabilities must be considered for purposes of determining solvency.[21]

*Liquidated Claims.* A good example of a liquidated claim is an ordinary promissory note. The principal amount owed is stated in the note, and the interest due as of a particular date is easily calculated.

*Contingent Claims.* The classic contingent claim is a guaranty signed by Company A for the debts of Company B. If, on the valuation date, Company B has not defaulted on the guaranteed debt and whether it will default is not yet known, then Company A's obligation is still contingent. Because something has to happen in the future (as compared to the valuation date), such a claim is contingent.

*Disputed Claims.* A lawsuit that has been filed and is being contested is a *disputed* claim. By contrast to a contingent claim, all the relevant facts have occurred (even though the plaintiff and the defendant may dispute what really happened, and the legal effect of what happened). If the lawsuit is not settled, it will be up to the fact finder (the jury or the judge) to decide what actually happened and, in light of the applicable law, whether the defendant is liable to the plaintiff and, if so, the amount of damages.

The courts usually respect these distinctions. "It is settled . . . that the terms disputed, contingent and liquidated have *different* meanings."[22] In *Loya v. Rapp (In re Loya)*,[23] the court stated:

> [T]he rule is clear that a contingent debt is one which the debtor will be called upon to pay only upon the occurrence or happening of an extrinsic event which will trigger the liability of the debtor to the alleged creditor.
>
> A tort claim ordinarily is not contingent as to liability; the events that give rise to the tort claim usually have occurred and liability is not dependent on some future event that may never happen. It is immaterial that the tort claim is not adjudicated or liquidated, or that the claim is disputed. . . .

How does an expert determine a fair valuation of these different sorts of claims?

The liquidated and undisputed claim is relatively easy: the amount due is known and easily determined (review the promissory note, or the balance sheet, which should have captured all liquidated and undisputed claims). One possible complication must be noted: debt is often traded, and in the case of a company in distress, it usually trades at a discount. In the case of public companies, a company's total enterprise value (TEV) is sometimes said to be the sum of its debts at such trading value plus the market capitalization of the common stock. However significant that calculation may be to investment bankers, the discounted or "trading" value of a company's debt should not be used when determining solvency or insolvency, because the holder of the claim, even if it has been acquired at a discount, can enforce it against the debtor in accordance with its terms.[24]

The contingent claim is harder because it is a contingent claim on the valuation date (and assuming that it is not any different on the opinion date). Most courts say that it doesn't make much sense to ignore it (and give a fair valuation of zero) or to assume the contingency will occur and the full amount will come due (and give it a fair valuation of 100 percent of the potential claim).[25] A well-known case, *Xonics Photochemical,* discussed this issue "at such length . . . to avoid creating the unsettling impression that contingent liabilities must for purposes of determining solvency be treated as definite liabilities even though the contingency has not occurred."[26] The court in *Xonics Photochemical* said that, to "value the contingent liability it is necessary to discount it by the probability that the contingency will occur and the liability become real."[27] As an example, the court went on to say:

> *Suppose that on the [relevant] date . . . there was a 1 percent chance that Xonics [the guarantor] . . . would ever be called on to yield up its assets to creditors of . . . Medical Systems [the company whose debts Xonics had guaranteed]. . . . Then the true measure of the liability created by these obligations on the date . . . would not be $28 million; it would be a paltry $17,000. . . . Discounted, the obligations would not make Xonics insolvent.*
>
> **In re Xonics Photochemical, Inc.,**
> **841 F.2d 198, 200 (7th Cir. 1988).**

The rule is easily stated, but its application can obviously be difficult. Determining the percentage chance that a guarantee of the debts of another company would be called could require a full analysis of the *other* company's financial condition. In discounting contingent liabilities, courts have sometimes limited the analysis to *foreseeable* events that might occur while the debtor is in business. Therefore, it is not necessary to discount a liability by *every* possible outcome, but only by those that are *foreseeable*.[28] When valuing a contingent liability, a court will attempt to consider the likelihood of the event occurring from an objective standpoint.[29] Arriving at a fair valuation of a disputed and unresolved claim may be harder still.

*Subsequent Events and Hindsight.* The fair valuation of a contingent or disputed claim can include another wrinkle when, *after* the valuation date but before the opinion date, the contingent claim becomes noncontingent (e.g., the guarantee is released, or a lawsuit is brought to collect the guaranty and a final judgment is entered that determines the amount due on the guaranty) or the disputed claim is resolved (e.g., the case is settled or tried, and a judgment for a specific amount is entered). How courts have addressed fair valuations of a contingent or disputed claim in these circumstances is discussed later in this chapter.

## INSOLVENCY TEST: THE VALUATION OF ASSETS

Valuation of the property or assets at a fair valuation requires the expert to value the debtor's business at the time of the transfer. The term *fair valuation* is frequently the subject of judicial gloss and academic commentary. *Fair valuation* has been defined by one commentator as the fair market value that "could be obtained by a capable and diligent businessman under no compulsion to sell."[30] One court has held that *fair valuation* refers to "the fair market value of the [d]ebtor's assets and liabilities within a reasonable time of the transfer."[31] Another court said the fair valuation standard contemplates a determination of what the debtor's assets ought to bring, that is, a going concern or market value.[32] Yet another put it this way: "The fair value of property is . . . determined . . . by estimating what debtor's assets would realize if sold in a prudent manner in current market condition."[33]

Here the expert can expect to be on familiar ground. Depending on the information available, the expert can use the asset approach, the income approach, or the market approach, to arrive at an opinion of value. For example, in *MFS/Sun Life Trust–High Yield Series v. Van Dusen Airport Servs. Co.*, 910 F. Supp. 913, 939, 942 (S.D.N.Y. 1995), in determining that an LBO was not a fraudulent transfer because the debtor was solvent after the transaction, the court relied on the discounted cash flow and market methods of valuation and reasoned as follows:

> *Both the plaintiffs and the defendants presented evidence of the value of VDAS based on discounted cash flow. This is an appropriate method of determining the going concern value of a company that is not in imminent danger of collapse. See Moody, 971 F.2d at 1067; Vadnais Lumber, 100 B.R. at 131-32 ("The proper standard of valuation to be applied in determination of solvency in a bankruptcy proceeding is the value of the business as a going concern,*

*not the liquidation value of its assets less its liabilities.").* The wide
variance in valuations is attributable to differences in initial earnings figures, in the growth rate applied to those figures, and in the
discount rate selected.

A number of the witnesses also performed valuations using
comparable companies or comparable transactions. Because there
is legitimate disagreement over how "comparable" one business is
to another, these analyses incorporate additional variables. Accordingly, they are best utilized to corroborate valuations obtained by
other methods.

## Going-Concern Valuation or Liquidation Valuation?

Before valuing assets, the court must determine whether a debtor was a
going concern. In valuation literature, this is the premise of the valuation.[34]
The bankruptcy cases that have addressed this issue have generally shown a
bias in favor of applying a going-concern valuation. For example, the Sev-
enth Circuit in the *In re Taxman Clothing Co.* case determined that, unless
a debtor was on its deathbed at the time of the subject transfer, fair valuation requires a going-concern valuation, not a liquidation valuation.[35]
Other courts have phrased the distinction in similar terms; one bankruptcy
court noted that assets are valued on a going-concern basis unless liquidation in bankruptcy was "clearly imminent on the date of the challenged
transfer."[36] And the Ninth Circuit in *Wolkowitz v. Am. Research Corp. (In
re DAK Indus.)* held that the bankruptcy court did not err in determining
that a debtor, which operated for two and a half years in Chapter 11 and
had ability to pay operating expenses during the same period, was a going
concern during the prebankruptcy preference period.[37] In another case, parties agreed that assets should be valued as going concern because, as of the
valuation date, the debtor planned to continue operations as usual.[38] In
the case of *Travelers International A.G. v. Trans World Airlines, Inc.
(In re Trans World Airlines, Inc.)*,[39] the Third Circuit, assuming that a
hypothetical sale of all of the debtor's assets could be accomplished in
12–18 months, valued the assets at a going-concern value, not distress-
sale value. The determination was specifically significant in the *TWA*
case because this allowed the court to *exclude* certain contingent liabilities from the solvency analysis that would have been triggered upon
liquidation.

But the decisions of the courts are not uniform. Sometimes they value
assets piecemeal and ignore any operating value that a particular business
may have.[40]

## Book Value of Assets

The book value of assets is often said to be irrelevant to the determination of fair valuation.[41] Courts generally will not rely on a book value showing of insolvency because book value may not reflect the property's fair value.[42] For example, goodwill and organizational expenses shown on a balance sheet, are not, in and of themselves, of any value that should be included when determining solvency.[43]

Courts that refer to or start from book value, will go beyond the book value of the assets and liabilities listed on the debtor's financial statements, and will determine the value of the company by hypothesizing a balance sheet as of the date of the transfer in question. "[A] court may modify balance sheet entries (i.e., increase/decrease the value of an asset or reduce/elevate the amount of the liability) in order to more accurately reflect the financial condition of the [d]ebtor."[44] Courts look beyond the book value of assets as listed by the debtor because accounting rules generally require assets to be reflected at their historical cost or face value. Moreover, concepts such as depreciation often have no relevance in determining the market value of a particular asset. Even mark-to-market book values may not always accurately reflect fair value of an asset. Nevertheless, the debtor's financial statements may provide evidence of the valuation of particular assets.[45] Despite the caselaw just referred to, some courts sometimes rely on balance-sheet and income-statement information to determine solvency/insolvency. For instance, in one case, a trustee proved insolvency even though debtor's bankruptcy *schedules* showed that assets exceeded liabilities by over $3.7 million, in part because the debtor's balance sheet (included in an SEC registration statement prepared by debtor the year prior to bankruptcy) showed that the debtor had a negative net worth at that time of over $9 million, and had continuing losses expected in the future, and the industry in which the debtor participated was described in the registration statement as operating at severely depressed levels.[46] From this, the court concluded that the debtor was a failing business in a failing industry.

## Purchase Price

Courts also often consider purchase price in valuation. For example, in *MFS/Sun Life Trust–High Yield Series v. Van Dusen Airport Servs. Co.*, 910 F. Supp. 913, 939 (S.D.N.Y. 1995), the court reasoned that, "Where a transaction is consummated after arms-length negotiations, and particularly where other potential purchasers expressed interest in buying the company on similar terms, the sale price is a good indicator of the value of the target's assets." The issue in *MFS/Sun Life* was whether an LBO was avoidable as a fraudulent conveyance. The District Court held that it was not avoidable because the debtor was solvent after the transaction. As noted earlier, the court also received expert testimony on the value of the company as a going concern based on use of the discounted cash flow approach to valuation and using the comparable sales approach.

## PROOF OF INSOLVENCY BY RETROJECTION

Although the statutory test of insolvency is clear, there are some cases in which a unique approach to proving insolvency has been allowed by the bankruptcy courts. For example, some courts have allowed insolvency to be proved by inference,[47] and others have applied a technique called retrojection. *Retrojection* is the process of working backwards from the time of the financial statement being used to the date of the transfer to show factors from which the debtor's insolvency may be established.[48] For instance, a debtor has been found insolvent when "debtor's balance sheet showed a negative equity and a continuous operation at a loss" and "a negative net worth for the year before the transfer" at issue.[49] When using retrojection to prove insolvency, however, the trustee must show the absence of any substantial or radical changes in the assets or liabilities of the debtor between the applicable dates.[50]

## THE INSOLVENCY TEST: COMPARING ASSETS AND DEBTS

Once debts and assets have been valued at a fair valuation, they are compared: if the sum of the debts exceeds the valuation, the debtor was insolvent; if debts are less than the value of the assets, the debtor was solvent.

## IS THE PUBLIC MARKET'S ASSESSMENT IN THE PAST CONCLUSIVE PROOF OF SOLVENCY, EVEN IF THE COMPANY LATER FAILS?

When a public company is being valued at a time in the past (the date of the alleged fraudulent transfer), several significant cases hold that the valuation may be determined: by the market's evaluation of the debtor's assets as a going concern at or about the time of the transfer. For example, in *In re VFB LLC*, 482 F.3d 624 (3d. Cir. 2007) the court considered claims arising out of a spinoff by Campbell Soup of a subsidiary (Vlassic Foods) alleging that it was a fraudulent transfer. The Third Circuit affirmed a determination that there had not been a fraudulent transfer because the subsidiary was solvent based on market capitalization several months after the transaction. With respect to the calculations performed by experts using a *post hoc* discounted cash flow analysis, the Third Circuit reasoned that "[A]bsent some reason to distrust it, the market price is 'a more reliable measure of the stock's value than the subjective estimates of one or two expert witnesses."'482 F.3d at 633.

*In re Iridium Operating LLC*[51] is another case in which market-based measures were key elements of the court's analysis. The question in *In re Iridium Operating LLC* was whether there had been a fraudulent conveyance (effected through payments totaling $3.7 billion under a contract for the development and deployment of a global satellite-based telecommunications system). The court's criticism of the experts and their inability to explain why the public markets had placed a value on *Iridium* and provided debt financing indicating liquidity and adequate capitalization led to the conclusion that the debtor was solvent and, therefore, there could be no constructively fraudulent transfer. The court criticized *post hoc* cash-flow projections where the public market obviously believed the debtor had value under its (ultimately highly inaccurate) business plan and business model:

> *[The expert's] opinions are also entitled to less weight because of his conscious disregard of . . . contemporaneous market evidence, including Iridium's stock price, which the courts view as a critical piece of information in valuing a company. Basing his opinion only on two DCF analyses, combined with [the expert's] inability to reconcile his conclusions of insolvency and inadequate capital with the market validation of Iridium's business plan and positive value at the time, leads to the conclusion that his opinions are of doubtful reliability.*
>
> *. . . [the expert's] conclusions of insolvency and inadequate capital do not correlate with the market validation of Iridium's business plans and the positive value attributed to the business during the relevant period. This failure of the Committee's experts to reconcile their conclusions with the prevailing market judgment or to cast serious doubt on the reliability of that market judgment pro-vides sufficient reason for this court to seriously question the reliability of their opinions.*[52]

## USE OF HINDSIGHT IN THE VALUATION PROCESS

Whether an expert can use hindsight when performing a valuation is a topic that has generated considerable debate over the years. The issue only arises, of course, when the expert must value a business or asset at a date in the past (the valuation date). The valuation date is always in the past whenever a fraudulent transfer claim or a preference claim is asserted, because liability depends on whether the debtor was insolvent when a prepetition transfer was made. By the time of trial (the opinion date), four or more years may have elapsed since the time of the transfer.

The specific issue can arise when valuing a disputed debt (or asset), or a contingent debt (or asset), or when the expert predicts the future earning capacity of a company at a time when the actual earnings are known.

## Using Hindsight to Determine the Fair Value of a Disputed Debt

A fact pattern common in fraudulent transfer cases neatly illustrates the problem. In many of these cases a lawsuit is filed against a debtor, and shortly thereafter the debtor makes a transfer of a valuable asset. At the time of the transfer, the underlying lawsuit has not been resolved, and is, therefore, a disputed claim. The transfer is later challenged as a fraudulent transfer. In many cases, by the time the fraudulent transfer case is actually tried, the underlying lawsuit will have been resolved (and is, therefore, no longer a disputed claim). Accordingly, the expert giving his or her opinion regarding solvency knows how the trial of the underlying lawsuit turned out. When determining solvency (which requires a fair valuation of the debtor's debts), does the expert take the judgment into account, or ignore it?

One answer is this: If a jury has determined the fair value of a disputed claim, how could the expert ignore that conclusive valuation? That was the approach of a leading case on this point, *SEC v Antar*,[53] in which the SEC prevailed on its claim that certain transfers by Sam M. Antar (Sam M.) were constructively fraudulent under fraudulent transfer law. To prevail, the SEC had to prove that Sam M. was insolvent at the time of the transfers:

> *The SEC asserts that as a result of its unliquidated securities fraud claim against Sam M., he was insolvent at the time of each and all of the 1991 and 1997 transfers.* The fact that the SEC's claim had not yet been reduced to judgment does not undermine Sam M.'s insolvent status.
>
> It is *now clear* that the value of the SEC's unliquidated claim against Sam M. was, and is, approximately $15 million, exclusive of prejudgment interest in the amount of approximately $42 million, as ordered by this court *[in a previous judgment]. Because the SEC's claim was based on Sam M.'s securities fraud in the 1980s,*

*Sam M. possessed this debt at the time of all the 1991 and 1997
transfers.*[54]

Other examples are easy to imagine: a contingent guarantee that existed
on the date of the transfer is called or released; a disputed claim is settled, or
the debtor wins at trial. As a practical matter, it's not clear why a court
would take the time (or allow experts to take the court's time) to determine
the fair value of a debt *that has already been determined*. Since the question
of fair valuation has been resolved in another lawsuit (or by settlement), no
one should be forced to make a theoretical determination of fair value.

In the case of a settlement of a lawsuit (as compared to a verdict), however, it has happened. In the case of *Advanced Telecommunication Network, Inc. v. Allen (In re Advanced Telecommunication Network, Inc.),*[55]
the court overlooked the critical distinction between contingent claims and
disputed claims. In 1995, one of ATN's competitors, WATS, filed a $39
million claim against ATN. While the WATS claim was pending, the two
principal owners of ATN were locked in a dispute for control of the company and, ultimately, the battle for control was settled by ATN's payment
of $6.25 million to one of the owners. Then, about a year later, ATN paid
WATS $10.5 million to settle the WATS claim. In 2003 ATN filed a Chap-
ter 11 bankruptcy case, and sued to recover the $6.25 million transferred to
the owner, alleging that it was a fraudulent transfer. A key issue was
whether ATN was solvent—specifically, Did the fair value of ATN's assets
exceed the fair value of its debts? To answer that question, the bankruptcy
court started with ATN's balance sheet and made several adjustments. The
bankruptcy court rejected the argument that, because the WATS settlement
was a plainly foreseeable liability, "the full amount of the [WATS] settlement" should be counted as a debt at the time of the transfer. Instead, the
"bankruptcy court found that ATN's obligation to WATS did not arise until *after* the transfer at issue in this case, could not have been reasonably
foreseen"[56] and adjusted the WATS claim to zero. The appeals court correctly found that the bankruptcy court made a mistake when it used the
*uncertainty about the ultimate resolution* of the WATS claim to assign "a
dollar value of zero to the liability (the equivalent of saying that there was
no chance whatsoever any liability would be incurred)."[57] However, the
appeals court then found "that the proper approach would have simply discounted the expected value of the judgment by the probability of its ever
occurring."[58] Following the reasoning of the *Xonics Photochemical* case,
discussed earlier, the appeals court stated:

*The "fair value" of a contingent liability, of course, should be dis-
counted according to the possibility of its ever becoming real. Thus*

*in this case the bankruptcy court should have estimated the
expected value of a judgment against ATN (ATN's own lawyers
had already placed it in the millions well before the case actually
settled for $10.5 million), and then multiplied that value by the
chance that ATN would face such a judgment (thus, for example,
halving the judgment's value if ATN faced only a fifty percent
chance of an adverse judgment).*

490 F.3d at 1335

But the appeals court apparently thought that the WATS claim was a
*contingent* claim, which it clearly was not. We submit that the proper result
would have been to allow hindsight. The parties that had the best ability to
value the dispute did so, by agreement, and settled the case for $10.5 mil-
lion. Had they done so the day before the transfer, the claim would have
been liquidated and this valuation issue would never have arisen. Had they
done so the day after the transfer was made, it would seem ridiculous to
ignore virtually contemporaneous evidence of the claim's fair valuation as
determined by the parties. A later settlement should be just as conclusive
and, in any event, has the benefit of taking at least one theoretical task off
the expert's already long list of judgment calls needed to come to an opinion
regarding solvency.

Courts have come to differing conclusions on this issue in the case of
companies burdened with asbestos claims. In *Official Comm. of Asbestos
Personal Injury Claimants v. Sealed Air Corp. (In re W.R. Grace &
Co.),*[59] the court allowed hindsight. In that case, the creditors' committee
brought a proceeding to avoid, as constructively fraudulent, the debtor's
prebankruptcy transfer of one of its divisions for less than reasonably
equivalent value, at a time when it was facing asbestos-related claims.
Some asbestos-related claims had already been asserted at the time of the
transfer, but, because of the lengthy time between exposure and diagno-
sis, there were an unknown number of claims at the time of the transfer
that had not been asserted, but would—inevitably—be asserted in the future. The defendants argued that the only asbestos-related liabilities that
should be considered to determine the debtor's solvency as of the transaction date were *those that were known on the date of the transfer or those
that the debtor reasonably should have known about at the time.* The
creditors' committee argued that the court was entitled to use *20/20 hindsight to determine the (later determined) actual value of those then-un-
known asbestos liabilities,* whether or not the debtor knew of these
liabilities on the transfer date.

The court found that the future claims were not contingent (the injury
had occurred prior to the transfer, even though the disease had not

manifested itself). Although the liability may have been unknown, and the best estimates may have reasonably erred, the debtors were aware of the existence of such liabilities. The court placed the risk of miscalculation of the value of the future asbestos liabilities at the feet of the defendant, for the reason that it could have easily protected itself from a fraudulent conveyance claim by paying reasonably equivalent value for the transferred assets. The court noted that an inquiry into the effect of future liabilities is not necessitated unless a transfer is made for less than reasonably equivalent value. This is sometimes referred to as the *wrongdoer rule* in damages cases.[60]

In *Diamond Power Intl. Inc. v. Babcock & Wilcox Co. (In re Babcock & Wilcox Co.)*,[61] the court came to the opposite conclusion. The court held that the burden of proof is on the plaintiffs to show that the debtor was insolvent at the time of the transfers based upon an objective estimate of future asbestos liabilities, irrespective of the subjective reasonableness of the debtor's estimates. The court rejected the argument that future liabilities must be assessed according to generally accepted accounting and auditing procedure, but the court also observed that:

> *Given the numerous variables involved in estimating exposure, latency periods, product identification etc., any estimation of asbestos liabilities is problematical, to say the least. Assumptions must be made that result in huge ranges of possible results. Predicting the future is always uncertain, and hindsight is perfect. Under the present circumstances in which the court is attempting to determine the amount of future asbestos liabilities for determining B & W's solvency . . . , the court cannot use hindsight and can only determine whether the predictions by B & W were reasonable under the circumstances existing at the time they were made.*

The court concluded that the asbestos claims were contingent on the transfer date and, therefore, that the debtor's estimation of the contingent liability was subject only to review for reasonableness. Applying that standard, the court held that the debtor's estimates were reasonable and, therefore, the plaintiffs failed to carry their burden of proving the debtor was insolvent at the time the transfer was made.

## Use of Hindsight to Determine Future Earning Capacity

When valuing a company at a time in the past and using the DCF method, courts frequently condemn the use of hindsight. For example, in *Mellon*

*Bank, N.A. v. Official Comm. of Unsecured Creditors of R.M.L., Inc. (In re R.M.L., Inc.),*[62] the court said that

> *[t]he use of hindsight to evaluate a debtor's financial condition for purposes of the [Bankruptcy] Code's "insolvency" element has been criticized by courts and commentators alike. . . . Far from "hindsight" or "post-hoc" analysis, a court looks at the circumstances . . . at the time of the alleged transfers.*

Similarly, in *MFS/Sun Life Trust–High Yield Series v. Van Dusen Airport Servs. Co.,*[63] the court said that

> *[p]laintiffs must prove that at the time of each of the transactions the "fair salable value" of its assets . . . was insufficient to pay its "probable" liabilities. . . . Moreover, solvency must be gauged at the time of the transfer and not with the benefit of hindsight.*

Valuation treatises and statement of valuation standards to be followed by experts often state the general rule that

> *The valuation date is the specific date at which the valuation analyst estimates the value of the subject interest and concludes on his or her estimation of value. Generally, the valuation analyst should consider only circumstances existing at the valuation date and events occurring up to the valuation date. An event that could affect the value may occur subsequent to the valuation date; such an occurrence is referred to as a* **subsequent event.** *Subsequent events are indicative of conditions that were not known or knowable at the valuation date, including conditions that arose subsequent to the valuation date. The valuation would not be updated to reflect those events or conditions. Moreover, the valuation report would typically not include a discussion of those events or conditions because a valuation is performed as of a point in time—the valuation date— and the events described in this subparagraph, occurring subsequent to that date, are not relevant to the value determined as of that date.*
> **Statement on Standards for Valuation Services, Issued by the AICPA Consulting Services Executive Committee**

The AICPA goes on to describe subsequent events that may be meaningful to the user of the valuation:

> *In situations in which a valuation is meaningful to the intended user beyond the valuation date, the events may be of such nature*

*and significance as to warrant disclosure (at the option of the valuation analyst) in a separate section of the report in order to keep users informed. Such disclosure should clearly indicate that information regarding the events is provided for informational purposes only and does not affect the determination of value as of the specified valuation date.*

**Statement on Standards for Valuation Services, Issued by the AICPA Consulting Services Executive Committee**

Generally, assets are valued as of the valuation date, based on the facts and circumstances available on that date without regard to hindsight. It should be noted that, in the tax context, according to *Estate of Jephson v. Commissioner,* 81 T.C. 999 (1983), postmortem events may be considered by the court for the limited purpose of establishing what the willing buyer and seller's expectations were as of valuation date and whether these expectations were reasonable and intelligent. In tax controversies the courts have ruled that subsequent events occurring after the valuation date may be considered if "reasonably foreseeable":[64]

*Serious objection was urged by [the government] to the admission in evidence of data as to events which occurred after [the valuation period]. It was urged that such facts were necessarily unknown on that date and hence could not be considered . . . . It is true that value . . . is not to be judged by subsequent events. There is, however, substantial importance of the reasonable expectations entertained on that date. Subsequent events may serve to establish that the expectations were entertained and also that such expectations were reasonable and intelligent. Our consideration of them has been confined to this purpose.*

**Couzens v. Comm'r, 11 B.T.A 1040 (1928)**

## Use of Hindsight in Damages Calculations

The argument for and against the use of hindsight have also been considered by some courts when calculating damages in patent or tort cases.

As one court so eloquently addressed the question in a leading patent case:

*At times the only evidence available may be that supplied by testimony of the experts as to the state of the art, the character of the improvement and the probable increase of efficiency or saving of*

*expense. . . . This will generally be the case if the trial follows quickly after the issue of the patent. But a different situation is presented if the years have gone by before the evidence is offered. Experience is then available to correct uncertain prophecy. Here is a book of wisdom that courts may not neglect. We find no rule of law that sets a clasp upon its pages, and forbids us to look within.*
Sinclair Refining v. Jenkins Petroleum Process, *289 U.S. 689, 698-99 (1933) (Cardozo, J.).*

Courts in England have made similar observations. For example, in *The Bwllfa and Merthyr Dare Steam Collieries (1891), Limited v. The Pontypridd Waterworks Company* [1903] AC 426, the claimant sought compensation following a ban on exploiting a profitable seam of coal. The court held that compensation was calculable by reference to actual market values known at the time of calculation. One of the judges asked, "Why should he [the arbitrator calculating the compensation] listen to conjecture on a matter which has become an accomplished fact? Why should he guess when he can calculate? With the light before him, why should he shut his eyes and grope in the dark?"

## CONCLUSION

The historical determinations of solvency in preference and fraudulent conveyance cases is almost always complicated because the valuation date is in the past. A logical, practical, and reasonable explanation of historical facts is essential to the ability to provide perspective and persuasion to your analysis and argument for a particular position.

## NOTES

1. 11 U.S.C. § 547(b).
2. 11 U.S.C. § 547(f), which provides, "For the purposes of this section, the debtor is presumed to have been insolvent on and during the 90 days immediately preceding the date of the filing of the petition."
3. 11 U.S.C. § 547(c)(1) provides that:

   *The trustee may not avoid under this section a transfer—(1) to the extent that such transfer was—(A) intended by the debtor and the creditor to or for whose benefit such transfer was made to be a contemporaneous exchange for new value given to the debtor; and (B) in fact a substantially contemporaneous exchange; . . . .*

4. 11 U.S.C. § 547(c)(2) provides that:

   *The trustee may not avoid under this section a transfer—. . . . (2) to the
   extent that such transfer was in payment of a debt incurred by the debtor
   in the ordinary course of business or financial affairs of the debtor and the
   transferee, and such transfer was—(A) made in the ordinary course of business or financial affairs of the debtor and the transferee; or (B) made
   according to ordinary business terms; . . . .*

5. Laws allowing creditors to avoid fraudulent transfers have a long history. Anglo-
   American fraudulent transfer law originated in sixteenth-century England with
   the Statute of Elizabeth, which deemed void any conveyance made with intent
   "to delay, hinder or defraud creditors and others of their just and lawful actions,
   suits, debts." Fraudulent Conveyances, 13 Eliz., ch. 5 (1571). The origins of
   fraudulent transfer law extend back even further, however: "Fraudulent conveyance laws extend over two thousand years to at least early Roman law . . . "
   *Glinka v. Bank of Vermont (In re Kelton Motors, Inc.)*, 130 BR 170, 177 (Bankr.
   D. Vt. 1991).

6. For example, § 550(e) of the Bankruptcy Code provides as follows with respect to
   the property recovered as an avoidable transfer:

   (1) *A good faith transferee from whom the trustee may recover under subsection (a) of this section has a lien on the property recovered to secure
   the lesser of—*
   A. *the cost, to such transferee, of any improvement made after the
   transfer, less the amount of any profit realized by or accruing to
   such transferee from such property; and*
   B. *any increase in the value of such property as a result of such improvement, of the property transferred.*

   (2) *In this subsection, "improvement" includes—*
   A. *physical additions or changes to the property transferred;*
   B. *repairs to such property;*
   C. *payment of any tax on such property;*
   D. *payment of any debt secured by a lien on such property that is su-
   perior or equal to the rights of the trustee; and*
   E. *preservation of such property.*

7. Section 544(b) of the Bankruptcy Code gives the trustee whatever avoiding powers an unsecured creditor with an allowable claim might have under applicable
   *state* or federal law, including the UFTA or UFCA, and Article 6 of the Uniform
   Commercial Code (bulk transfers; bulk sales).

8. The predecessor to UFTA was the Uniform Fraudulent Conveyance Act
   ("UFCA"). Currently, UFCA is the law in only five states, so we will not discuss it
   separately. In any event, most of the concepts and principles are the same as those
   found in UFTA and the Bankruptcy Code. Accordingly, court decisions constru-
   ing UFCA are often persuasive when interpreting UFTA or the Bankruptcy Code.

9. The Bankruptcy Abuse Prevention and Consumer Protection Act of 2005 ("BAPCPA") extended the reach-back period for fraudulent transfers from one year to two years. However, this provision of BAPCPA applies only to cases filed one year after the enactment of the BAPCPA statute. Thus, for cases filed after April 20, 2006, the look-back period under § 548 is two years; for cases commenced on or before April 20, 2006, the look-back period is one year.
10. § 9(a) or (b) of UFTA.
11. UFTA § 4(b). References to fraudulent obligations have been omitted.
12. Bankruptcy Code § 101(32).
13. UFTA § 2(a).
14. The Bankruptcy Code's full definition of *insolvency* is as follows:

> *(32) The term "insolvent" means—*
> > *(A) with reference to an entity other than a partnership and a municipality, financial condition such that the sum of such entity's debts is greater than all of such entity's property, at a fair valuation, exclusive of—*
> > > *(i) property transferred, concealed, or removed with intent to hinder, delay, or defraud such entity's creditors; and*
> > > *(ii) property that may be exempted from property of the estate under section 522 of this title;*
> > *(B) with reference to a partnership, financial condition such that the sum of such partnership's debts is greater than the aggregate of, at a fair valuation—*
> > > *(i) all of such partnership's property, exclusive of property of the kind specified in subparagraph (A)(i) of this paragraph; and*
> > > *(ii) the sum of the excess of the value of each general partner's nonpartnership property, exclusive of property of the kind specified in subparagraph (A) of this paragraph, over such partner's nonpartnership debts; and*
> > *(C) with reference to a municipality, financial condition such that the municipality is—*
> > > *(i) generally not paying its debts as they become due unless such debts are the subject of a bona fide dispute; or*
> > > *(ii) unable to pay its debts as they become due.*

UFTA's full definition of *insolvency* is as follows:
> (a) A debtor is insolvent if the sum of the debtor's debts is greater than all of the debtor's assets, at a fair valuation.
> (b) A debtor who is generally not paying his [or her] debts as they become due is presumed to be insolvent.
> (c) A partnership is insolvent under subsection (a) if the sum of the partnership's debts is greater than the aggregate of all of the partnership's assets, at a fair valuation, and the sum of the excess of the value of each general partner's nonpartnership assets over the partner's nonpartnership debts.

(d) Assets under this section do not include property that has been transferred, concealed, or removed with intent to hinder, delay, or defraud creditors or that has been transferred in a manner making the transfer voidable under this [Act].

(e) Debts under this section do not include an obligation to the extent it is secured by a valid lien on property of the debtor not included as an asset.

15. 11 U.S.C. § 547(g); *see ABB Vecto Gray, Inc. v. First Nat'l Bank of Bethany, Oklahoma (In re Robinson Bros. Drilling, Inc.),* 9 F.3d 871, 874 (10th Cir. 1993); *Ralar Distribs., Inc. v. Rubbermaid, Inc. (In re Ralar Distribs. Inc.),* 4 F.3d 62, 67 (1st Cir. 1993).

16. *See Lawson v. Ford Motor Co. (In re Roblin Indus., Inc.),* 78 F.3d 30, 34 (2d Cir. 1996); *Arrow Electronics v. Justus (In re Kaypro),* 218 F.3d 1070 (9th Cir. 2000) ("To prove insolvency, the trustee must show by a preponderance of the evidence that the debtor's liabilities exceeded its assets.")

17. *Orix Credit Alliance, Inc. v. Harvey (In re Lamar Haddox Contractor, Inc.),* 40 F.3d 118, 121 (5th Cir. 1994).

18. UFTA § 2(b).

19. There can be, of course, debts shown on a balance sheet that will never be called on to be paid, such as some accounts payable.

20. UFTA § 1(3). Section 101(5) of the Bankruptcy Code defines *claim* as follows:

The term *"claim"* means—
(A) *right to payment, whether or not such right is reduced to judgment, liquidated, unliquidated, fixed, contingent, matured, unmatured, disputed, undisputed, legal, equitable, secured, or unsecured; or*
(B) *right to an equitable remedy for breach of performance if such breach gives rise to a right to payment, whether or not such right to an equitable remedy is reduced to judgment, fixed, contingent, matured, unmatured, disputed, undisputed, secured, or unsecured.*

21. UFTA § 1(3) and § 2(a), or § 101(5) and (32) of the Bankruptcy Code, as applicable.

22. *Nicholes v. Johnny Appleseed of Wash. (In re Nicholes),* 184 B.R. 82, 88 (B.A.P. 9th Cir. 1995).

23. *Loya v. Rapp (In re Loya),* 123 B.R. 338, 340 (B.A.P. 9th Cir. 1991).

24. *Travelers International A.G. v. Trans World Airlines, Inc. (In re Trans World Airlines, Inc.),* 134 F.3d 188 (3d Cir. 1998) (Third Circuit declined to apply the fair valuation requirement of § 101(32)(A) of the Bankruptcy Code to public debt, which it measured at face value).

25. *See, e.g., Credit Managers Ass'n of S. Cal. v. Fed. Co.,* 629 F. Supp. 175 (C.D. Cal. 1985); *Ohio Corrugating Co. v. DPAC, Inc. (In re Ohio Corrugating Co.),* 91 B.R. 430, 438-39 (Bankr. N.D. Ohio 1988).

26. *In re Xonics Photochemical, Inc.,* 841 F.2d 198, 201 (7th Cir. 1988).

27. *In re Xonics Photochemical, Inc.,* 841 F.2d 198, 200 (7th Cir. 1988).

28. *See Travelers Int'l AG v. Trans World Airlines, Inc. (In re Trans World Airlines, Inc.),* 134 F.3d 188, 197-198 (3d Cir. 1998) (valuing a contingent liability in a

preference action); *Federal Deposit Ins. Corp. v. Bell*, 106 F.3d 258, 264 (8th Cir. 1997).

29. *See Mellon Bank, N.A. v. Official Comm. of Unsecured Creditors of R.M.L., Inc. (In re R.M.L., Inc.)*, 92 F.3d 139, 155-156 (3d Cir. 1996); but *see Tri-Continental Leasing Corp. v. Zimmerman*, 485 F. Supp. 495 (N.D. Cal. 1980).

30. Kevin J. Liss, Note, *Fraudulent Conveyance Law and Leveraged Buyouts*, 87 Colum. L. Rev. 1491, 1505 (1987).

31. *Ohio Corrugating Co. v. DPAC, Inc. (In re Ohio Corrugating Co.)*, 91 B.R. 430, 436 (Bankr. N.D. Ohio 1988).

32. *Consove v. Cohen* (In re Roco Corp.), 701 F.2d. at 978, 983 (1st Circ. 1983).

33. *Orix Credit Alliance, Inc. v. Harvey (In re Lamar Haddox Contractor, Inc.)*, 40 F.3d 118, 121 (5th Cir. 1994).

34. Pratt, *Valuing a Business*, at p. 41.

35. 905 F.2d 166, 170 (7th Cir. 1990).

36. *WRT Creditors Liquidation Trust v. WRT Bankruptcy Litigation Master File Defendants (In re WRT Energy Corp.)*, 282 B.R. 343 (Bankr. W.D.La. 2001) (collecting cases); *see Moody v. Sec. Pac. Bus. Credit, Inc.*, 971 F.2d 1056, 1067-1069 (3d Cir. 1992) (valuation of assets on going-concern basis is not improper); *see also Kupetz v. Wolf*, 845 F.2d 842 (9th Cir. 1988) (focusing on going-concern value not improper); 2 Alan N. Resnick & Henry J. Sommer, *Collier on Bankruptcy* ¶ 101.31[5] (15th ed. rev. 2005) (assets should be valued at going-concern value).

37. 170 F.3d 1197 (9th Cir. 1999).

38. *In re Lids Corporation*, 281 B.R. 535, 541.

39. *Travelers Int'l AG v. Trans World Airlines, Inc. (In re Trans World Airlines, Inc.)*, 134 F.3d 188, 197-198 (3d Cir. 1998).

40. *See Wieboldt Stores, Inc. v. Schottenstein*, 94 B.R. 488, 505 (N.D. Ill. 1988) (ignore going-concern value in solvency analysis); *Murphy v. Meritor Sav. Bank (In re O'Day Corp.)*, 126 B.R. 370, 403 (Bankr. D. Mass. 1991) (same).

41. *Excello Press, Inc. v. Bowers, Inc. (In re Excello Press, Inc.)*, 96 B.R. 840 (Bankr. N.D. Ill. 1989)

42. *Orix Credit Alliance, Inc. v. Harvey (In re Lamar Haddox Contractor, Inc.)*, 40 F.3d 118, 121 (5th Cir. 1994). Similarly, it should be noted that in introducing evidence in support of a showing of insolvency, an accountant's "conclusory opinion testimony . . . without any [supporting] evidence" will be insufficient when there are "substantial questions . . . as to the fair value of the debtor's property." *Id.* at 122.

43. *See Kendall v. Sorani (In re Richmond Produce Co.)*, 151 B.R. 1012, 1019 (Bankr. N.D. Cal. 1993) ("[T]he inquiry [into the solvency issue] must be to what extent an asset would have value for a creditor attempting to satisfy its claim. Goodwill and organization expense could not be sold to satisfy a creditor's claim."), *aff'd*, 195 B.R. 455 (N.D. Cal. 1996).

44. *See, e.g., Ohio Corrugating Co. v. DPAC, Inc. (In re Ohio Corrugating Co.)*, 91 B.R. 430, 438 n.11 (Bankr. N.D. Ohio 1988).

45. *See Consove v. Cohen (In re Roco Corp.)*, 701 F.2d 978 (1st Cir. 1983); *Rubin v. Mfrs. Hanover Trust Co.*, 661 F.2d 979, 991 (2d Cir. 1981).

46. *Lawson v. Ford Motor Co. (In re Roblin Indus., Inc.)*, 78 F.3d 30, 35-38 (2nd Cir. 1996).

47. *Constructora Maza, Inc. v. Banco d. Ponce*, 616 F.2d. 573 (1st Cir. 1980).

48. See *Briden v. Foley*, 776 F.2d 379, 382 (1st Cir. 1985); *Misty Management Corp. v. Lockwood*, 539 F.2d 1205, 1213 (9th Cir. 1976) ("Alternatively, the February 22, 1967 balance sheet attached to Misty's Chapter X petition provided a basis from which Misty's insolvency as of August 25, 1966 could be shown. Such 'retrojection' is permissible insofar as care is taken to account for all changes in financial position between the date of the financial statement and the date upon which insolvency is in question.")

49. See *Margraff v. Gruber Bottling Works, Inc. (In re Gruber Bottling Works, Inc.)*, 16 B.R. 348 (Bankr. E.D. Pa. 1982) (preference action).

50. *Foreman Indus., Inc. v. Broadway Sand & Gravel (In re Foreman Indus., Inc.)*, 59 B.R. 145 (Bankr. S.D. Ohio 1986); *Kanasky v. Randolph (In re R. Purbeck & Assocs., Ltd.)*, 27 B.R. 953 (Bankr. D. Conn. 1983)

51. 373 B.R. 283 (Bankr. S.D.N.Y. 2007).

52. 373 B.R. at 352.

53. 120 F. Supp. 2d 431 (D.N.J. 2000).

54. 120 F. Supp. 2d at 443 (citations omitted; emphasis added). Other cases have taken the same approach; *see, e.g., Tri-Continental Leasing Corp. v. Zimmerman*, 485 F. Supp. 495, 500 (N.D. Cal. 1980) (citing with approval the case of *Baker v. Geist*, 321 A.2d 634 (Pa. 1974), where "the court held that the mere assertion of a claim for personal injuries arising out of an automobile accident constitutes an existing debt even prior to the filing of the lawsuit. The court apparently looked to the amount of the ultimate judgment for its estimate of the probable liability on the debt at the time of the conveyance.").

55. 490 F.3d 1325 (11th Cir. 2007).

56. 490 F.3d at 1334-1335.

57. *Id.* at 1336.

58. *Id.* at 1335.

59. 281 B.R. 852 (Bankr. D. Del. 2002).

60. See Chapter 8 of Wagner, Dunbar, and Weil, *Litigation Services Handbook, The Role of the Financial Expert, 4th edition:* John Wiley & Sons; *see also Gillman v. Scientific Research Prods., Inc. (In re Mama D'Angelo, Inc.)*, 55 F.3d 552, 556 (10th Cir. 1995) (courts may consider information originating subsequent to the transfer date if it tends to shed light on a fair and accurate assessment of the asset or liability of the pertinent date).

61. 274 B.R. 230 (Bankr. E.D. La. 2002).

62. 92 F.3d 139, 155-56 (3d Cir. 1996). *See also Lippe v. Bairnco Corp.*, 249 F. Supp. 2d 357, 379-80 (S.D.N.Y. 2003), *aff'd*, 99 Fed. App'x 274 (2d Cir. 2004).

63. 910 F. Supp. 913, 938 (S.D.N.Y. 1995).

64. See *Estate of Jephson v. Commissioner*, 81 T.C. 999 (1983), *Ithaca Trust Co. v. United States*, 279 U.S. 151 (1929); *Estate of Van Horne v. Commissioner*, 720 F.2d 1114, 1116 (9th Cir. 1983), *affg.* 78 T.C. 728 (1982), *cert. denied* 466 U.S. 980 (1984); *Guggenheim v. Helvering*, 117 F.2d 469 (2d Cir. 1941), *cert. denied* 314 U.S. 621 (1941); *Couzens v. Commissioner*, 11 B.T.A. 1040, 1165 (1928).

# CHAPTER 9

# Solvency Opinions

## INTRODUCTION

For the purpose of this text a solvency opinion is a report or opinion prepared or issued close to the time of a corporate capital transaction, which provides a measure of assurance to a transaction participant that the parties to the transaction are financially solvent prior to a transaction and/or that a combined or resulting company will be solvent following completion of the transaction.

## WHO USES SOLVENCY OPINIONS?

Solvency opinions are used to obtain a measure of confidence that a company will be able to meet its financial obligations as they come due. The requirement that one or both parties obtain a solvency opinion is frequently included in purchase or merger agreements as a closing condition. The buyer may require a solvency opinion to ensure that a combined company will be able to service the debt associated with a transaction, and that equity value will not be impaired.

Occasionally a participant in a merger or acquisition may obtain a solvency opinion as a measure of protection against the *impact* of a fraudulent conveyance action, not simply as a potential legal defense. By way of example, a lender may want to be sure that in the event of a finding that a transaction constitutes a fraudulent conveyance, there is sufficient liquidity in a company to permit unwinding of the transaction.

Another user of solvency opinions is a private equity firm completing a dividend recapitalization. A dividend recapitalization transaction, which effectively levers a company to pay dividends to owners, is a tool used by private equity owners to increase equity returns. Under a dividend recapitalization, a company takes on additional debt for the purpose of paying a dividend to its equity investors. Although this may enhance returns to shareholders, increased leverage poses a risk to the borrower and could result in financial instability, default, or bankruptcy. As a result, many private equity firms will obtain a solvency opinion prior to completing a dividend recapitalization. Whether issued by an investment banking advisor, a lender, or other expert, a solvency opinion can be an important tool for the private equity firm if it is later sued by creditors who suffer losses in a bankruptcy.

> *An LBO lender is obligated to consider the solvency of the post-transaction creditor when lending funds that will flow out of the borrower to equity holders, i.e. a dividend recapitalization. Simple good faith on the part of the lender is not sufficient to avoid a finding of fraudulent convenience.*
>
> *The Court found that "If a conveyance is made without fair consideration, and the transferor will be left insolvent, will be left with an unreasonably small capital or intends or believes that it will incur debts beyond its ability to pay as they mature, it is fraudulent without regard to the actual intent of the transferor or the transferee."*
>
> **Crowthers McCall Pattern, Inc. v. Lewis, 129 B.R. 992, 997 (SDNY 1991) (citations omitted)**

In addition, private equity firms also may use solvency opinions as part of the due diligence process to determine how much additional debt can be assumed by the borrower without risking insolvency.

Solvency opinions also are helpful to sellers of private companies where the purchase price is paid as a combination of cash and equity earn-out. In a leveraged buyout transaction, the buyer will use the target company's debt capacity to fund a portion of the purchase price. A company that takes on too much debt to pay for its own acquisition risks insolvency and destruction of potential earn-out value.

Solvency opinions can serve as an effective defense in the event of an action alleging that the transaction was a fraudulent transfer. In the context of a bankruptcy following a leveraged acquisition, unsecured creditors may allege that a company took on too much debt to pay for the acquisition, taking assets from a company that otherwise would have been available to pay the creditors in the normal course of business. A solvency opinion prepared at the time of the acquisition would document the preparer's belief that the amount of debt taken on to fund the acquisition was not so high as to adversely impact the company's ability to meet its obligations as they come due.

> *Delaware courts have established that boards of directors are entitled to rely on solvency opinions: "[Smith's Food and Drug Centers] hired the investment firm . . . to examine the transactions and render a solvency opinion. [The firm] eventually issued a report to the SFD Board replete with assurances that the transactions would not endanger SFD's solvency, and would not impair SFD's capital in violation of 8 Del.C. § 160 . . . We interpret 8 Del.C. § 172 to entitle boards to rely on experts . . . to determine compliance with 8 Del.C. § 160."*
> *Klang v. Smith's Food and Drug Centers, Inc.*
> 702 A.2d 150 (Del. 1997)

Solvency opinions also can be prepared as part of *ex-post* examination of a failed transaction or litigation, where one party alleges that there was sufficient information *before* the transaction that would have allowed the parties to ascertain beforehand that the contemplated transaction would result in an insolvent combined entity.

## SOLVENCY OPINION PREPARATION

When preparing a solvency opinion, the valuation professional typically asks the following questions:

- Does the fair value of the assets exceed the fair value of the liabilities and obligations after consideration of all post-transaction debt?
- Can the company meet its debt obligations as they come due?
- Is the company adequately capitalized on the date of the subject transaction?

An important element of the solvency opinion is an examination of the company's projected operating cash flows. This projection encompasses revenue, expenses, and required investment in fixed and working capital. It takes into consideration past performance and expectations about the future (new customers, potential cost reductions, new facilities).

In addition, it considers the post-transaction capital structure. In other words, after a transaction is completed and the new debt has been assumed by a company, debt service requirements become a priority claim on the assets of the company. The projections will be used to assess whether the company will be able to service its debt and still have sufficient capital to fund the ongoing needs of its business without impairing its ability to pay creditors.

The following should be considered in preparation of the solvency opinion, all of which are considered to be requirements, when the veracity of the opinion and the extent to which it can be relied upon are evaluated by experts and courts:

- Exercise proper due diligence in the evaluation of the company generally. This is a broad standard that requires the preparer to understand the business dynamics, including industry issues, management, customers, and suppliers and operating history.
- Thoroughly review all transaction agreements. This requirement encompasses merger, financing, and management agreements, and any other documents that will be executed as part of the contemplated transaction.
- Pressure test management's projections. Management's projections should not be relied upon as is; they must be subjected to testing and review. The preparer should evaluate the sensitivity of the projections to outside pressures such as industry or general economic conditions, and assess the likelihood that the revenue and expense targets will be achieved.
- Properly evaluate capital structure, including an assessment of the impact of the new capital structure on the operations of the company.

In addition, the valuation professional should consider the need for, and availability of, outside capital as a factor in achieving the projections:

- To what extent is external capital required to achieve the projections, and is external capital expected to be available in the market?
- To what extent is the sale of assets necessary to achieve the projections? Is there likely to be a market for the assets contemplated to be sold? Are the assumptions related to proceeds associated with sold assets reasonable?

Each of these considerations must be evaluated in light of current market conditions, especially when general and company-specific economic drivers are in a state of deterioration. Economic trends must be considered when evaluating and refining projections used to assess a company's cash-flow sufficiency. In addition, capital market conditions and the availability of credit may have a significant impact on whether the subject company will be able to pay its debts when they come due. In other words, the preparer must consider the maturities of the debts and evaluate the likelihood of successful refinancing at the appropriate time.

This issue can be extremely sensitive in the case of bridge financing used to fund an acquisition of a company or a piece of real estate. In rapidly changing credit and valuation environments, it is particularly important to compare the expected durations of the assets and the liabilities, and understand the risks associated with bridge financing.

For instance, in late 2006, at the height of the real-estate boom, Equity Office Properties, a publicly traded REIT, agreed to sell its office property portfolio to buyout firm The Blackstone Group, which then disassembled the portfolio and sold pieces to different buyers. The New York properties were acquired by Macklowe Properties using *short-term bridge financing* with the expectation that replacement permanent financing would be available. Immediately thereafter, however, the credit markets tightened, Macklowe was unable to refinance out of the bridge debt, and was forced to restructure its entire portfolio, including the surrender of certain properties to the lender. Macklowe found itself in a situation in which its long-term assets, the buildings, could not be liquidated quickly enough to fund repayment of its short-term debts.

## SOLVENCY METRICS

In preparing a solvency opinion, the preparer should review and evaluate a range of financial ratios that are indicators of a company's general solvency:

**Current Ratio**

> Also known as the working capital ratio, this is the ratio of current assets to current liabilities. It is a basic liquidity measure that is useful in measuring a company's ability to meet obligations to trade and other current creditors.

**Quick/Acid-Test Ratio**

> This is a higher-level version of the current ratio, and is calculated as the ratio of current assets *excluding inventories* to current liabilities. It is considered more conservative because it removes from consideration any risk (time, market, valuation, etc.) that a company might face in the liquidation of its inventories while attempting to satisfy its current liabilities.

### Debt/Equity Ratio

Calculated as total liabilities divided by shareholder equity, this ratio measures the extent to which a company has been financing its growth through debt as opposed to new equity investment or retention of earnings. This is a very important factor in a solvency opinion since it will be affected doubly by dividends or any other distribution of assets funded by incurrence of new debt: debt increases *at the same time* that equity decreases.

### Debt/Total Assets Ratio

This ratio measures the extent to which a company's assets have been financed by debt rather than by equity. It is calculated as total assets divided by total liabilities. A low multiple indicates a very conservative and highly solvent company. A ratio of 1.0 indicates that half of a company's balance sheet is financed by debt. A ratio in excess of 1.0 might give some creditors concern and should indicate the need for even greater focus on projected cash flows and ability to meet upcoming financing obligations.

### Liquidity Index

This ratio measures how long it will take to convert receivables and inventory into cash or, in other words, how many days removed from cash a company is. This ratio is calculated as

$$[(\text{Accounts receivable} \times \text{Collection period}) + (\text{Inventory} \times \text{Cycle period})] / (\text{Cash} + \text{Accounts receivable} + \text{Inventory})$$

where collection period is the number of days, on average, it would take to collect the receivables balance, and cycle period is the number of days, on average, it would take to sell down the on-hand inventory. A smaller number of days indicates stronger liquidity.

### Solvency Ratio

Calculated as (After tax net profits + Depreciation)/Total liabilities, this form of cash flow coverage ratio measures a company's ability to meet its ongoing obligations. As a general rule, a ratio greater than 20 percent is an indicator of general financial health.

## CASE STUDIES

As discussed earlier, the use of solvency opinions can be divided into three broad categories: preemptive defense of a fraudulent transfer claim; a responsible exercise in pretransaction due diligence; or an after-the-fact forensic examination tool. As one might expect, the use as a due diligence tool is even more critical when either company in a transaction is stressed before the deal, either for reasons specific to a company or for general economic reasons.

In 2008, as the multiyear buyout boom was ending and the global economy was slowing, two major transactions failed to close, largely over issues of solvency opinions. We examine these transactions here, together with the intended purpose of the solvency opinion as well as how its use ultimately led to the transaction not being completed.

> *Shopping for a solvency opinion, especially when the first firm asked was unable to provide one, may not give investors a greater level of comfort. "If two doctors give you an opinion about your stage-four colon cancer, and one says it's in remission, and the other says it isn't, this might be helpful information . . . . In this case, the deal is no more likely to close than it was four hours ago, whatever the rising stock quote might tell you. Why would Citigroup (C) (one of the four lead LBO lenders), for example, agree to dispense with the first solvency opinion?"*[1]

**BCE Inc. (Bell Canada) leveraged buyout**

In June 2007, BCE Inc., parent company of Bell Canada, announced that it would be taken private in a C$50 billion (US$41 billion) leveraged buyout, the largest in history. The proposed buyer was a large Canadian pension plan in partnership with several private equity firms. The deal was contingent on Bell Canada obtaining a solvency opinion confirming that a company would remain solvent after the transaction. A deadline of December 2008 was imposed for the opinion; otherwise, the proposed transaction would lapse.

The merger agreement specifically required a solvency opinion prepared by KPMG LLC, a large accounting and consulting firm. However, after conducting its analysis, KPMG refused to issue an opinion. In mid-December, KPMG announced it would hire a competitor, PricewaterhouseCoopers, to issue an opinion, though PwC's opinion would be nonbinding according to the terms of the merger agreement, which required a clean solvency opinion from KPMG. Although PwC issued the sought-after solvency opinion, the lenders still refused to fund the transaction.

The proposed transaction was terminated in December 2008. As of this writing, BCE is pursuing litigation over a $1.2 billion breakup fee.

> *By seeking and obtaining an "Insolvency" Opinion that was not otherwise required by a merger agreement, and then sharing such opinion with proposed lenders, the Court found that " . . . Hexion had knowingly and intentionally breached its covenants and obligations under the merger agreement. . . . [T]here is only one point in time at which it is necessary to make a determination of solvency—at (or as of) closing."*
>
> *In other words, a solvency opinion cannot in and of itself be used as reason to terminate a transaction.*
>
> **Hexion Specialty Chems., Inc., et al. v. Huntsman Corp.,**
> **965 A. 28 715, 756, 578 (Del. Ch. 2008).**

In July 2007, Hexion Specialty Chemicals, a subsidiary of private equity firm Apollo Management, agreed to buy Huntsman Corp. for $6.5 billion. Huntsman's results continued to deteriorate in 2007 and the first quarter of 2008, causing Hexion to have second thoughts about the transaction. After Huntsman released its 2007 results, Hexion tried to walk away from the deal. However, the merger agreement did not provide a way for Hexion to walk other than via a very narrowly drawn Material Adverse Change clause.

In this case, the solvency opinion requirement was in the financing commitment letter, not the merger agreement. In addition, the requirement was that the opinion be issued "by a reputable appraisal firm, or the finance head of either Huntsman or Hexion."[2]

Apollo Management, Hexion's parent, hired Duff & Phelps to conduct a solvency analysis and, unofficially, to provide an opinion of *insolvency*. Once it received the Duff & Phelps opinion letter, it publicized the contents broadly, including to the two committed lenders, who then refused to fund the transaction.

The issue: was Apollo's engagement of Duff & Phelps a prudent pre-transaction due diligence move, or was it a maneuver to find a way to scuttle the deal? The merger agreement required Hexion, the buyer, to use its best efforts to provide a solvency certificate to the banks.

In response to the Duff & Phelps report, Huntsman shopped around for an opinion of its own, and eventually provided a solvency opinion prepared by American Appraisal. However, the proposed lenders found the opinion unsatisfactory, and used their rejection of the opinion as the basis for a decision not to fund. In announcing their decision, the banks said that "Aspects of the methodology, assumptions and depth of information utilized in the solvency analysis have left the banks with serious reservations about whether a customary and reasonably satisfactory certificate could be delivered at this time." In other words, a clean second opinion failed to convince the lenders that the earlier warning sign opinion was any less valid about the proposed borrower's ability to remain solvent.

In September 2008, a Delaware court found that Hexion deliberately scuttled the financing by publicizing the Duff & Phelps insolvency opinion, which caused banks to refuse to fund, and also turned away bidders for certain Huntsman assets that were to be divested for antitrust purposes following the merger. The vice chancellor ordered Hexion to use its best efforts to raise the funding necessary to honor the merger agreement. The transaction was terminated in December 2008 after the banks refused to fund, citing the Duff & Phelps report, and Hexion was unable to arrange alternative financing, despite exercising its best efforts

On a separate note, the Vice Chancellor also commented on the projections used in preparation of the insolvency opinion. Whereas due care requires that the prudent preparer pressure test the projections provided by management, in *Huntsman*, the preparer erred in the other direction; Duff & Phelps never requested *any* information from Huntsman, relying instead on information and projections provided by Hexion, the projected acquirer. The projections reflected a projected earnings number that was 20–30 percent below Huntsman's own projections, further leading the court to find that Hexion had been seeking an insolvency opinion where none was required by the transaction documents.

## CONCLUSION

In summary, a solvency opinion is an independent expert opinion on a borrower's ability to remain solvent after the addition of debt associated with a transaction, to pay debts as they mature, and to continue operations as a going concern.

## NOTES

1. Mark McQueen: BCE Takeover: Why I'm Ignoring PWC's Competing Solvency Opinion, Seeking Alpha, December 9, 2008. http://seekingalpha.com/article/109801-bce-takeover-why-i-m-ignoring-pwc-s-competing-solvency-opinion.
2. Euan Rocha & Megan Davies, *Update 4-Banks Balk at Funding Huntsman-Hexion Deal*, Oct. 25, 2008, http://www.reuters.com/article/euMergersNews/idUSN2837221520081028.

CHAPTER **10**

# Daubert

## CHALLENGES TO EXPERTS OR THEIR TESTIMONY

The two key cases dealing with challenges to the admission of expert testimony are the Supreme Court's decisions in *Daubert v. Merrell Dow Pharmaceuticals, Inc.*, 509 U.S. 579 (1993) and *Kumho Tire Co. Ltd. v. Carmichael*, 526 U.S. 137 (1999).

### The Trial Judge as Gatekeeper— The *Daubert* Case

The *Daubert* case focused on the provisions of Federal Rule of Evidence 702 pertaining to the use of *scientific* evidence in the context of a case in which expert testimony was offered in support of alleged causation of birth defects from the use of Bendectin, a prescription antinausea medicine.[1] The Supreme Court's decision focused on the difference between "the quest for truth in the courtroom and the quest for truth in the laboratory . . . " and noted that science is subject to "perpetual revisions," whereas the law is focused on finality and timeliness of judgment *Id*, at 596–97. The ultimate holding was that the trial judge in federal court was to be the gatekeeper of the admission of expert testimony. That function is met by determining whether the expert is presenting scientific knowledge, which necessarily requires a "preliminary assessment of whether the reasoning or methodology underlying the testimony is scientifically valid" and can be applied to the facts of the case *Id*, at 592–93. The focus of the judge's assessment is on "principles and methodology, not on the conclusions that they generate." *Id*, at 580. It was also noted that scientific knowledge must be subject to being tested empirically, and have been "subjected to peer review and publication," which, although it will not guarant admissibility, is a significant factor. *Id*, at 593. Similarly, general acceptance in the scientific community is helpful, but not determinative.

## *Kumho Tire* Case

*Kumho Tire* applied the *Daubert* principles to engineers and other experts who are not scientists. Its analysis is clearly applicable to business valuations offered by experts. The key is whether the testimony has "a reliable basis in the knowledge and experience of [the relevant] discipline." 526 U.S. at 138.

## *Daubert* Challenges to Financial Experts

Financial expert witnesses are often subjected to *Daubert* challenges. Lack of reliability, lack of relevance, and lack of qualifications are frequent reasons to exclude the testimony of an expert witness. A successful *Daubert* challenge sometimes results in the complete exclusion of the expert's testimony; in other cases, only a portion is excluded.

This chapter reviews some illustrative cases applying *Daubert* to financial and other commercial experts, usually in the area of valuations. There are many instances in which the court rigorously examines the expert or the expert's proposed testimony in excruciating detail and excludes the expert's testimony. The reported cases can highlight the kinds of weaknesses in an expert's qualifications or testimony that have prompted courts to exclude, in whole or in part, proffered financial expert testimony.

## Lack of Qualifications—Formal Training or Sufficient Experience

At least one appellate court has stated that the qualifications requirement is to be construed liberally. A lack of formal training or certification may not automatically disqualify a financial expert facing a *Daubert* challenge, but such an expert will need sufficient experience in the field at issue to overcome a lack of formal training and certification. For example, an accountant has been found qualified to perform a discounted present-value calculation of lost future earnings. Experience and training qualified the witness as an expert in reconstructive accounting.

As one court noted, the "principle of *Daubert* is merely that if an expert witness is to offer an opinion based on science, it must be real science, not junk science. [The expert witness, an] accountant, did not purport to be doing science. He was doing accounting. From financial information furnished by [the plaintiff company] and assumptions given him by counsel of the effect of the termination on [the plaintiff company's] sales, the accountant calculated the discounted present value of the lost future earnings that [the plaintiff company] would have had had it not been terminated. This was a calculation well within the competence of a C.P.A." *Tuf Racing Products, Inc. v. American Suzuki Motor Corp.,* 223 F.3d 585, 591 (7th Cir. 2000).

This cannot be taken too far. Someone who must admit that "he has no formal education or training in business valuation";[2] that "he has no experience in preparing valuation reports";[3] and who states "I'm not a certified valuation expert, and I don't issue valuation reports"[4] will not pass the *Daubert* test in a case requiring a business valuation.

## Lack of Qualifications—Narrowly Focused Qualifications Not Required

Some cases involve arcane assets or businesses and their valuation. Quite likely, there will be situations in which an expert is asked to value a type of business that the expert has never had direct experience with. Does that disqualify the expert? Probably not. In one case, an expert was retained to testify about market prices for a hedge fund's leveraged investments in collateralized mortgage obligations (CMOs). The expert had extensive background and qualifications in the economic analysis of securities prices and interest rates but had no prior experience in valuing CMOs. However, he did teach a course at Harvard that had included a segment on CMOs and their valuation, and had performed consulting work and advised on a Ph.D. thesis that involved CMO valuation. The court stated that the contention that the expert was not qualified suggests that only specialists in a particular field could be considered experts. The court stated that the law does not insist that only someone who specializes in CMOs could qualify as an expert on the subject, and allowed the testimony.

## Lack of Qualifications—Bias or Other Ethical Conflict

Not surprisingly, an expert may be disqualified if he or she is biased. Perhaps surprisingly, courts have concluded that an expert is biased based *solely* on the way in which adjustments are made or methodologies are applied—because all the adjustments and choices were made in the direction that would be helpful to the position of the expert's client. One court stated that "the deliberate, manifest, pervasive and systematic bias on [the expert's] part in applying the standard methodologies for estimating the total enterprise value of [the company] warrants disqualifying him and his report on the principal ground of unreliability. The Court has taken considerable pains to point out the myriad ways in which *[the expert] deliberately drove his adjustments of the discount rate and other variables toward the lowest order of value in order to accomplish his client's implicit bidding*, notwithstanding his protestations of objectivity." *Med Diversified II*, 346 B.R. at 626.

A prior connection to a case can create bias. One court decision demonstrates that an expert who has a prior connection to matters relevant to his opinion may have *no ability* to avoid disqualification. The court observed: "either [the expert's] testimony is biased because he had formed a preconception of [the transactions from his role as a 'fraud auditor' in an earlier case]; or . . . [he] deliberately chose not to apply his existing knowledge when it was directly relevant to issues he knew had been raised in this case." *Med Diversified I*, 334 B.R. at 98.

Another way that an expert can be disqualified is by agreeing to be paid on a contingency basis (i.e., getting paid only if the client obtains a recovery and getting paid a percentage of the recovery). In such a case, one court stated that this "highly unusual contingent fee for an expert witness raises obvious issues of credibility," and that a court "was entitled to discredit anything [the expert] said on the basis of this unusual arrangement." *In re Oneida Ltd.*, 351 B.R. 79, 92 (Bankr. S.D.N.Y. 2006).

In complex bankruptcy cases, however, it is often the case that the financial advisor to the debtor, the creditors' committee, or the equity committee will be engaged to perform a variety of roles that are needed to negotiate a plan of reorganization, and it is typical for financial advisors to be paid, in part, a "success" or "transaction" fee if a plan is confirmed. Courts have not disqualified experts that are members of, or employed by, such financial advisory firms as a result of such compensation arrangements.[5]

## Lack of Reliability—Lack of Peer Review

Some courts state that the peer-review portion of *Daubert* has little or no application to nonscientific testimony.[6] This is fortunate indeed because it is almost inconceivable that any expert's opinion of value of a particular business or asset would ever be subject to "peer review," at least in the same way that scientific papers are.

Somewhat surprisingly, at least one court has not dismissed the factor out of hand; just because the expert's opinion is "specifically focused on a particular fact situation that it is likely to be of little interest within academic circles" a court may still conclude that "it [is] difficult to say that it [is] so much more obscure than other matters of interest within academia [such] that questions of peer review and publication would not even apply. . . . Nonetheless, while peer review and publication can be a very important consideration, like any other factor it is not a prerequisite of admissibility."[7]

## Opinion Developed Expressly for Purposes of Testifying

Unlike scientific research that may be published in a peer-reviewed journal, an expert has no reason to perform a valuation of a particular business unless one of the parties to the private dispute pays them to do so. Nevertheless, in such cases experts are sometimes challenged on the basis that the expert's opinion was developed expressly for purposes of testifying. As long as there is "sufficient other indicia of reliability," such a challenge should not be sustained.[8]

## Opinion Based on Subjective Judgment

Usually, courts recognize that the application of the expert's judgment is appropriate. As one court stated:

> *That an expert injects personal judgment in the course of offering his testimony is hardly grounds for excluding that testimony.* Judgments must inevitably be made *in the use of loss reserve calculations, and no actuarial method is so accurate as to eliminate some use of subjective judgment in the estimation of future claims.*
> **Crowley, V. Chait 322, F. Supp. 2d 530, 549 (D.N.J. 2004)**
> **(emphasis added)**

At least one court has looked to professional valuation literature to defend the ability of an expert to make judgment calls, stating (in response to a complaint that the expert "failed to justify the particular valuation approach . . . she utilized . . . ."[9]):

> *"Professional judgment must be used to select the approach(es) and the method(s) that best indicate the value of the business interest." NACVA [National Association of Certified Valuation Analysts] Professional Standards, PX 419, § 3.6. "The approaches/methods used within a given assignment are a matter that must be determined by the business appraiser's professional judgment. The task is generally decided through consideration of the approaches/methods that are conceptually most appropriate and those for which the most reliable data is available." Business Appraisal Standards promulgated by The Institute of Business Appraisers, Inc. (Publication P-311c) (2001), Defendants' Exhibit ("DX") 484, at § 1.16. "No single valuation method is universally applicable to all appraisal purposes.*

*The context in which the appraisal is to be used is a critical factor."*
*S. PRATT, R. REILLY & R. SCHWEIHS, VALUING A BUSI-*
*NESS-THE ANALYSIS AND APPRAISAL OF CLOSELY HELD*
*COMPANIES (4th ed. 2000) ("Pratt"), PX 396, at 27.*

There is no precise guideline or quantitative formula for selecting which approach or approaches are most applicable in a
given situation. . . . [C]ommon factors to be considered by the
analyst when selecting among alternative valuation approaches
[include]:

1. The quantity and quality of the available financial and operational data.
2. The degree of the analyst's access to the available financial and
operational data.
3. The supply of industry private sale transactional data.
4. The supply of industry publicly traded company data.
5. The type of business, nature of business assets, and type of industry subject to valuation.
6. The nature of the business interest subject to valuation.
7. Statutory, judicial, and administrative considerations.
8. The informational needs of the valuation audience.
9. The purpose and objective of the valuation.
10. The professional judgment, technical expertise and experienced common sense of the analyst.

Pratt, PX 396, at 439. Because the choice of approach is a matter
of professional judgment upon which reasonable experts can differ,
Ms. Eggleston's decision to use a particular approach to the exclusion of others, standing alone, does not render her opinion
unreliable.

**In re Commercial Fin. Servs.,** 350 B.R. 520,
(Bankr. N.D. Okla. 2005) at 532

In another case, however, various judgment calls, including assigning
various weights to different factors of a valuation analysis[10] or to different
methods of valuation,[11] were criticized individually or cumulatively, as
showing "pervasive bias."[12]

## Failure to Use an Accepted Valuation Method

There are a variety of approaches used to value a business and, typically, all
applicable approaches are used by experts. Although the expert may

conclude that one approach or the other is the most reliable (e.g., because of the quality of the data available), even the less reliable method can provide a "check" of the other methods.[13]

Several courts have disqualified valuation experts (or their valuation opinion) because the expert failed to use one of the common methods. In particular, a failure to use the DCF method of valuation has been the basis for a disqualification under *Daubert*. One court explained it this way:

> *The methodology used by Mr. Peltz in determining the value of Addus consisted of two separate valuation techniques: (1) a Guideline Company Multiple Approach ("Company Approach") and (2) a Guideline Transaction Multiple Approach ("Transaction Approach"). Yet the leading authorities on business valuation, including the authority most cited by the parties, Dr. Shannon Pratt, "recognize that the most reliable method for determining the value of a business is the Discounted Cash Flow ('DCF') Method."* Lippe v. Bairnco Corp., 288 B.R. 678 (S.D.N.Y.2003) *(citing Shannon P. Pratt et. al., Valuing A Business: The Analysis and Appraisal of Closely Held Companies 154 (4th ed. 2000) ("Regardless of what valuation approach is used, in order for it to make rational economic sense from a financial point of view, the results should be compatible with what would result if a well-supported discounted economic income analysis were carried out."))*, aff'd, 99 Fed. Appx. 274 (2d Cir.2004). *During his testimony, even Mr. Peltz recognized that the DCF method is commonly used to value 100% of the equity of a privately held company. Yet he did not use the DCF method in determining the value of the Addus shares.*
>
> *In* Lippe, *the court excluded the testimony of a business valuation expert based, in part, on the expert's failure to use the DCF method in determining the value of the business. The court held "[b]y failing to use the DCF method and relying solely on the comparable companies method, [the expert] did not have an ability to do a 'check' on his determinations."* Lippe, 288 B.R. at 689. *Accordingly, the expert's testimony was excluded as unreliable.* Id. at 701.
>
> *For essentially the same reason, Mr. Peltz's failure to use the DCF method amounts to a material flaw in his methodology sufficient to bar his testimony as an expert witness because his conclusions lack "good grounds." . . . Although Mr. Peltz used two methods in determining the value of Addus, both approaches are considered "market" approaches which apply a multiple computed from data derived from other alleged comparable companies. In*

*contrast, the DCF method is considered an "income" approach to valuation that uses data derived from the target company itself to compute the current value of the projected future economic benefit of owning the company. Mr. Peltz never determined that the DCF method was inappropriate as a valuation method under the circumstances, and he even considered using the DCF method, stating at one point in his testimony: "[t]he methodology is appropriate. No question." For some unknown reason, Mr. Peltz did not use the DCF method and he failed to offer an adequate explanation why he did not do so. Instead, he testified that he simply ascertained the method he used was reliable. As in* Lippe, *this Court finds that Mr. Peltz's use of only two "comparable companies" methods simply did not provide the necessary "check" on the value he arrived at that would render that value a reliable measure of the company's worth.*

**Med Diversified I at 98 (some citations omitted)**

But other cases have acknowledged that "it would be wrong to conclude that there is a categorical requirement that any valuation analysis must be supported by DCF calculations" and that "[t]he need for conducting a DCF analysis as a check on other methods is not as critical in instances where the initial analysis is more trustworthy."[14] Said another way, "[t]he choice of a valuation approach constitutes the exercise of professional judgment, which may be evaluated at trial in assessing the weight to accord the testimony based thereon."[15]

Where the issues that the expert is opining on are unique, however, an inability to cite to a particular accounting or other financial standard by which the opinions are evaluated may not defeat reliability.[16]

## Use of a Valuation Method Not Recognized in Industry

An expert was not allowed to use a valuation method that has been accepted—but only as a method to value options for a *minority* of the shares of *publicly traded* companies—in order to value *100 percent* of the shares of a *private* company.[17]

But, where "comparable securities-based pricing is accepted within the industry" even if an expert's *precise* method is not the same as the methods employed in the industry, testimony can support a conclusion that the expert's methodology is "sufficiently reliable to be admitted."[18] In particular, when an expert has "combined analytical tools in a particular way which has not gained general acceptance," this may not be sufficient to disqualify the expert where the "essential principles of his technique do have general acceptance" and the expert used tests to assess the "meaning and accuracy of his results."[19]

## Improper or Inconsistent Use of Valuation Methods

An expert that tosses out data from a particular company as an outlier for one set of calculations but included data from that company for another calculation puts his testimony at risk on reliability grounds.[20]

## Failure to Consider Reliable Data

An expert's opinion can be thrown into doubt if the expert does not take into account data that would appear to be relevant to the valuation at hand. For instance, an expert was attacked because his computer-generated prices for CMOs did not take into account the actual prices of these CMOs—but since one of the issues in the case was the legitimacy of those actual prices, there was a logical basis for the expert to exclude that data."[21]

By contrast, an expert in another case[22] disregarded actual prices for $CO_2$ because he concluded that market prices could not be observed, as most of the sales "moves within, not between, firms."[23] Affirming the exclusion of the expert's testimony, the Tenth Circuit observed that "expert testimony based on hypothesis can (and sometimes must) be used to establish market value, courts tend to prefer evidence derived from actual sales."[24] The reasons given by the expert for not considering prices obtained in comparable markets were deemed inadequate by the trial court, and the appellate court refused to reverse in light of the "abuse-of-discretion standard applicable to its review."[25]

## Reliance on Unreliable Data or Unverified Data

An expert's testimony was excluded when (among other things), he acknowledged that he relied on a document but admitted that "he did not know what the document was, who created it, or how it was created."[26] The failure of an expert to do independent analysis of data from databases he relied on was one of many reasons that the opinion of one expert was excluded.[27] Reliance on a "very small database of publicly held companies" was part of the reason that one court found an expert's opinion, about the value of a privately held company, unreliable.[28]

## Reliance on Evidence Preselected by Counsel

Experts "should conduct independent analyses. . . . The information upon which an expert bases his testimony must be reliable, and the selective furnishing of information by counsel . . . runs afoul of Fed. R. Evid. 703, which, in addition to Rule 702, must be considered by a court for *Daubert* purposes. . . . Any parts of that [expert's] report which rely on the preselected deposition testimony . . . is barred."[29]

Similarly, an expert's reliance on "a sampling of tapes that were selected by an attorney for [a party]" was one of several facts cited when a court properly excluded an expert's testimony.[30]

An expert is well-advised to document the breadth of materials reviewed in connection with her opinion so that any such allegation of bias or spoon feeding can be rebutted. The following is a good example of what an expert wants to be able to say if such an allegation is made:

> *Chase falsely claims that [the expert's] opinions are based exclusively upon information provided by CFS general counsel . . . , and that her "wholesale reliance" on one "biased" source "is basis alone to find her testimony unreliable." As is demonstrated by the lists of documents and sources appended to her expert reports, [the expert] reviewed thousands of boxes of documents containing CFS's and NGU's business and financial records, culling out for particular reliance documents reflecting circumstances reasonably contemporaneous with the valuation dates, and reviewed testimony given and documents produced by CFS's employees, lawyers, accountants, advisors, bankers, and other professionals, before offering her opinions on CFS's and NGU's solvency. There is no evidence that [the expert] simply repackaged information and opinions fed to her by [counsel].*
>
> *Commercial Fin. Servs.*, 350 B.R. at 531 n.6
> (citations omitted)

## Reliance on Unreasonable Assumptions

An expert's opinion of a decedent's future earning capacity were rejected when they were wholly speculative.[31] The expert "simply made up new lines of work for Mr. Joy."[32] His estimate of the future value of the decedent's real estate investments was similarly speculative, because it was based on "a single piece of property in the Virgin Islands without ascertaining the experience of investors in [that] market."[33]

Similarly, a court found no meaningful support for projections of future revenue at about 5 percent a year when in prior years the *actual* revenue increases were 34 percent and 11 percent,[34] and found no justification for increasing the interest rate payable on debt simply because of an absence of a guaranty in the case of a purchase by a third party.[35]

## Failure to Check Reasonableness of Results or to Test Model

An expert who relies on a computer model to derive valuations should test the meaningfulness and accuracy of the results obtained from the use of the model.[36] When the expert used two methods to demonstrate that his model was meaningful and accurate, and one was "not precisely a 'test,' [but] was 'a rough cross-check of reasonableness,'" and the other test captured a "general indication in the . . . market as a whole," the testing techniques were sufficient, even though they were not without their limitations.[37]

In the context of a valuation report, however, one court discounted the necessity or value of a sensitivity analysis, as follows:

> *Chase argues that failing to conduct a sensitivity analysis to test the effect of varying some of Ms. Eggleston's [the expert] key assumptions "violates valuation practices and standards." In support, Chase cites AICPA's Draft Statement of Standards for Valuation Services No. 1 (2002) ("Draft Statement"), which suggests the consideration of a sensitivity analysis, which is described in the Draft Statement as "a summary of the effect on discounted cash flow results from varying key assumptions (such as the discount rate, commodity pricing and/or major operating assumptions)" when performing a valuation using the discounted cash flow method. Ms. Eggleston states (and Chase does not refute) that the Draft Statement was widely criticized and was withdrawn and that no replacement draft was in circulation at the time of her reports.*
>
> *Chase also relies on THE HANDBOOK OF ADVANCED BUSINESS VALUATION, which states "in order to make a determination as to whether a company has adequate capital and is likely to be able to pay its debts as they come due, one should examine the company's financial performance under a range of possible performance scenarios." Also, in an article in* Viewpoints *on Value, the authors suggest using sensitivity analyses to "help valuators and managers isolate distressed companies' key value*

*drivers." These excerpts do not convince the Court that conducting a sensitivity analysis to identify "key value drivers" is mandatory (or even necessary) to a sound solvency analysis.*

*Common sense indicates that when performing calculations involving large numbers, changes in variables like discount rates, prices of charged off loans, and cost allocations will shift the final result of the calculation in one direction or the other. A more relevant concern is whether Ms. Eggleston is able to articulate a reasonable basis in fact for choosing a particular variable, not whether changing the variable may alter the result (it always will). Ms. Eggleston explained her reasons for selecting a relatively safe discount rate for discounting liabilities, expressed in excruciating detail all the reasons she chose to include or exclude certain income streams or expenses (account by account) in her calculation of CFS's servicing liability, and identified some evidence to support her decision to value purchased receivables at eight percent of their face value. Even if Ms. Eggleston performed sensitivity analyses on those variables, as suggested (and performed) by Chase's expert, Chase does not explain how that analysis could alter the facts on which Ms. Eggleston relied when selecting the particular variables or demonstrate that Ms. Eggleston's assumptions are per se unreasonable.*

**Commercial Fin. Servs., 350 B.R. at 554–55**
(internal cites omitted).

Advance testing *may* be useful to defend judgment calls or assumptions made by the expert, but at least one court has dismissed such an argument (in the case in which the expert applied a low control premium), as follows:

*Chartwell argues that even if the control premium was not applied, Cimasi's valuation analysis would not significantly differ, so a flawed application of the control premium should not materially alter this Court's determination. Chartwell misses the point. As a gatekeeper, this Court must look to the methodology used and its application, not the ultimate outcome, and where application of the methodology is fatally flawed, as here, the Court must exclude the evidence, regardless of its effect on the ultimate outcome.*

**Med Diversified II, 346 B.R. at 638**
(emphasis added).

## Reliance on Opinions of Other Experts

An expert can, and often must, rely on the opinion of other experts.

An expert, however, may not simply repeat or adopt the findings of another expert without attempting to assess the validity of the opinions relied upon. *In re TMI Litig.*, 193 F.3d 613, 715-16 (3d Cir. 1999) (finding blind reliance by expert on other expert opinions demonstrates flawed methodology under *Daubert*). . . . [C]ourts must ensure an expert witness is sufficiently familiar with the reasoning or methodology behind the information to permit cross-examination.[38]

## Correction of Errors

"[T]he fact that [the expert] reviewed his original report and made certain corrections to it does not show that his methodology was unreliable—revisions are consistent with the scientific method."[39]

"*Daubert* does not require that an expert's testimony be excluded simply because he admitted and corrected his own mistakes or retracted his false statements. In fact, one of the very purposes of a *Daubert* hearing . . . is to give experts a chance to explain and even correct errors. . . . There is no stigma attached to such error correction, nor should there be. If anything, it strengthens the quality of the expert report."[40]

## LACK OF RELEVANCE

An expert will not be allowed to testify about a breach of contract, breach of the implied covenant of good faith, or whether conduct was commercially unreasonable, where the expert "relies almost exclusively" on the interpretation of deposition testimony. "In so doing, he . . . seeks to supplant the role of counsel in making argument at trial, and the role of the jury interpreting the evidence." This is true even though an expert can testify to customs and standards of an industry, and how a party's conduct measures up to such standards.[41]

## PRACTICAL LESSONS FROM *DAUBERT* CASES FOR EXPERTS AND LAWYERS

A lawyer should give—and the expert should demand—access to all of the exhibits and all of the deposition testimony. It should be left to the expert or the expert's staff to decide what can and cannot be ignored. Lawyers should get their experts involved in requests for production of documents: What does the expert need to see? What sort of documents are typically kept by a company in a situation like the one you are dealing with?

Lawyers should make the expert explain *everything* to the lawyer. This will have several benefits:

- Sometimes making the expert explain what he is doing (or is planning to do) will cause an expert to recognize a gap in his reasoning.
- If the lawyer doesn't fully understand what the expert is doing, the lawyer won't be able to explain it to the judge at the *Daubert* stage, or to the judge or jury at trial.
- If the lawyer doesn't "get it" after the expert explains it, the judge or the jury won't "get it" after the expert testifies.
- Things that don't add up means that something is wrong. Sometimes it may be that the expert realizes that a step in his analysis needs work; sometimes it's a matter of using a better way to explain the analysis.
- In working with the expert, asking questions is appropriate: *guiding* the expert by suggesting a modification in the approach being taken or methodologies being used, or that should not be used, is not. The expert is the person with the training and who will be on the witness stand, and the financial expert's independence, knowledge, and judgment should shine through at all times.

Do appropriate reality checks. For example, if valuation is the issue, was there an arm's-length sale that can be used to check a later valuation? Are the sales assumptions consistent with other market data? Are the profit margins consistent with industry averages?

The lawyer and the expert should frankly confront any shortcomings and weaknesses in the expert's analysis, and how the expert overcame them. Is there a better way to do so?

The expert should document every key step in the logic of the opinion, from the ultimate opinion all the way back to (1) the treatises that qualify the methods used, (2) the exhibits that contain the underlying facts, and (3) the publications relied on for market data.

Proof the report and the demonstratives for stupid errors. You will find them.

Don't lose sight of the fact that you may have different audiences at different times: the judge, if there is a *Daubert* hearing (delving into more detail), and the judge or jury at trial (engaging on some technical matters, as necessary, but connecting to the big issues of the case and showing the seriousness and reliability of the analysis).

## CONCLUSION

*Daubert* issues for business valuation experts can be considered to go to the core of your competence and professionalism in doing your job. The same level of technical knowledge, thoroughness, and independent expertise that will reflect itself in the quality of your written work and your testimony on the witness stand will also help you deal with any challenge to the admissibility of your work as a valuation expert where your focus is not on the result of your analysis, but on the process of your analysis and the result the process leads you to.

## NOTES

1. Federal Rule of Evidence 702 provides as follows:

   *Rule 702. Testimony by Experts: If scientific, technical, or other specialized knowledge will assist the trier of fact to understand the evidence or to determine a fact in issue, a witness qualified as an expert by knowledge, skill, experience, training, or education, may testify thereto in the form of an opinion or otherwise, if (1) the testimony is based upon sufficient facts or data, (2) the testimony is the product of reliable principles and methods, and (3) the witness has applied the principles and methods reliably to the facts of the case.*

2. In re *Med Diversified*, Inc., 334 B.R. 89, 96 (Bankr. E.D.N.Y. 2005) [Med Diversified I].
3. *Id.* at 97.
4. *Id.* at 96 n. 13.
5. *See, e.g., In re Zenith Electronics Corp.,* 241 B.R. 92 (Bankr. D/Del. 1999).
6. *See, e.g., Smithkline Beecham Corp. v. Eastern Applicators, Inc.,* No. 99-CV-6552, 2001 WL 1526273 at *3 (E.D. Pa. Nov. 29, 2001) (bid rigging case, commercial roofers with practical experience used as experts to calculate a competitive bid).
7. *Primavera Familienstiftung v. Askin,* 130 F.Supp.2d 450, 525–26 (S.D.N.Y. 2001).
8. *Primavera Familienstiftung v. Askin,* 130 F.Supp.2d 450, 528 (S.D.N.Y. 2001).
9. In re *Commercial Fin. Servs.,* Inc., 350 B.R. 529, at 532 (Bankr. N.D. Okla 2005).
10. *Med Diversified I,* 334 B.R. at 100–01 (footnote omitted):

    *Mr. Peltz failed to explain adequately why in his application of the Company Approach he gave the value he arrived at using the EV/CFO multiple a weight of 67.7%, 2/3 greater than the value he arrived at using the EV/R multiple, which was significantly higher than the EV/CFO value. Absent a sufficient explanation for the weights assigned to these two values, Mr. Peltz's entire analysis is questionable because had he assigned different weights in applying the Company Approach, the value he arrived at may have been significantly divergent from the value he arrived at using the Transaction Approach.*

11. *In re Med Diversified*, Inc., 346 B.R. 621, 632–33 (Bankr. E.D.N.Y. 2006) [Med Diversified II] (emphasis added) (footnote omitted):

   *Using the DCF method, Cimasi determined that the value of 100% of the shares of Addus was $18,772,961. This figure constituted 60% of his final determination that Addus was only worth $21 million . . . . By the by, he* offers no adequate explanation why this Court should not require equal weights to the results obtained by each of the three standardized methods. See In re Exide Technologies, *303 B.R. 48, 65 (Bankr. D. Del. 2003). It has not escaped the Court's attention to the fact that the values derived from applying the other two methods were higher than that from the DCF method. By reducing the weights of the results from the other methods, once again he shoved the data to a lower value.*

   But compare this statement from In re Oneida, Ltd., *351 B.R. 79, 88 (Bankr. S. D.N.Y. 2006) (emphasis added)*

   *In order to arrive at a current value for the Debtors, all three valuations rely on a discounted cash flow analysis ("DCF analysis"), a comparable (or selected) company analysis and a precedent transaction (or selected acquisition) analysis. The comparable company analyses and the precedent transaction analyses were not heavily disputed. The experts also generally agreed that the DCF analysis was the most probative as to value.*

12. *See Med Diversified II*, quoted above at footnote 11.
13. *But see* footnote 11.
14. *Celebrity Cruises Inc. v. Essef Corp.*, 434 F. Supp. 2d 169, 179-80 (S.D.N.Y. 2006).
15. *Commercial Fin. Servs.*, 350 B.R. at 534. The court noted, for instance, that "Ms. Eggleston rejected the market approach due to the absence of sales of comparable companies during the relevant time period, citing documentary evidence to support her conclusion." *Id.* at 533.
16. *ProtoComm Corp. v. Novell Advanced Servs., Inc.*, 171 F. Supp. 2d 473, 480 (E.D. Pa. 2001):

   *Defendants prime argument is that Pakter fails to articulate an accounting or other financial standard by which his opinions were evaluated. My analysis of this contention follows: this case, however, is unique. Simple accounting standards may not explain the full nature of the transaction at issue here. Pakter based his opinions on personal knowledge and experience, as well as a seemingly copious review of a multitude of relevant business documents. He and his firm conducted their own evaluations based on the materials before them and such knowledge and experience. It is not for this Court to decide whether those opinions are in fact accurate, only that they a [sic] based on a reliable method. If defendants believe Pakter's testimony to be flimsy, they can challenge his opinions through "[v]igorous cross-examination, presentation of contrary evidence, and careful instruction on the burden of proof . . . " Daubert, 509 U.S. at 596, 113 S.Ct. at 2798. I therefore conclude that plaintiff has shown by a preponderance of the evidence that Pakter employs a reliable method to support his conclusions.*

17. *Med Diversified I*, 334 B.R. at 102-03 (footnote omitted):

   *[T]he parties have not cited a single case, either in a federal bankruptcy or federal district court, in which that court accepted as a recognized methodology the application of the Black-Scholes Method to valuing an option in 100% of controlled shares in a privately held company. This Court is not prepared to embark on a cruise down this unexplored river in the heart of the jungle in order to discover the application of this Method outside the principal context in which it has been customarily applied, namely, to valuing an option for a minority of publicly traded shares.*

18. *Primavera*, 130 F. Supp. 2d at 526.
19. *Id.* at 527. *But see Med Diversified I*, 334 B.R. at 101 n. 20 (citations omitted):

   *Mr. Peltz stated, in effect, that he is free to develop any reliable measure for use in placing a value on a company, regardless of whether Dr. Pratt has included that same measure in his book [recognized by the parties as an authoritative reference book on valuation]. The problem is that Mr. Peltz has not shown his measure to be reliable.*

20. *Med Diversified I*, 334 B.R. at 102 ("Mr. Peltz never adequately explained to this Court's satisfaction why Gentiva was an outliner for the EBITDA calculation but was not an outliner for the net cash flow from operations calculation, casting even more doubt on the reliability of his methods.")
21. *Primavera* 130 F.Supp.2d at 524.
22. *Atlantic Richfield Co. v. Farm Credit Bank of Wichita*, 226 F.3d 1138 (10th Cir. 2000).
23. 226 F.3d at 1165.
24. 226 F.3d at 1167. The Court went on to reason as follows:

   *For instance, in* Ashland Oil, Inc. v. Phillips Petroleum Co., *554 F.2d 381 (10th Cir.1975), we intimated that "comparable sales or current market price is the best" and "by far the preferable method" for determining value. Id. at 387; see also id. (commenting that the expert testimony presented in the case, "[n]o matter how interesting" as a matter of theory, was "only opinion evidence" and did not "establish facts"); cf. Brooke Group Ltd. v. Brown & Williamson Tobacco Corp., 509 U.S. 209, 242, 113 S.Ct. 2578, 125 L.Ed.2d 168 (1993) ("Expert testimony is useful as a guide to interpreting market facts, but it is not a substitute for them."). Accordingly, even if the relevant market is not perfectly competitive, "it still makes better sense to begin with the collective judgment expressed in the market price" than to start with "a wholly subjective pronouncement of worth."* Campbell v. United States, 228 Ct. Cl. 661, 661 F.2d 209, 221 (1981). *By the same token, when determining market value "[c]ompletely comparable sales are not likely to be found" and "[s]ales that have some different characteristics must be considered."* Piney Woods Country Life Sch. v. Shell Oil Co., 726 F.2d 225, 239 (5th Cir.1984); see also id. *(suggesting that a court "should not dismiss fairly comparable sales out of hand because of certain incomparable qualities").*

*Judged by these standards, the district court's conclusion that Smith strayed too far from the available sales data cannot be described as "manifestly unreasonable." For example, the prices received by ARCO from several $CO_2$ sales in the early 1980s conceivably could serve as the basis for a "market value" calculation. The record indicates that between 1982 and 1984, ARCO made several sales to "working interest" owners in West Texas who were not $CO_2$ suppliers. The defendants do not contest that during this time ARCO sold or delivered approximately 55% of its $CO_2$ to third parties. The record also indicates that between 1983 and 1989 ARCO sold or delivered an average of 37% of its $CO_2$ to third parties. In light of this evidence, it was not "arbitrary, capricious, or whimsical" for the district court to conclude that, at least during the early 1980s, ARCO's purported incentive to depress $CO_2$ prices was substantially blunted.*

25. *Id.* at 1168. The Court noted:

*Suffice it to say that our standard of review plays a major role in the disposition of this issue. Whether the existence of other markets and the sales data presented by ARCO fatally undermine Smith's theory is eminently debatable. If our review were de novo, we might very well conclude that Smith's theory explains or otherwise accounts for these markets and data.*

26. *Montgomery County v. Microvote Corp.*, 320 F.3d 440, 448–49 (3d Cir. 2003).

27. *Med Diversified I*, 334 B.R. at 100 (internal cites omitted):

*Moreover, in deriving a value for Addus using both the Company and Transaction approaches, Mr. Peltz depended on databases of research findings of only ten allegedly comparable privately held companies engaged in home health care and related industries. Mr. Peltz testified that he did not do any independent analysis of these companies, and did not independently analyze the data from the databases from which he derived his figures— "Mergerstat" and "Factset." In choosing the companies and transactions upon which his analysis is based, Mr. Peltz admittedly never considered the nature or products of the businesses, or the market in which these*

*businesses operated. Thus, the data on which Mr. Peltz's conclusions are
based is simply inadequate.*

28. *Med Diversified II*, 346 B.R. at 631-32 (footnotes omitted):

   *Unfortunately, Cimasi's benchmarking analysis relied heavily on a very
   small database of publicly held companies and was applied in a manner
   that was skewed to disfavor Addus, thereby rendering not only the benchmarking analysis unreliable, but also tainting his DCF and GCV analyses.*

   . . .

   *Cimasi did not satisfy the Court that the "peer-reviewed literature" accepts
   a sample size of carefully selected public or private companies as few as
   three or four. But more fundamental is the Court's skepticism that it is
   methodogically sound to compare the data from public companies with
   that of a closely held private business. That is a huge quantum leap that
   this Court is unwilling to make. The literature cited by Cimasi is severely
   limited and little of it appears to satisfy the rigorous standard of peer-
   reviewed publications.*

29. *Crowley*, 322 F. Supp. 2d at 542 (citation and footnote omitted).
30. *Microvote*, 320 F.3d at 449.
31. *Joy v. Bell Helicopter Textron, Inc.*, 999 F.2d 549 (D.C. Cir. 1993).
32. *Id.* at 569.
33. *Id.*, see also, *Eymard v. Pan Am. World Airways (In re Air Crash Disaster)*, 795
    F.2d 1230 (5th Cir. 1986), where, among other things, the expert assumed that
    the decedent would begin saving at the rate of up to 20% a year, despite the fact
    that he had virtually no savings at his death.
34. *Med Diversified II*, 346 B.R. at 633–34 (footnotes omitted):

   *While the actual increase in revenue for Addus was 34.76% from 1999 to
   2000, and 11.24% from 2000 to 2001, his projected revenue increases for
   the prospective 5 year period were: 4.94% for years 1 & 2, 3.95% for year
   3, and around 5% for years 4 & 5. He calculated projected revenue for
   Addus by applying these percentage increases to Addus's actual and projected revenue figures.*

   *The record is devoid of any meaningful support for use of these varia-
   bles to project future revenue.*

35. *Med Diversified II*, 346 B.R. at 636 (footnote omitted):

   *The actual cost of Addus' debt was 4.28 %. Cimasi added 12% to that
   number to account for the fact that Addus' debt was personally guaranteed
   by its principal, Andrew Wright. According to Cimasi, "it is reasonable to
   assume that in the absence of those guarantees that there would be an incremental rise in the cost of debt attributable to the hypothetical sale of*

*[Addus]." Cimasi Report, Section 5, p. 19 or 28. Thus, the cost of debt used in his WACC calculation was 16.28 %.*

*There is simply no justification for the addition of 12% to the cost of Addus's debt simply because Wright personally guaranteed the debt. There is no reason to believe that a hypothetical purchaser would pay an additional 12% to extend the same credit to Addus. Indeed, other than Cimasi's testimony that the going rate for a company like Addus would have been around 16%, there is no other evidence to support the conclusion that 12% should be added to the cost of debt because of Addus's debt structure.*

*Moreover, there is nothing in the literature that sets forth the criteria for imposing any adjustments for a personal guaranty when comparing the cost of debt for a public company with the cost of debt for the subject private company. In this respect, there is no peer recognized technical knowledge for computing the cost of debt when there is or is not a guarantee by the controlling shareholder(s).*

36. *Primavera*, 130 F. Supp. 2d at 525.
37. *Id.* at 525 n75.
38. *In re Polypropylene Carpet Antitrust Litig.*, 93 F. Supp. 2d 1348, 1357 (N.D. Ga. 2000).
39. *Primavera*, 130 F. Supp. 2d at 527.
40. *Crowley*, 322 F. Supp. 2d at 540.
41. *Primavera*, 130 F. Supp. 2d at 529.

# AICPA Statement on Standards for Valuation Services No. 1, Valuation of a Business, Business Ownership Interest, Security, or Intangible Asset

# Contents of Statement

# Foreword

## Why Issued

Valuations of businesses, business ownership interests, securities, or intangible assets (hereinafter collectively referred to in this foreword as *business valuations*) may be performed for a wide variety of purposes including the following:

1. Transactions (or potential transactions), such as acquisitions, mergers, leveraged buyouts, initial public offerings, employee stock ownership plans and other share based plans, partner and shareholder buy-ins or buyouts, and stock redemptions.

2. Litigation (or pending litigation) relating to matters such as marital dissolution, bankruptcy, contractual disputes, owner disputes, dissenting shareholder and minority ownership oppression cases, and employment and intellectual property disputes.

3. Compliance-oriented engagements, including (*a*) financial reporting and (*b*) tax matters such as corporate reorganizations; S corporation conversions; income, estate, and gift tax compliance; purchase price allocations; and charitable contributions.

4. Planning oriented engagements for income tax, estate tax, gift tax, mergers and acquisitions, and personal financial planning.

In recent years, the need for business valuations has increased significantly. Performing an engagement to estimate value involves special knowledge and skill.

Given the increasing number of members of the AICPA who are performing business valuation engagements or some aspect thereof, the AICPA Consulting Services Executive Committee has written this standard to improve the consistency and quality of practice among AICPA members performing business valuations. AICPA members will be required to follow this standard when they perform engagements to estimate value that culminate in the expression of a conclusion of value or a calculated value.

The Consulting Services Executive Committee is a body designated by AICPA Council to promulgate technical standards under Rule 201, *General Standards* (AICPA, *Professional Standards*, vol. 2, ET sec. 201.01), and Rule 202, *Compliance With Standards* (AICPA, *Professional Standards*, vol. 2, ET sec. 202.01), of the AICPA *Code of Professional Conduct*.

# Valuation of a Business, Business Ownership Interest, Security, or Intangible Asset

## Introduction and Scope

1. This Statement establishes standards for AICPA members (hereinafter referred to in this Statement as *members*) who are engaged to, or, as part of another engagement, estimate the value of a **business**,[1] *business ownership interest, security*, or **intangible asset** (hereinafter collectively referred to in this Statement as *subject interest*). For purposes of this Statement, the definition of a *business* includes not-for-profit entities or activities.

2. As described in this Statement, the term **engagement to estimate value** refers to an engagement or any part of an engagement (for example, a tax, litigation, or acquisition-related engagement) that involves estimating the value of a subject interest. An engagement to estimate value culminates in the expression of either a **conclusion of value** or a **calculated value** (see paragraph 21). A member who performs an engagement to estimate value is referred to, in this Statement, as a **valuation analyst**.

3. Valuation analysts should be aware of any governmental regulations and other professional standards applicable to the engagement, including the AICPA *Code of Professional Conduct* and the Statement on Standards for Consulting Services (SSCS) No. 1, *Consulting Services: Definitions and Standards* (AICPA, *Professional Standards*, vol. 2, CS sec. 100), and the extent to which they apply to engagements to estimate value. Compliance is the responsibility of the valuation analyst.

---

[1] This Statement includes two glossaries. Appendix B is the International Glossary of Business Valuation Terms (IGBVT), jointly developed by the AICPA, the American Society of Appraisers (ASA), the Canadian Institute of Chartered Business Valuators, the National Association of Certified Valuation Analysts, and the Institute of Business Appraisers. The IGBVT is reproduced verbatim in Appendix B, "International Glossary of Business Valuation Terms." Appendix C provides definitions for terms included in this Statement, but not defined in the IGBVT. The terms defined in Appendix B are in boldface type the first time they appear in this Statement; the terms defined in Appendix C are in italicized boldface type the first time they appear in this Statement.

4. In the process of estimating value as part of an engagement, the valuation analyst applies **valuation approaches** and **valuation methods**, as described in this Statement, and uses professional judgment. The use of professional judgment is an essential component of estimating value.

## Exceptions from this Statement

5. This Statement is not applicable to a member who participates in estimating the value of a subject interest as part of performing an attest engagement defined by Rule 101 of the AICPA Code of Professional Conduct (for example, as part of an audit, review, or compilation engagement).

6. This Statement is not applicable when the value of a subject interest is provided to the member by the client or a third party, and the member does not apply valuation approaches and methods, as discussed in this Statement.

7. This Statement is not applicable to internal use assignments from employers to employee members not in the *practice of public accounting*, as that term is defined in the AICPA *Code of Professional Conduct* (AICPA, *Professional Standards*, vol. 2, ET sec. 92. 25). (Interpretation No. 1, "Scope of Applicable Services" of *Statement on Standards for Valuation Services*, Illustrations 24 and 25).

8. This Statement is not applicable to engagements that are exclusively for the purpose of determining economic damages (for example, lost profits) unless those determinations include an engagement to estimate value. See also Interpretation No. 1, Illustrations 1, 2, and 3.

9.(a) This Statement is not applicable to mechanical computations that do not rise to the level of an engagement to estimate value; that is, when the member does not apply valuation approaches and methods and does not use professional judgment. See Interpretation No. 1, Illustration 8.

(b) This Statement is not applicable when it is not practical or not reasonable to obtain or use relevant information; as a result, the member is unable to apply valuation approaches and methods that are described in this Statement.[2]

---

[2] Unless prohibited by statute or by rule, a member may use the client's estimates for compliance reporting to a third party if the member determines that the estimates are reasonable (based on the facts and circumstances known to the member). See Interpretation No. 1, "Scope of Applicable Services" of *Statement on Standards for Valuation Services* and *Statement for Standards on Tax Services* No. 4.

## Jurisdictional Exception

10. If any part of this Statement differs from published governmental, judicial, or accounting authority, or such authority specifies valuation development procedures or valuation reporting procedures, then the valuation analyst should follow the applicable published authority or stated procedures with respect to that part applicable to the valuation in which the member is engaged. The other parts of this Statement continue in full force and effect (Valuation Services Interpretation No. 1).

# Overall Engagement Considerations

## Professional Competence

11. Rule 201A, *Professional Competence*, of the AICPA *Code of Professional Conduct* (AICPA, *Professional Standards*, vol. 2, ET. sec. 201.01), states that a member shall "undertake only those professional services that the member or the member's firm can reasonably expect to be completed with professional competence." Performing a valuation engagement with professional competence involves special knowledge and skill. A valuation analyst should possess a level of knowledge of valuation principles and theory and a level of skill in the application of such principles that will enable him or her to identify, gather, and analyze data, consider and apply appropriate valuation approaches and methods, and use professional judgment in developing the estimate of value (whether a single amount or a range). An in-depth discussion of valuation theory and principles, and how and when to apply them, is not within the scope of this Statement.

12. In determining whether he or she can reasonably expect to complete the valuation engagement with professional competence, the valuation analyst should consider, at a minimum, the following:

*a.* Subject entity and its industry

*b.* Subject interest

*c.* **Valuation date**

*d.* Scope of the valuation engagement

   *i.* Purpose of the valuation engagement

    *ii.* ***Assumptions and limiting conditions*** expected to apply to the valuation engagement (paragraph 18)

    *iii.* Applicable **standard of value** (for example, *fair value* or **fair market value**), and the applicable **premise of value** (for example, going concern)

    *iv.* Type of valuation report to be issued (paragraph 48), intended use and users of the report, and restrictions on the use of the report

  *e.* Governmental regulations or other professional standards that apply to the subject interest or to the valuation engagement

## Nature and Risks of the Valuation Services and Expectations of the Client

13. In understanding the nature and risks of the ***valuation services*** to be provided, and the expectations of the client, the valuation analyst should consider the matters in paragraph 12, and in addition, at a minimum, the following:

*a.* The proposed terms of the valuation engagement

*b.* The identity of the client

*c.* The nature of the interest and ownership rights in the business, business interest, security, or intangible asset being valued, including **control** characteristics and the degree of **marketability** of the interest

*d.* The procedural requirements of a valuation engagement and the extent, if any, to which procedures will be limited by either the client or circumstances beyond the client's or the valuation analyst's control

*e.* The use of and limitations of the report, and the conclusion or calculated value

*f.* Any obligation to update the valuation

## Objectivity and Conflict of Interest

14. The AICPA *Code of Professional Conduct* requires objectivity in the performance of all professional services, including valuation engagements. Objectivity is a state of mind. The principle of objectivity imposes the obligation to be impartial, intellectually honest, disinterested, and free from conflicts of interest. If necessary, where

a potential conflict of interest may exist, a valuation analyst should make the disclosures and obtain consent as required under Interpretation No. 102-2, "Conflicts of Interest," under Rule 102, *Integrity and Objectivity* (AICPA, *Professional Standards*, vol. 2, ET sec. 102.03).

## Independence and Valuation

15.  If valuation services are performed for a client for which the valuation analyst or valuation analyst's firm also performs an attest engagement (defined by Rule 101 of the AICPA Code of Professional Conduct), the valuation analyst should meet the requirements of Interpretation No. 101-3, "Performance of Nonattest Services," under Rule 101, *Independence* (AICPA, *Professional Standards*, vol. 2, ET sec. 101.05), so as not to impair the member's independence with respect to the client.

## Establishing an Understanding with the Client

16.  The valuation analyst should establish an understanding with the client, preferably in writing, regarding the engagement to be performed. If the understanding is oral, the valuation analyst should document that understanding by appropriate memoranda or notations in the working papers. (If the engagement is being performed for an attest client, AICPA Ethics Interpretation 101-3 requires the engagement understanding to be in writing.) Regardless of whether the understanding is written or oral, the valuation analyst should modify the understanding if he or she encounters circumstances during the engagement that make it appropriate to modify that understanding.

17.  The understanding with the client reduces the possibility that either the valuation analyst or the client may misinterpret the needs or expectations of the other party. The understanding should include, at a minimum, the nature, purpose, and objective of the valuation engagement, the client's responsibilities, the valuation analyst's responsibilities, the applicable assumptions and limiting conditions, the type of report to be issued, and the standard of value to be used.

### Assumptions and Limiting Conditions

18.  Assumptions and limiting conditions are common to valuation engagements. Examples of typical assumptions and limiting

conditions for a business valuation are provided in Appendix A, "Illustrative List of Assumptions and Limiting Conditions for a Business Valuation." The assumptions and limiting conditions should be disclosed in the valuation report (paragraphs 52(l), 68(g), and 71(m)).

### Scope Restrictions or Limitations

19. A restriction or limitation on the scope of the valuation analyst's work, or the data available for analysis, may be present and known to the valuation analyst at the outset of the valuation engagement or may arise during the course of a valuation engagement. Such a restriction or limitation should be disclosed in the valuation report (paragraphs 52(m), 68(e), and 71(n)).

### Using the Work of Specialists in the Engagement to Estimate Value

20. In performing an engagement to estimate value, the valuation analyst may rely on the work of a third party specialist (for example, a real estate or equipment appraiser). The valuation analyst should note in the assumptions and limiting conditions the level of responsibility, if any, being assumed by the valuation analyst for the work of the third party specialist. At the option of the valuation analyst, the written report of the third party specialist may be included in the valuation analyst's report.

## Development

### Types of Engagement

21. There are two types of engagements to estimate value—a *valuation engagement* and a *calculation engagement*. The valuation engagement requires more procedures than does the calculation engagement. The valuation engagement results in a conclusion of value. The calculation engagement results in a calculated value. The type of engagement is established in the understanding with the client (paragraphs 16 and 17):

a. *Valuation engagement*—A valuation analyst performs a valuation engagement when (1) the engagement calls for the valuation analyst to estimate the value of a subject interest and (2) the valuation analyst estimates the value (as outlined in paragraphs 23–45) and is free to apply the valuation approaches and methods he or she deems appropriate in the circumstances. The valuation analyst expresses the results of the valuation as a conclusion of value; the conclusion may be either a single amount or a range.

b. *Calculation engagement*—A valuation analyst performs a calculation engagement when (1) the valuation analyst and the client agree on the valuation approaches and methods the valuation analyst will use and the extent of procedures the valuation analyst will perform in the process of calculating the value of a subject interest (these procedures will be more limited than those of a valuation engagement) and (2) the valuation analyst calculates the value in compliance with the agreement. The valuation analyst expresses the results of these procedures as a calculated value. The calculated value is expressed as a range or as a single amount. A calculation engagement does not include all of the procedures required for a valuation engagement (paragraph 46).

## Hypothetical Conditions

22.  Hypothetical conditions affecting the subject interest may be required in some circumstances. When a valuation analyst uses hypothetical conditions during a valuation or calculation engagement, he or she should indicate the purpose for including the hypothetical conditions and disclose these conditions in the valuation or calculation report (paragraphs 52(n), 71(o), and 74).

## Valuation engagement

23.  In performing a valuation engagement, the valuation analyst should:

- Analyze the subject interest (paragraphs 25–30)
- Consider and apply appropriate valuation approaches and methods (paragraphs 31–42)
- Prepare and maintain appropriate documentation (paragraphs 44–45)

24.  Even though the list in paragraph 23 and some requirements and guidance in this Statement are presented in a manner that suggests a sequential valuation process, valuations involve an ongoing process of gathering, updating, and analyzing information. Accordingly, the sequence of the requirements and guidance in this

Statement may be implemented differently at the option of the valuation analyst.

### Analysis of the Subject Interest

25. The analysis of the subject interest will assist the valuation analyst in considering, evaluating, and applying the various valuation approaches and methods to the subject interest. The nature and extent of the information needed to perform the analysis will depend on, at a minimum, the following:

- Nature of the subject interest
- Scope of the valuation engagement
- Valuation date
- Intended use of the valuation
- Applicable standard of value
- Applicable **premise of value**
- Assumptions and limiting conditions
- Applicable governmental regulations or other professional standards

26. In analyzing the subject interest, the valuation analyst should consider financial and nonfinancial information. The type, availability, and significance of such information vary with the subject interest.

### Nonfinancial information

27. The valuation analyst should, as available and applicable to the valuation engagement, obtain sufficient nonfinancial information to enable him or her to understand the subject entity, including its:

- Nature, background, and history
- Facilities
- Organizational structure
- Management team (which may include officers, directors, and key employees)
- Classes of **equity** ownership interests and rights attached thereto
- Products or services, or both
- Economic environment
- Geographical markets

- Industry markets
- Key customers and suppliers
- Competition
- **Business risks**
- Strategy and future plans
- Governmental or regulatory environment

## Ownership Information

28. The valuation analyst should obtain, where applicable and available, ownership information regarding the subject interest to enable him or her to:

- Determine the type of ownership interest being valued and ascertain whether that interest exhibits control characteristics
- Analyze the different ownership interests of other owners and assess the potential effect on the value of the subject interest
- Understand the classes of equity ownership interests and rights attached thereto
- Understand the rights included in, or excluded from, each intangible asset
- Understand other matters that may affect the value of the subject interest, such as:
  — *For a business, business ownership interest, or security:* shareholder agreements, partnership agreements, operating agreements, voting trust agreements, buy-sell agreements, loan covenants, restrictions, and other contractual obligations or restrictions affecting the owners and the subject interest
  — *For an intangible asset:* legal rights, licensing agreements, sublicense agreements, nondisclosure agreements, development rights, commercialization or exploitation rights, and other contractual obligations

## Financial Information

29. The valuation analyst should obtain, where applicable and available, financial information on the subject entity such as:

- Historical financial information (including annual and interim financial statements and key financial statement ratios and statistics) for an appropriate number of years

- Prospective financial information (for example, budgets, forecasts, and projections)
- Comparative summaries of financial statements or information covering a relevant time period
- Comparative common size financial statements for the subject entity for an appropriate number of years
- Comparative common size industry financial information for a relevant time period
- Income tax returns for an appropriate number of years
- Information on compensation for owners including benefits and personal expenses
- Information on key man or officers' life insurance
- Management's response to inquiry regarding:
  — Advantageous or disadvantageous contracts
  — Contingent or off-balance-sheet assets or liabilities
  — Information on prior sales of company stock

30. The valuation analyst should read and evaluate the information to determine that it is reasonable for the purposes of the engagement.

### Valuation Approaches and Methods

31. In developing the valuation, the valuation analyst should consider the three most common valuation approaches:

- **Income (Income-based) approach**
- **Asset (Asset-based) approach** (used for businesses, business ownership interests, and securities) or **cost approach** (used for intangible assets)
- **Market (Market-based) approach**

32. The valuation analyst should use the valuation approaches and methods that are appropriate for the valuation engagement. General guidance on the use of approaches and methods appears in paragraphs 33–41, but detailed guidance on specific valuation approaches and methods and their applicability is outside the scope of this Statement.

33. *Income Approach.* Two frequently used valuation methods under the income approach include the **capitalization of benefits**

**method** (for example, earnings or cash flows) and the **discounted future benefits method** (for example, earnings or cash flows). When applying these methods, the valuation analyst should consider a variety of factors, including but not limited to, the following:

a. *Capitalization of benefits (for example, earnings or cash flows) method.* The valuation analyst should consider the following:
   - *Normalization* adjustments
   - Nonrecurring revenue and expense items
   - Taxes
   - **Capital structure** and financing costs
   - Appropriate capital investments
   - Noncash items
   - Qualitative judgments for risks used to compute discount and **capitalization rates**
   - Expected changes (growth or decline) in future benefits (for example, earnings or cash flows)

b. *Discounted future benefits method (for example, earnings or cash flows).* In addition to the items in item *a* above, the valuation analyst should consider:
   - Forecast/projection assumptions
   - Forecast/projected earnings or cash flows
   - **Terminal value**

c. For an intangible asset, the valuation analyst should also consider, when relevant:
   - Remaining useful life
   - Current and anticipated future use of the intangible asset
   - Rights attributable to the intangible asset
   - Position of intangible asset in its life cycle
   - Appropriate discount rate for the intangible asset
   - Appropriate **capital or contributory asset charge**, if any
   - Research and development or marketing expense needed to support the intangible asset in its existing state
   - Allocation of income (for example, **incremental income, residual income**, or **profit split income**) to intangible asset

- Whether any tax amortization benefit would be included in the analysis
- Discounted multi-year excess earnings
- Market royalties
- Relief from royalty

### Asset Approach and Cost Approach

34. A frequently used method under the asset approach is the adjusted net asset method. When using the adjusted net asset method in valuing a business, business ownership interest, or security, the valuation analyst should consider, as appropriate, the following information related to the premise of value:

- Identification of the assets and liabilities
- Value of the assets and liabilities (individually or in the aggregate)
- Liquidation costs (if applicable)

35. When using methods under the cost approach to value intangible assets, the valuation analyst should consider the type of cost to be used (for example, reproduction cost or replacement cost), and, where applicable, the appropriate forms of depreciation and obsolescence and the remaining useful life of the intangible asset.

### Market Approach

36. Three frequently used valuation methods under the market approach for valuing a business, business ownership interest, or security are:

- **Guideline public company method**
- *Guideline company transactions method*
- Guideline sales of interests in the subject entity, such as business ownership interests or securities

Three frequently used market approach valuation methods for intangible assets are:

- Comparable uncontrolled transactions method (which is based on arm's-length sales or licenses of guideline intangible assets)
- Comparable profit margin method (which is based on comparison of the profit margin earned by the subject entity that owns or

operates the intangible asset to profit margins earned by guide-line companies)

- ***Relief from royalty method*** (which is based on the royalty rate, often expressed as a percentage of revenue that the subject entity that owns or operates the intangible asset would be obligated to pay to a hypothetical third-party licensor for the use of that intangible asset)

For the methods involving guideline intangible assets (for example, the comparable profit margin method), the valuation analyst should consider the subject intangible asset's remaining useful life relative to the remaining useful life of the guideline intangible assets, if available.

37. In applying the methods listed in paragraph 36 or other methods to determine valuation pricing multiples or metrics, the valuation analyst should consider:

- Qualitative and quantitative comparisons
- Arm's-length transactions and prices
- The dates and, consequently, the relevance of the market data

38. The valuation analyst should set forth in the report the rationale and support for the valuation methods used (paragraph 47).

39. *Rules of Thumb.* Although technically not a valuation method, some valuation analysts use rules of thumb or industry benchmark indicators (hereinafter, collectively referred to as **rules of thumb**) in a valuation engagement. A rule of thumb is typically a reasonableness check against other methods used and should generally not be used as the only method to estimate the value of the subject interest.

### Valuation Adjustments

40. During the course of a valuation engagement, the valuation analyst should consider whether valuation adjustments (discounts or premiums) should be made to a **pre-adjustment** value. Examples of valuation adjustments for valuation of a business, business ownership interest, or security include a **discount for lack of marketability or liquidity** and a **discount for lack of control**. An example of a valuation adjustment for valuation of an intangible asset is obsolescence.

# # 198

41. When valuing a controlling ownership interest under the income approach, the value of any **nonoperating assets**, nonoperating liabilities, or *excess or deficient operating assets* should be excluded from the computation of the value based on the operating assets and should be added to or deleted from the value of the operating entity. When valuing a noncontrolling ownership interest under the income approach, the value of any nonoperating assets, nonoperating liabilities, or excess or deficient operating assets may or may not be used to adjust the value of the operating entity depending on the valuation analyst's assessment of the influence exercisable by the noncontrolling interest. In the asset-based or cost approach, it may not be necessary to separately consider nonoperating assets, nonoperating liabilities, or excess or deficient operating assets.

### Conclusion of Value

42. In arriving at a conclusion of value, the valuation analyst should:

a. Correlate and reconcile the results obtained under the different approaches and methods used.

b. Assess the reliability of the results under the different approaches and methods using the information gathered during the valuation engagement.

c. Determine, based on items a and b, whether the conclusion of value should reflect (1) the results of one valuation approach and method or (2) a combination of the results of more than one valuation approach and method.

### Subsequent Events

43. The valuation date is the specific date at which the valuation analyst estimates the value of the subject interest and concludes on his or her estimation of value. Generally, the valuation analyst should consider only circumstances existing at the valuation date and events occurring up to the valuation date. An event that could affect the value may occur subsequent to the valuation date; such an occurrence is referred to as a *subsequent event*. Subsequent events are indicative of conditions that were not known or knowable at the valuation date, including conditions that arose subsequent to the valuation date. The valuation would not be updated to reflect those events or conditions. Moreover, the valuation report would typically not

include a discussion of those events or conditions because a valuation is performed as of a point in time—the valuation date—and the events described in this subparagraph, occurring subsequent to that date, are not relevant to the value determined as of that date. In situations in which a valuation is meaningful to the intended user beyond the valuation date, the events may be of such nature and significance as to warrant disclosure (at the option of the valuation analyst) in a separate section of the report in order to keep users informed (paragraphs 52(p), 71(r), and 74). Such disclosure should clearly indicate that information regarding the events is provided for informational purposes only and does not affect the determination of value as of the specified valuation date.

## Documentation

44. Documentation is the principal record of information obtained and analyzed, procedures performed, valuation approaches and methods considered and used, and the conclusion of value. The quantity, type, and content of documentation are matters of the valuation analyst's professional judgment. Documentation may include:

- Information gathered and analyzed to obtain an understanding of matters that may affect the value of the subject interest (paragraphs 25–30)
- Assumptions and limiting conditions (paragraph 18)
- Any restriction or limitation on the scope of the valuation analyst's work or the data available for analysis (paragraph 19)
- Basis for using any *valuation assumption* during the valuation engagement
- Valuation approaches and methods considered
- Valuation approaches and methods used including the rationale and support for their use
- If applicable, information relating to subsequent events considered by the valuation analyst (paragraph 43)
- For any rule of thumb used in the valuation, source(s) of data used, and how the rule of thumb was applied (paragraph 39)
- Other documentation considered relevant to the engagement by the valuation analyst

45.  The valuation analyst should retain the documentation for a period of time sufficient to meet the needs of applicable legal, regulatory, or other professional requirements for records retention.

## Calculation engagement

46.  In performing a calculation engagement, the valuation analyst should consider, at a minimum, the following:

a.  Identity of the client

b.  Identity of the subject interest

c.  Whether or not a business interest has ownership control characteristics and its degree of marketability

d.  Purpose and intended use of the calculated value

e.  Intended users of the report and the limitations on its use

f.  Valuation date

g.  Applicable premise of value

h.  Applicable standard of value

i.  Sources of information used in the calculation engagement

j.  Valuation approaches or valuation methods agreed upon with the client

k.  Subsequent events, if applicable (paragraph 43)

In addition, the valuation analyst should comply with the documentation requirements listed in paragraphs 44 and 45. The quantity, type, and content of documentation are matters of the valuation analyst's professional judgment.

## The Valuation Report

47.  A valuation report is a written or oral communication to the client containing the conclusion of value or the calculated value of the subject interest. Reports issued for purposes of certain controversy proceedings are exempt from this reporting standard (paragraph 50).

48.  The three types of written reports that a valuation analyst may use to communicate the results of an engagement to estimate value are: for a valuation engagement, a detailed report or a summary report; and for a calculation engagement, a calculation report.

*For a Valuation Engagement*

a. *Detailed Report:* This report may be used only to communicate the results of a valuation engagement (conclusion of value); it should not be used to communicate the results of a calculation engagement (calculated value) (paragraph 51).

b. *Summary Report:* This report may be used only to communicate the results of a valuation engagement (conclusion of value); it should not be used to communicate the results of a calculation engagement (calculated value) (paragraph 71).

For a valuation engagement, the determination of whether to prepare a detailed report or a summary report is based on the level of reporting detail agreed to by the valuation analyst and the client.

*For a Calculation Engagement*

c. *Calculation Report:* This type of report should be used only to communicate the results of a calculation engagement (calculated value); it should not be used to communicate the results of a valuation engagement (conclusion of value) (paragraph 73).

49. The valuation analyst should indicate in the valuation report the restrictions on the use of the report (which may include restrictions on the users of the report, the uses of the report by such users, or both) (paragraph 65(d)).

## Reporting Exemption for Certain Controversy Proceedings

50. A valuation performed for a matter before a court, an arbitrator, a mediator or other facilitator, or a matter in a governmental or administrative proceeding, is exempt from the reporting provisions of this Statement. The reporting exemption applies whether the matter proceeds to trial or settles. The exemption applies only to the reporting provisions of this Statement (paragraphs 47–49 and 51–78). The developmental provisions of the Statement (paragraphs 21–46) still apply whenever the valuation analyst expresses a conclusion of value or a calculated value (Valuation Services Interpretation No. 1).

## Detailed Report

51. The *detailed report* is structured to provide sufficient information to permit intended users to understand the data, reasoning, and analyses underlying the valuation analyst's conclusion of value. A

detailed report should include, as applicable, the following sections titled using wording similar in content to that shown:

- Letter of transmittal
- Table of contents
- Introduction
- Sources of information
- Analysis of the subject entity and related nonfinancial information
- Financial statement/information analysis
- Valuation approaches and methods considered
- Valuation approaches and methods used
- Valuation adjustments
- Nonoperating assets, nonoperating liabilities, and excess or deficient operating assets (if any)
- Representation of the valuation analyst
- Reconciliation of estimates and conclusion of value
- Qualifications of the valuation analyst
- Appendices and exhibits

The above listed report sections and the detailed information within the sections described in the following paragraphs 52–77 may be positioned in the body of the report or elsewhere in the report at the discretion of the valuation analyst.

## Introduction

52. This section should provide an overall description of the valuation engagement. The information in the section should be sufficient to enable the intended user of the report to understand the nature and scope of the valuation engagement, as well as the work performed. The introduction section may include, among other things, the following information:

a. Identity of the client
b. Purpose and intended use of the valuation
c. Intended users of the valuation
d. Identity of the subject entity
e. Description of the subject interest

*f.* Whether the business interest has ownership control characteristics and its degree of marketability

*g.* Valuation date

*h.* Report date

*i.* Type of report issued (namely, a detailed report) (paragraph 51)

*j.* Applicable premise of value

*k.* Applicable standard of value

*l.* Assumptions and limiting conditions (alternatively, these often appear in an appendix) (paragraph 18)

*m.* Any restrictions or limitations in the scope of work or data available for analysis (paragraph 19)

*n.* Any hypothetical conditions used in the valuation engagement, including the basis for their use (paragraph 22)

*o.* If the work of a specialist was used in the valuation engagement, a description of how the specialist's work was relied upon (paragraph 20)

*p.* Disclosure of subsequent events in certain circumstances (paragraph 43)

*q.* Any application of the jurisdictional exception (paragraph 10)

*r.* Any additional information the valuation analyst deems useful to enable the user(s) of the report to understand the work performed

If the above items are not included in the introduction, they should be included elsewhere in the valuation report.

### Sources of Information

53. This section of the report should identify the relevant sources of information used in performing the valuation engagement. It may include, among other things, the following:

*a.* For valuation of a business, business ownership interest, or security, whether and to what extent the subject entity's facilities were visited

*b.* For valuation of an intangible asset, whether the legal registration, contractual documentation, or other tangible evidence of the asset was inspected

*c.* Names, positions, and titles of persons interviewed and their relationships to the subject interest *d.* Financial information (paragraphs 54 and 56)

*e.* Tax information (paragraph 55)

*f.* Industry data

*g.* Market data

*h.* Economic data

*i.* Other empirical information

*j.* Relevant documents and other sources of information provided by or related to the entity

54. If the financial information includes financial statements that were reported on (audit, review, compilation, or attest engagement performed under the Statements on Standards for Attestation Engagements [SSAEs]) by the valuation analyst's firm, the valuation report should disclose this fact and the type of report issued. If the valuation analyst or the valuation analyst's firm did not audit, review, compile, or attest under the SSAEs to the financial information, the valuation analyst should so state and should also state that the valuation analyst assumes no responsibility for the financial information.

55. The financial information may be derived from or may include information derived from tax returns. With regard to such derived information and other tax information (paragraph 53(e)), the valuation analyst should identify the tax returns used and any existing relationship between the valuation analyst and the tax preparer. If the valuation analyst or the valuation analyst's firm did not audit, review, compile, or attest under the SSAEs to any financial information derived from tax returns that is used during the valuation engagement, the valuation analyst should so state and should also state that the valuation analyst assumes no responsibility for that derived information.

56. If the financial information used was derived from financial statements prepared by management that were not the subject of an audit, review, compilation, or attest engagement performed under the SSAEs, the valuation report should:

- Identify the financial statements
- State that, as part of the valuation engagement, the valuation analyst did not audit, review, compile, or attest under the SSAEs to the financial information and assumes no responsibility for that information

## Analysis of the Subject Entity and Related Nonfinancial Information

57. The valuation analyst should include a description of the relevant nonfinancial information listed and discussed in paragraph 27.

## Financial Statement / Information Analysis

58. This section should include a description of the relevant information listed in paragraph 29. Such description may include:

*a.* The rationale underlying any normalization or **control adjustments** to financial information

*b.* Comparison of current performance with historical performance

*c.* Comparison of performance with industry trends and norms, where available

## Valuation Approaches and Methods Considered

59. This section should state that the valuation analyst has considered the valuation approaches discussed in paragraph 31.

## Valuation Approaches and Methods Used

60. In this section, the valuation analyst should identify the valuation methods used under each valuation approach and the rationale for their use.

61. This section should also identify the following for each of the three approaches (if used):

*a.* Income approach:

- Composition of the representative benefit stream
- Method(s) used, and a summary of the most relevant risk factors considered in selecting the appropriate **discount rate**, the capitalization rate, or both
- Other factors as discussed in paragraph 33

*b.* Asset-based approach or cost approach:

- *Asset-based approach:* Any adjustments made by the valuation analyst to the relevant balance sheet data
- *Cost approach:* The type of cost used, how this cost was estimated, and, if applicable, the forms of and costs associated with depreciation and obsolescence used under the approach and how those costs were estimated

*c.* Market approach:
  - For the guideline public company method:
    - o The selected guideline companies and the process used in their selection
    - o The pricing multiples used, how they were used, and the rationale for their selection. If the pricing multiples were adjusted, the rationale for such adjustments
  - For the guideline company transactions method, the sales transactions and pricing multiples used, how they were used, and the rationale for their selection. If the pricing multiples were adjusted, the rationale for such adjustments
  - For the guideline sales of interests in the subject entity method, the sales transactions used, how they were used, and the rationale for determining that these sales are representative of arm's length transactions

62. When a rule of thumb is used in combination with other methods, the valuation report should disclose the source(s) of data used and how the rule of thumb was applied (paragraph 39).

### Valuation Adjustments

63. This section should (*a*) identify each valuation adjustment considered and determined to be applicable, for example, discount for lack of marketability, (*b*) describe the rationale for using the adjustment and the factors considered in selecting the amount or percentage used, and (*c*) describe the pre-adjustment value to which the adjustment was applied (paragraph 40).

### Nonoperating Assets and Excess Operating Assets

64. When the subject interest is a business, business ownership interest, or security, the valuation report should identify any related nonoperating assets, nonoperating liabilities, or excess or deficient operating assets and their effect on the valuation (paragraph 41).

### Representation of the Valuation Analyst

65. Each written report should contain the representation of the valuation analyst. The representation is the section of the report wherein the valuation analyst summarizes the factors that guided his or her work during the engagement. Examples of these factors include the following:

a. The analyses, opinions, and conclusion of value included in the valuation report are subject to the specified assumptions and limiting conditions (see paragraph 18), and they are the personal analyses, opinions, and conclusion of value of the valuation analyst.

b. The economic and industry data included in the valuation report have been obtained from various printed or electronic reference sources that the valuation analyst believes to be reliable (any exceptions should be noted). The valuation analyst has not performed any corroborating procedures to substantiate that data.

c. The valuation engagement was performed in accordance with the American Institute of Certified Public Accountants Statement on Standards for Valuation Services.

d. The parties for which the information and use of the valuation report is restricted are identified; the valuation report is not intended to be and should not be used by anyone other than such parties (paragraph 49).

e. The analyst's compensation is fee-based or is contingent on the outcome of the valuation.

f. The valuation analyst used the work of one or more outside specialists to assist during the valuation engagement. (An outside specialist is a specialist other than those employed in the valuation analyst's firm.) If the work of such a specialist was used, the specialist should be identified. The valuation report should include a statement identifying the level of responsibility, if any, the valuation analyst is assuming for the specialist's work.

g. The valuation analyst has no obligation to update the report or the opinion of value for information that comes to his or her attention after the date of the report.

h. The valuation analyst and the person(s) assuming responsibility for the valuation should sign the representation in their own name(s). The names of those providing significant professional assistance should be identified.

### Representations Regarding Information Provided to the Valuation Analyst

66. It may be appropriate for the valuation analyst to obtain written representations regarding information that the subject entity's management provides to the valuation analyst for purposes of his or her performing the valuation engagement. The decision whether to

obtain a representation letter is a matter of judgment for the valuation analyst.

### Qualifications of the Valuation Analyst

67. The report should contain information regarding the qualifications of the valuation analyst.

### Conclusion of Value

68. This section should present a reconciliation of the valuation analyst's estimate or various estimates of the value of the subject interest. In addition to a discussion of the rationale underlying the conclusion of value, this section should include the following or similar statements:

a. A valuation engagement was performed, including the subject interest and the valuation date.

b. The analysis was performed solely for the purpose described in this report, and the resulting estimate of value should not be used for any other purpose.

c. The valuation engagement was conducted in accordance with the Statement(s) on Standards for Valuation Services of the American Institute of Certified Public Accountants.

d. A statement that the estimate of value resulting from a valuation engagement is expressed as a conclusion of value.

e. The scope of work or data available for analysis is explained, including any restrictions or limitations (paragraph 19).

f. A statement describing the conclusion of value, either a single amount or a range.

g. The conclusion of value is subject to the assumptions and limiting conditions (paragraph 18) and to the valuation analyst's representation (paragraph 65).

h. The report is signed in the name of the valuation analyst or the valuation analyst's firm.

i. The date of the valuation report is included.

j. The valuation analyst has no obligation to update the report or the conclusion of value for information that comes to his or her attention after the date of the report.

69. The following is an example of report language that could be used, but is not required, when reporting the results of a valuation engagement:

> We have performed a *valuation engagement*, as that term is defined in the Statement on Standards for Valuation Services (SSVS) of the American Institute of Certified Public Accountants, of [*DEF Company, GHI business ownership interest of DEF Company, GHI security of DEF Company, or GHI intangible asset of DEF Company*] as of [*valuation date*]. This valuation was performed solely to assist in the matter of [*purpose of the valuation*]; the resulting estimate of value should not be used for any other purpose or by any other party for any purpose. This valuation engagement was conducted in accordance with the SSVS. The estimate of value that results from a valuation engagement is expressed as a conclusion of value.

> [*If applicable*] We were restricted or limited in the scope of our work or data available for analysis as follows: [*describe restrictions or limitations*].

> Based on our analysis, as described in this valuation report, the estimate of value of [*DEF Company, GHI business ownership interest of DEF Company, GHI security of DEF Company, or GHI intangible asset of DEF Company*] as of [*valuation date*] was [*value, either a single amount or a range*]. This conclusion is subject to the Statement of Assumptions and Limiting Conditions found in [*reference to applicable section of valuation report*] and to the Valuation Analyst's Representation found in [*reference to applicable section of valuation report*]. We have no obligation to update this report or our conclusion of value for information that comes to our attention after the date of this report.

> [*Signature*]

> [*Date*]

## Appendices and Exhibits

70. Appendices or exhibits may be used for required information or information that supplements the detailed report. Often, the assumptions and limiting conditions and the valuation analyst's representation are provided in appendices to the detailed report.

## Summary Report

71. A summary report is structured to provide an abridged version of the information that would be provided in a detailed report,

and therefore, need not contain the same level of detail as a detailed report. However, a summary report should, at a minimum, include the following:

a. Identity of the client

b. Purpose and intended use of the valuation

c. Intended users of the valuation

d. Identity of the subject entity

e. Description of the subject interest

f. The business interest's ownership control characteristics, if any, and its degree of marketability

g. Valuation date

h. Valuation report date

i. Type of report issued (namely, a summary report) (paragraph 48)

j. Applicable premise of value

k. Applicable standard of value

l. Sources of information used in the valuation engagement

m. Assumptions and limiting conditions of the valuation engagement (paragraph 18)

n. The scope of work or data available for analysis including any restrictions or limitations (paragraph 19)

o. Any hypothetical conditions used in the valuation engagement, including the basis for their use (paragraph 22)

p. If the work of a specialist was used in the valuation (paragraph 20), a description of how the specialist's work was used, and the level of responsibility, if any, the valuation analyst is assuming for the specialist's work

q. The valuation approaches and methods used

r. Disclosure of subsequent events in certain circumstances (paragraph 43)

s. Any application of the jurisdictional exception (paragraph 10)

t. Representation of the valuation analyst (paragraph 65)

u. The report is signed in the name of the valuation analyst or the valuation analyst's firm

v. A section summarizing the reconciliation of the estimates and the conclusion of value as discussed in paragraphs 68 and 69 *w.* A statement that the valuation analyst has no obligation to update the report or the calculation of value for information that comes to his or her attention after the date of the valuation report

72. Appendices or exhibits may be used for required information (paragraph 70) or information that supplements the summary report. Often, the assumptions, limiting conditions, and the valuation analyst's representation are provided in appendices to the summary report.

## Calculation Report

73. As indicated in paragraph 48, a calculation report is the only report that should be used to report the results of a calculation engagement. The report should state that it is a calculation report. The calculation report should include the representation of the valuation analyst similar to that in paragraph 65, but adapted for a calculation engagement.

74. The calculation report should identify any hypothetical conditions used in the calculation engagement, including the basis for their use (paragraph 22), any application of the jurisdictional exception (paragraph 10), and any assumptions and limiting conditions applicable to the engagement (paragraph 18). If the valuation analyst used the work of a specialist (paragraph 20), the valuation analyst should describe in the calculation report how the specialist's work was used and the level of responsibility, if any, the valuation analyst is assuming for the specialist's work. The calculation report may also include a disclosure of subsequent events in certain circumstances (paragraph 43).

75. Appendices or exhibits may be used for required information (paragraph 72) or information that supplements the calculation report. Often, the assumptions and limiting conditions and the valuation analyst's representation are provided in appendices to the calculation report.

76. The calculation report should include a section summarizing the calculated value. This section should include the following (or similar) statements:

*a.* Certain calculation procedures were performed; include the identity of the subject interest and the calculation date.

*b.* Describe the calculation procedures and the scope of work performed or reference the section(s) of the calculation report in which the calculation procedures and scope of work are described.

*c.* Describe the purpose of the calculation procedures, including that the calculation procedures were performed solely for that purpose and that the resulting calculated value should not be used for any other purpose or by any other party for any purpose.

*d.* The calculation engagement was conducted in accordance with the Statement on Standards for Valuation Services of the American Institute of Certified Public Accountants.

*e.* A description of the business interest's characteristics, including whether the subject interest exhibits control characteristics, and a statement about the marketability of the subject interest.

*f.* The estimate of value resulting from a calculation engagement is expressed as a calculated value.

*g.* A general description of a calculation engagement is given, including that (1) a calculation engagement does not include all of the procedures required for a valuation engagement and (2) had a valuation engagement been performed, the results may have been different.

*h.* The calculated value, either a single amount or a range, is described.

*i.* The report is signed in the name of the valuation analyst or the valuation analyst's firm.

*j.* The date of the valuation report is given.

*k.* The valuation analyst has no obligation to update the report or the calculation of value for information that comes to his or her attention after the date of the report.

77. The following is an example of report language that could be used, but is not required, in reporting a calculation engagement:

> We have performed a *calculation engagement*, as that term is defined in the Statement on Standards for Valuation Services (SSVS) of the American Institute of Certified Public Accountants. We performed certain calculation procedures on [*DEF Company, GHI business ownership interest of DEF Company, GHI security of DEF Company, or GHI intangible asset of DEF Company*] as of [*calculation date*]. The specific calculation procedures are detailed in para-

graphs [*reference to paragraph numbers*] of our calculation report. The calculation procedures were performed solely to assist in the matter of [*purpose of valuation procedures*], and the resulting calculation of value should not be used for any other purpose or by any other party for any purpose. This calculation engagement was conducted in accordance with the SSVS. The estimate of value that results from a calculation engagement is expressed as a calculated value.

In a calculation engagement, the valuation analyst and the client agree on the specific valuation approaches and valuation methods the valuation analyst will use and the extent of valuation procedures the valuation analyst will perform to estimate the value of the subject interest. A calculation engagement does not include all of the procedures required in a *valuation engagement*, as that term is defined in the SVSS. Had a valuation engagement been performed, the results might have been different.

Based on our calculations, as described in this report, which are based solely on the procedures agreed upon as referred to above, the resulting calculated value of [*DEF Company, GHI business ownership interest of DEF Company, GHI security of DEF Company, or GHI intangible asset of DEF Company*] as of [*valuation date*] was [*calculated value, either a single amount or a range*]. This calculated value is subject to the Statement of Assumptions and Limiting Conditions found in [*reference to applicable section of valuation report*] and to the Valuation Analyst's Representation found in [*reference to applicable section of valuation report*]. We have no obligation to update this report or our calculation of value for information that comes to our attention after the date of this report.

[*Signature*]

[*Date*]

## Oral Report

78. An oral report may be used in a valuation engagement or a calculation engagement. An oral report should include all information the valuation analyst believes necessary to relate the scope, assumptions, limitations, and the results of the engagement so as to limit any misunderstandings between the analyst and the recipient of the oral report. The member should document in the working papers the substance of the oral report communicated to the client.

## Effective Date

79. This Statement applies to engagements to estimate value accepted on or after January 1, 2008. Earlier application is encouraged.

# APPENDIX A

# Illustrative List of Assumptions and Limiting Conditions for a Business Valuation

The valuation report or calculation report should include a list of assumptions and limiting conditions under which the engagement was performed. This appendix includes an illustrative list of assumptions and limiting conditions that may apply to a business valuation.

### Illustrative List of Assumptions and Limiting Conditions

1. The conclusion of value arrived at herein is valid only for the stated purpose as of the date of the valuation.

2. Financial statements and other related information provided by [ABC Company] or its representatives, in the course of this engagement, have been accepted without any verification as fully and correctly reflecting the enterprise's business conditions and operating results for the respective periods, except as specifically noted herein. [Valuation Firm] has not audited, reviewed, or compiled the financial information provided to us and, accordingly, we express no audit opinion or any other form of assurance on this information.

3. Public information and industry and statistical information have been obtained from sources we believe to be reliable. However, we make no representation as to the accuracy or completeness of such information and have performed no procedures to corroborate the information.

4. We do not provide assurance on the achievability of the results forecasted by [ABC Company] because events and circumstances frequently do not occur as expected; differences between actual and expected results may be material; and achievement of the forecasted results is dependent on actions, plans, and assumptions of management.

5. The conclusion of value arrived at herein is based on the assumption that the current level of management expertise and effectiveness would continue to be maintained, and that the character and integrity of the enterprise through any sale, reorganization, exchange, or diminution of the owners' participation would not be materially or significantly changed.

6. This report and the conclusion of value arrived at herein are for the exclusive use of our client for the sole and specific purposes as noted herein. They may not be used for any other purpose or by any other party for any purpose. Furthermore the report and conclusion of value are not intended by the author and should not be construed by the reader to be investment advice in any manner whatsoever. The conclusion of value represents the considered opinion of [*Valuation Firm*], based on information furnished to them by [*ABC Company*] and other sources.

7. Neither all nor any part of the contents of this report (especially the conclusion of value, the identity of any valuation specialist(s), or the firm with which such valuation specialists are connected or any reference to any of their professional designations) should be disseminated to the public through advertising media, public relations, news media, sales media, mail, direct transmittal, or any other means of communication without the prior written consent and approval of [*Valuation Firm*].

8. Future services regarding the subject matter of this report, including, but not limited to testimony or attendance in court, shall not be required of [*Valuation Firm*] unless previous arrangements have been made in writing.

9. [*Valuation Firm*] is not an environmental consultant or auditor, and it takes no responsibility for any actual or potential environmental liabilities. Any person entitled to rely on this report, wishing to know whether such liabilities exist, or the scope and their effect on the value of the property, is encouraged to obtain a professional environmental assessment. [*Valuation Firm*] does not conduct or provide environmental assessments and has not performed one for the subject property.

10. [*Valuation Firm*] has not determined independently whether [*ABC Company*] is subject to any present or future liability relating to environmental matters (including, but not limited to CERCLA/Superfund liability) nor the scope of any such liabilities. [*Valuation Firm*]'s valuation takes no such liabilities into account, except as they have been reported to [*Valuation Firm*] by [*ABC Company*] or by an environmental consultant working for [*ABC Company*], and then only to the extent that the liability was reported to us in an actual or estimated dollar amount. Such matters, if any, are noted in the report. To the extent such information has been reported to us, [*Valuation Firm*] has relied

on it without verification and offers no warranty or representation as to its accuracy or completeness.

11. [*Valuation Firm*] has not made a specific compliance survey or analysis of the subject property to determine whether it is subject to, or in compliance with, the American Disabilities Act of 1990, and this valuation does not consider the effect, if any, of noncompliance.

12. [Sample wording for use if the jurisdictional exception is invoked.] The conclusion of value (or the calculated value) in this report deviates from the Statement on Standards for Valuation Services as a result of published governmental, judicial, or accounting authority.

13. No change of any item in this appraisal report shall be made by anyone other than [*Valuation Firm*], and we shall have no responsibility for any such unauthorized change.

14. Unless otherwise stated, no effort has been made to determine the possible effect, if any, on the subject business due to future Federal, state, or local legislation, including any environmental or ecological matters or interpretations thereof.

15. If prospective financial information approved by management has been used in our work, we have not examined or compiled the prospective financial information and therefore, do not express an audit opinion or any other form of assurance on the prospective financial information or the related assumptions. Events and circumstances frequently do not occur as expected and there will usually be differences between prospective financial information and actual results, and those differences may be material.

16. We have conducted interviews with the current management of [*ABC Company*] concerning the past, present, and prospective operating results of the company.

17. Except as noted, we have relied on the representations of the owners, management, and other third parties concerning the value and useful condition of all equipment, real estate, investments used in the business, and any other assets or liabilities, except as specifically stated to the contrary in this report. We have not attempted to confirm whether or not all assets of the business are free and clear of liens and encumbrances or that the entity has good title to all assets.

# APPENDIX B

# International Glossary of Business Valuation Terms*

To enhance and sustain the quality of business valuations for the benefit of the profession and its clientele, the below identified societies and organizations have adopted the definitions for the terms included in this glossary.

The performance of business valuation services requires a high degree of skill and imposes upon the valuation professional a duty to communicate the valuation process and conclusion in a manner that is clear and not misleading. This duty is advanced through the use of terms whose meanings are clearly established and consistently applied throughout the profession.

If, in the opinion of the business valuation professional, one or more of these terms needs to be used in a manner which materially departs from the enclosed definitions, it is recommended that the term be defined as used within that valuation engagement.

This glossary has been developed to provide guidance to business valuation practitioners by further memorializing the body of knowledge that constitutes the competent and careful determination of value and, more particularly, the communication of how that value was determined.

Departure from this glossary is not intended to provide a basis for civil liability and should not be presumed to create evidence that any duty has been breached.

**American Institute of Certified Public Accountants**
**American Society of Appraisers**
**Canadian Institute of Chartered Business Valuators**
**National Association of Certified Valuation Analysts**
**The Institute of Business Appraisers**

---

* Reproduced verbatim from the International Glossary of Business Valuation Terms (the Glossary), which appears at http://bvfls.aicpa.org/Resources/Business+Valuation/ Tools+and+ Aids/Definitions+and+Terms/International+Glossary+of+Business+Valuation+Terms.htm. Note that the phrase, "we discourage the use of this term," that appears herein is also reproduced verbatim.

**Adjusted Book Value Method**–a method within the asset approach whereby all assets and liabilities (including off-balance sheet, intangible, and contingent) are adjusted to their fair market values. {NOTE: In Canada on a going concern basis}

**Adjusted Net Asset Method**–see **Adjusted Book Value Method**.

**Appraisal**–see **Valuation**.

**Appraisal Approach**–see **Valuation Approach**.

**Appraisal Date**–see **Valuation Date**.

**Appraisal Method**–see **Valuation Method**.

**Appraisal Procedure**–see **Valuation Procedure**.

**Arbitrage Pricing Theory**–a multivariate model for estimating the cost of equity capital, which incorporates several systematic risk factors.

**Asset (Asset-Based) Approach**–a general way of determining a value indication of a business, business ownership interest, or security using one or more methods based on the value of the assets net of liabilities.

**Beta**–a measure of systematic risk of a stock; the tendency of a stock's price to correlate with changes in a specific index.

**Blockage Discount**–an amount or percentage deducted from the current market price of a publicly traded stock to reflect the decrease in the per share value of a block of stock that is of a size that could not be sold in a reasonable period of time given normal trading volume.

**Book Value**–see **Net Book Value**.

**Business**–see **Business Enterprise**.

**Business Enterprise**–a commercial, industrial, service, or investment entity (or a combination thereof) pursuing an economic activity.

**Business Risk**–the degree of uncertainty of realizing expected future returns of the business resulting from factors other than financial leverage. See **Financial Risk**.

**Business Valuation**—the act or process of determining the value of a business enterprise or ownership interest therein.

**Capital Asset Pricing Model (CAPM)**—a model in which the cost of capital for any stock or portfolio of stocks equals a risk-free rate plus a risk premium that is proportionate to the systematic risk of the stock or portfolio.

**Capitalization**—a conversion of a single period of economic benefits into value.

**Capitalization Factor**—any multiple or divisor used to convert anticipated economic benefits of a single period into value.

**Capitalization of Earnings Method**—a method within the income approach whereby economic benefits for a representative single period are converted to value through division by a capitalization rate.

**Capitalization Rate**—any divisor (usually expressed as a percentage) used to convert anticipated economic benefits of a single period into value.

**Capital Structure**—the composition of the invested capital of a business enterprise; the mix of debt and equity financing.

**Cash Flow**—cash that is generated over a period of time by an asset, group of assets, or business enterprise. It may be used in a general sense to encompass various levels of specifically defined cash flows. When the term is used, it should be supplemented by a qualifier (for example, "discretionary" or "operating") and a specific definition in the given valuation context.

**Common Size Statements**—financial statements in which each line is expressed as a percentage of the total. On the balance sheet, each line item is shown as a percentage of total assets, and on the income statement, each item is expressed as a percentage of sales.

**Control**—the power to direct the management and policies of a business enterprise.

**Control Premium**—an amount or a percentage by which the pro rata value of a controlling interest exceeds the pro rata value of a noncontrolling interest in a business enterprise to reflect the power of control.

**Cost Approach**–a general way of determining a value indication of an individual asset by quantifying the amount of money required to replace the future service capability of that asset.

**Cost of Capital**–the expected rate of return that the market requires in order to attract funds to a particular investment.

**Debt-Free**–*we discourage the use of this term.* See **Invested Capital**.

**Discount for Lack of Control**–an amount or percentage deducted from the pro rata share of value of 100% of an equity interest in a business to reflect the absence of some or all of the powers of control.

**Discount for Lack of Marketability**–an amount or percentage deducted from the value of an ownership interest to reflect the relative absence of marketability.

**Discount for Lack of Voting Rights**–an amount or percentage deducted from the per share value of a minority interest voting share to reflect the absence of voting rights.

**Discount Rate**–a rate of return used to convert a future monetary sum into present value.

**Discounted Cash Flow Method**–a method within the income approach whereby the present value of future expected net cash flows is calculated using a discount rate.

**Discounted Future Earnings Method**–a method within the income approach whereby the present value of future expected economic benefits is calculated using a discount rate.

**Economic Benefits**–inflows such as revenues, net income, net cash flows, etc.

**Economic Life**–the period of time over which property may generate economic benefits.

**Effective Date**–see **Valuation Date**.

**Enterprise**–see **Business Enterprise**.

**Equity**–the owner's interest in property after deduction of all liabilities.

**Equity Net Cash Flows**—those cash flows available to pay out to equity holders (in the form of dividends) after funding operations of the business enterprise, making necessary capital investments, and increasing or decreasing debt financing.

**Equity Risk Premium**—a rate of return added to a risk-free rate to reflect the additional risk of equity instruments over risk free instruments (a component of the cost of equity capital or equity discount rate).

**Excess Earnings**—that amount of anticipated economic benefits that exceeds an appropriate rate of return on the value of a selected asset base (often net tangible assets) used to generate those anticipated economic benefits.

**Excess Earnings Method**—a specific way of determining a value indication of a business, business ownership interest, or security determined as the sum of *a*) the value of the assets derived by capitalizing excess earnings and *b*) the value of the selected asset base. Also frequently used to value intangible assets. See **Excess Earnings**.

**Fair Market Value**—the price, expressed in terms of cash equivalents, at which property would change hands between a hypothetical willing and able buyer and a hypothetical willing and able seller, acting at arms length in an open and unrestricted market, when neither is under compulsion to buy or sell and when both have reasonable knowledge of the relevant facts. {NOTE: In Canada, the term *"price"* should be replaced with the term *"highest price"*.}

**Fairness Opinion**—an opinion as to whether or not the consideration in a transaction is fair from a financial point of view.

**Financial Risk**—the degree of uncertainty of realizing expected future returns of the business resulting from financial leverage. See **Business Risk**.

**Forced Liquidation Value**—liquidation value, at which the asset or assets are sold as quickly as possible, such as at an auction.

**Free Cash Flow**—*we discourage the use of this term.* See **Net Cash Flow**.

**Going Concern**—an ongoing operating business enterprise.

**Going Concern Value**–the value of a business enterprise that is expected to continue to operate into the future. The intangible elements of Going Concern Value result from factors such as having a trained work force, an operational plant, and the necessary licenses, systems, and procedures in place.

**Goodwill**–that intangible asset arising as a result of name, reputation, customer loyalty, location, products, and similar factors not separately identified.

**Goodwill Value**–the value attributable to goodwill.

**Guideline Public Company Method**–a method within the market approach whereby market multiples are derived from market prices of stocks of companies that are engaged in the same or similar lines of business and that are actively traded on a free and open market.

**Income (Income-Based) Approach**–a general way of determining a value indication of a business, business ownership interest, security, or intangible asset using one or more methods that convert anticipated economic benefits into a present single amount.

**Intangible Assets**–nonphysical assets such as franchises, trademarks, patents, copyrights, goodwill, equities, mineral rights, securities, and contracts (as distinguished from physical assets) that grant rights and privileges and have value for the owner.

**Internal Rate of Return**–a discount rate at which the present value of the future cash flows of the investment equals the cost of the investment.

**Intrinsic Value**–the value that an investor considers, on the basis of an evaluation or available facts, to be the "true" or "real" value that will become the market value when other investors reach the same conclusion. When the term applies to options, it is the difference between the exercise price and strike price of an option and the market value of the underlying security.

**Invested Capital**–the sum of equity and debt in a business enterprise. Debt is typically (*a*) all interest-bearing debt or (*b*) long-term, interest-bearing debt. When the term is used, it should be supplemented by a specific definition in the given valuation context.

**Invested Capital Net Cash Flows**–those cash flows available to pay out to equity holders (in the form of dividends) and debt investors (in the form of principal and interest) after funding operations of the business enterprise and making necessary capital investments.

**Investment Risk**–the degree of uncertainty as to the realization of expected returns.

**Investment Value**–the value to a particular investor based on individual investment requirements and expectations. {NOTE: in Canada, the term used is *"Value to the Owner"*.}

**Key Person Discount**–an amount or percentage deducted from the value of an ownership interest to reflect the reduction in value resulting from the actual or potential loss of a key person in a business enterprise.

**Levered Beta**–the beta reflecting a capital structure that includes debt.

**Limited Appraisal**–the act or process of determining the value of a business, business ownership interest, security, or intangible asset with limitations in analyses, procedures, or scope.

**Liquidity**–the ability to quickly convert property to cash or pay a liability.

**Liquidation Value**–the net amount that would be realized if the business is terminated and the assets are sold piecemeal. Liquidation can be either "orderly" or "forced."

**Majority Control**–the degree of control provided by a majority position.

**Majority Interest**–an ownership interest greater than 50% of the voting interest in a business enterprise.

**Market (Market-Based) Approach**–a general way of determining a value indication of a business, business ownership interest, security, or intangible asset by using one or more methods that compare the subject to similar businesses, business ownership interests, securities, or intangible assets that have been sold.

**Market Capitalization of Equity**–the share price of a publicly traded stock multiplied by the number of shares outstanding.

**Market Capitalization of Invested Capital**–the market capitalization of equity plus the market value of the debt component of invested capital.

**Market Multiple**–the market value of a company's stock or invested capital divided by a company measure (such as economic benefits, number of customers).

**Marketability**–the ability to quickly convert property to cash at minimal cost.

**Marketability Discount**–see **Discount for Lack of Marketability**.

**Merger and Acquisition Method**–a method within the market approach whereby pricing multiples are derived from transactions of significant interests in companies engaged in the same or similar lines of business.

**Mid-Year Discounting**–a convention used in the Discounted Future Earnings Method that reflects economic benefits being generated at midyear, approximating the effect of economic benefits being generated evenly throughout the year.

**Minority Discount**–a discount for lack of control applicable to a minority interest.

**Minority Interest**–an ownership interest less than 50% of the voting interest in a business enterprise.

**Multiple**–the inverse of the capitalization rate.

**Net Book Value**–with respect to a business enterprise, the difference between total assets (net of accumulated depreciation, depletion, and amortization) and total liabilities as they appear on the balance sheet (synonymous with Shareholder's Equity). With respect to a specific asset, the capitalized cost less accumulated amortization or depreciation as it appears on the books of account of the business enterprise.

**Net Cash Flows**–when the term is used, it should be supplemented by a qualifier. See **Equity Net Cash Flows** and **Invested Capital Net Cash Flows**.

**Net Present Value**–the value, as of a specified date, of future cash inflows less all cash outflows (including the cost of investment) calculated using an appropriate discount rate.

**Net Tangible Asset Value**—the value of the business enterprise's tangible assets (excluding excess assets and nonoperating assets) minus the value of its liabilities.

**Nonoperating Assets**—assets not necessary to ongoing operations of the business enterprise. {NOTE: in Canada, the term used is *"Redundant Assets"*.}

**Normalized Earnings**—economic benefits adjusted for nonrecurring, noneconomic, or other unusual items to eliminate anomalies and/or facilitate comparisons.

**Normalized Financial Statements**—financial statements adjusted for nonoperating assets and liabilities and/or for nonrecurring, noneconomic, or other unusual items to eliminate anomalies and/or facilitate comparisons.

**Orderly Liquidation Value**—liquidation value at which the asset or assets are sold over a reasonable period of time to maximize proceeds received.

**Premise of Value**—an assumption regarding the most likely set of transactional circumstances that may be applicable to the subject valuation; for example, going concern, liquidation.

**Present Value**—the value, as of a specified date, of future economic benefits and/or proceeds from sale, calculated using an appropriate discount rate.

**Portfolio Discount**—an amount or percentage deducted from the value of a business enterprise to reflect the fact that it owns dissimilar operations or assets that do not fit well together.

**Price/Earnings Multiple**—the price of a share of stock divided by its earnings per share.

**Rate of Return**—an amount of income (loss) and/or change in value realized or anticipated on an investment, expressed as a percentage of that investment.

**Redundant Assets**—see **Nonoperating Assets**.

**Report Date**—the date conclusions are transmitted to the client.

**Replacement Cost New**—the current cost of a similar new property having the nearest equivalent utility to the property being valued.

**Reproduction Cost New**–the current cost of an identical new property.

**Required Rate of Return**–the minimum rate of return acceptable by investors before they will commit money to an investment at a given level of risk.

**Residual Value**–the value as of the end of the discrete projection period in a discounted future earnings model.

**Return on Equity**–the amount, expressed as a percentage, earned on a company's common equity for a given period.

**Return on Investment**–See **Return on Invested Capital** and **Return on Equity**.

**Return on Invested Capital**–the amount, expressed as a percentage, earned on a company's total capital for a given period.

**Risk-Free Rate**–the rate of return available in the market on an investment free of default risk.

**Risk Premium**–a rate of return added to a risk-free rate to reflect risk.

**Rule of Thumb**–a mathematical formula developed from the relationship between price and certain variables based on experience, observation, hearsay, or a combination of these; usually industry specific.

**Special Interest Purchasers**–acquirers who believe they can enjoy post-acquisition economies of scale, synergies, or strategic advantages by combining the acquired business interest with their own.

**Standard of Value**–the identification of the type of value being utilized in a specific engagement; for example, fair market value, fair value, investment value.

**Sustaining Capital Reinvestment**–the periodic capital outlay required to maintain operations at existing levels, net of the tax shield available from such outlays.

**Systematic Risk**–the risk that is common to all risky securities and cannot be eliminated through diversification. The measure of systematic risk in stocks is the beta coefficient.

**Tangible Assets**–physical assets (such as cash, accounts receivable, inventory, property, plant and equipment, etc.).

**Terminal Value**–See **Residual Value**.

**Transaction Method**–See **Merger and Acquisition Method**.

**Unlevered Beta**–the beta reflecting a capital structure without debt.

**Unsystematic Risk**–the risk specific to an individual security that can be avoided through diversification.

**Valuation**–the act or process of determining the value of a business, business ownership interest, security, or intangible asset.

**Valuation Approach**–a general way of determining a value indication of a business, business ownership interest, security, or intangible asset using one or more valuation methods.

**Valuation Date**–the specific point in time as of which the valuator's opinion of value applies (also referred to as "Effective Date" or "Appraisal Date").

**Valuation Method**–within approaches, a specific way to determine value.

**Valuation Procedure**–the act, manner, and technique of performing the steps of an appraisal method.

**Valuation Ratio**–a fraction in which a value or price serves as the numerator and financial, operating, or physical data serve as the denominator.

**Value to the Owner**–see **Investment Value**.

**Voting Control**–*de jure* control of a business enterprise.

**Weighted Average Cost of Capital (WACC)**–the cost of capital (discount rate) determined by the weighted average, at market value, of the cost of all financing sources in the business enterprise's capital structure.

# APPENDIX C

# Glossary of Additional Terms

**Assumptions and Limiting Conditions.** Parameters and boundaries under which a valuation is performed, as agreed upon by the valuation analyst and the client or as acknowledged or understood by the valuation analyst and the client as being due to existing circumstances. An example is the acceptance, without further verification, by the valuation analyst from the client of the client's financial statements and related information.

**Business Ownership Interest.** A designated share in the ownership of a business (business enterprise).

**Calculated Value.** An estimate as to the value of a business, business ownership interest, security, or intangible asset, arrived at by applying valuation procedures agreed upon with the client and using professional judgment as to the value or range of values based on those procedures.

**Calculation Engagement.** An engagement to estimate value wherein the valuation analyst and the client agree on the specific valuation approaches and valuation methods that the valuation analyst will use and the extent of valuation procedures the valuation analyst will perform to estimate the value of a subject interest. A calculation engagement generally does not include all of the valuation procedures required for a valuation engagement. If a valuation engagement had been performed, the results might have been different. The valuation analyst expresses the results of the calculation engagement as a calculated value, which may be either a single amount or a range.

**Capital or Contributory Asset Charge.** A fair return on an entity's *contributory assets*, which are tangible and intangible assets used in the production of income or cash flow associated with an intangible asset being valued. In this context, *income or cash flow* refers to an applicable measure of income or cash flow, such as net income, or operating cash flow before taxes and capital expenditures. A capital charge may be expressed as a percentage return on an economic rent associated with, or a profit split related to, the contributory assets.

**Capitalization of Benefits Method.** A method within the income approach whereby expected future benefits (for example, earnings or cash flow) for a representative single period are converted to value through division by a capitalization rate.

**Comparable Profits Method.** A method of determining the value of intangible assets by comparing the profits of the subject entity with those of similar uncontrolled companies that have the same or similar complement of intangible assets as the subject company.

**Comparable Uncontrolled Transaction Method.** A method of determining the value of intangible assets by comparing the subject transaction to similar transactions in the market place made between independent (uncontrolled) parties.

**Conclusion of Value.** An estimate of the value of a business, business ownership interest, security, or intangible asset, arrived at by applying the valuation procedures appropriate for a valuation engagement and using professional judgment as to the value or range of values based on those procedures.

**Control Adjustment.** A valuation adjustment to financial statements to reflect the effect of a controlling interest in a business. An example would be an adjustment to owners' compensation that is in excess of market compensation.

**Engagement to Estimate Value.** An engagement, or any part of an engagement (for example, a tax, litigation, or acquisition-related engagement), that involves determining the value of a business, business ownership interest, security, or intangible asset. Also known as *valuation service*.

**Excess Operating Assets.** Operating assets in excess of those needed for the normal operation of a business.

**Fair Value.** In valuation applications, there are two commonly used definitions for fair value:

(1)  For financial reporting purposes only, the price that would be received to sell an asset or paid to transfer a liability in an orderly transaction between market participants at the measurement date. *Source:* Financial Accounting Standards Board definition in Statement of Financial Accounting Standards (SFAS) No. 157, *Fair Value Measurements*, as used in the context of Generally Accepted Accounting Principles (GAAP) (Effective 2008).

(2) For state legal matters only, some states have laws that use the term *fair value* in shareholder and partner matters. For state legal matters only, therefore, the term may be defined by statute or case law in the particular jurisdiction.

**Guideline Company Transactions Method.** A method within the market approach whereby market multiples are derived from the sales of entire companies engaged in the same or similar lines of business.

**Hypothetical Condition.** That which is or may be contrary to what exists, but is supposed for the purpose of analysis.

**Incremental Income.** Additional income or cash flow attributable to an entity's ownership or operation of an intangible asset being valued, as determined by a comparison of the entity's income or cash flow with the intangible asset to the entity's income or cash flow without the intangible asset. In this context, *income or cash flow* refers to an applicable measure of income or cash flow, such as license royalty income or operating cash flow before taxes and capital expenditures.

**Normalization.** See *Normalized Earnings* in Appendix B, "International Glossary of Business Valuation Terms."

**Pre-adjustment Value.** The value arrived at prior to the application, if appropriate, of valuation discounts or premiums.

**Profit Split Income.** With respect to the valuation of an intangible asset of an entity, a percentage allocation of the entity's income or cash flow whereby (1) a split (or percentage) is allocated to the subject intangible and (2) the remainder is allocated to all of the entity's tangible and other intangible assets. In this context, *income or cash flow* refers to an applicable measure of income or cash flow, such as net income or operating cash flow before taxes and capital expenditures.

**Relief from Royalty Method.** A valuation method used to value certain intangible assets (for example, trademarks and trade names) based on the premise that the only value that a purchaser of the assets receives is the exemption from paying a royalty for its use. Application of this method usually involves estimating the fair market value of an intangible asset by quantifying the present value of the stream of market-derived royalty payments that the owner of the intangible asset is exempted from or "relieved" from paying.

**Residual Income.** For an entity that owns or operates an intangible asset being valued, the portion of the entity's income or cash flow remaining after subtracting a capital charge on all of the entity's tangible and other intangible assets. *Income or cash flows* can refer to any appropriate measure of income or cash flow, such as net income or operating cash flow before taxes and capital expenditures.

**Security.** A certificate evidencing ownership or the rights to ownership in a business enterprise that (1) is represented by an instrument or by a book record or contractual agreement, (2) is of a type commonly dealt in on securities exchanges or markets or, when represented by an instrument, is commonly recognized in any area in which it is issued or dealt in as a medium for investment, and (3) either one of a class or series or, by its terms, is divisible into a class or series of shares, participations, interests, rights, or interest-bearing obligations.

**Subject Interest.** A business, business ownership interest, security, or intangible asset that is the subject of a valuation engagement.

**Subsequent Event.** An event that occurs subsequent to the valuation date.

**Valuation Analyst.** For purposes of this Statement, an AICPA member who performs an engagement to estimate value that culminates in the expression of a conclusion of value or a calculated value.

**Valuation Assumptions.** Statements or inputs utilized in the performance of an engagement to estimate value that serve as a basis for the application of particular valuation methods.

**Valuation Engagement.** An engagement to estimate value in which a valuation analyst determines an estimate of the value of a subject interest by performing appropriate valuation procedures, as outlined in the AICPA Statement on Standards for Valuation Services, and is free to apply the valuation approaches and methods he or she deems appropriate in the circumstances. The valuation analyst expresses the results of the valuation engagement as a conclusion of value, which may be either a single amount or a range.

**Valuation Service.** See **Engagement to Estimate Value**.

# Interpretation No. 1-01, "Scope of Applicable Services" of *Statement on Standards for Valuation Services No. 1*, Valuation of a Business, Business Ownership Interest, Security, or Intangible Asset

## Background

1. The Statement on Standards for Valuation Services (SSVS) establishes standards of performance and reporting for all AICPA members performing those valuation services that are within the scope of the Statement. When originally proposed on March 30, 2005, the Exposure Draft contained a list of questions and answers (Appendix A of the March 30, 2005 Exposure Draft) that were intended to assist members in determining if an engagement, particularly with regard to litigation or tax engagements, fell within the scope of the Statement. Through the Exposure Draft process, it was determined that the questions and answers were an integral part of the Statement and should be made authoritative. This Interpretation is part of the AICPA's continuing efforts at self-regulation of its members in valuation practice, and its desire to provide guidance to members when providing valuation services. The Interpretation does not change or elevate any level of conduct prescribed by any standard. Its goal is to clarify existing standards.

## General Interpretation

2. The SSVSs apply to an engagement to estimate value if, as all or as part of another engagement, a member determines the value of a business, business ownership interest, security, or intangible asset (SSVS paragraphs 1 and 2). In the process of estimating value, professional judgment is used to apply valuation approaches and valuation methods as described in the SSVSs (SSVS paragraph 4).

3. In determining whether a particular service falls within the scope of the Statement, a member should consider those services that are specifically excluded:

- Audit, review, and compilation engagements (SSVS paragraph 5)
- Use of values provided by the client or a third party (SSVS paragraph 6)
- Internal use assignments from employers to employee members not in the *practice of public accounting* (SSVS paragraph 7)
- Engagements that are exclusively for the purpose of determining economic damages (for example, lost profits) and that do not include an engagement to estimate value (SSVS paragraph 8)
- Mechanical computations that do not rise to the level of an engagement to estimate value (SSVS paragraph 9(a))
- Engagements where it is not practical or reasonable to obtain or use relevant information and, therefore, the member is unable to apply valuation approaches and methods described in this Statement. (SSVS paragraph 9(b))
- Engagements meeting the jurisdictional exception (SSVS paragraph 10)

4. A member should be diligent in determining if an engagement falls within the scope of the Statement. Unless specifically excluded by the SSVS, if the engagement requires a member to apply valuation approaches and methods, and use professional judgment in applying those approaches and methods, the SSVS would apply. In determining the scope and requirements of the engagement, a member should consider the client's needs, or the requirements of a third party for which the valuation is intended, including governmental, judicial, and accounting authorities. In addition, a member should consider other professional standards that might apply.

## Specific Illustrations

5. The following illustrations address general fact patterns. Accordingly, the application of the guidance discussed in the "General Interpretation" section to variations in general facts, or to particular facts and circumstances, may lead to different conclusions. In each illustration, there is no authority other than that indicated.

## Illustrations Relating to Litigation Engagements and Certain Controversy Proceedings

6. *Illustration 1.* Do lost profits damage computations fall within the scope of the Statement?

7. *Conclusion.* No, unless the computations are undertaken as part of an engagement to estimate value (SSVS paragraphs 1, 2, and 8).

8. *Illustration 2.* Is an economic damages computation that incorporates a terminal value within the scope of the Statement?

9. *Conclusion.* The use of a terminal value exclusively for the determination of lost profits is not within the scope of this statement unless that determination will be used as part of an engagement to estimate value (Illustration 1).

10. *Illustration 3.* If a start-up business is destroyed, is the economic damages computation within the scope of the Statement?

11. *Conclusion.* There are two common measures of damages: lost profits and loss of value. If a valuation analyst performs an engagement to estimate value to determine the loss of value of a business or intangible asset, the Statement applies. Otherwise, the Statement does not apply (*Illustration 1*). In order to determine whether the Statement applies, a member acting as an expert witness should evaluate whether the particular damages calculation constitutes an engagement to estimate value with respect to the business, business interest, security, or intangible asset or whether it constitutes a lost-profits computation.

12. *Illustration 4.* Does the Statement include any exceptions relating to litigation or controversy proceedings?

13. *Conclusion.* Yes, the Statement includes a reporting exemption for certain controversy proceedings (SSVS paragraph 50); however, there is no litigation or controversy proceeding exemption from the developmental provisions of the Statement (SSVS paragraphs 21–46) in circumstances in which an engagement to estimate value is performed (*Illustration 1*).

14. *Illustration 5.* Is the Statement's reporting exemption for litigation or controversy proceedings (see SSVS paragraph 50) the same as the "litigation exemption" in the AICPA attestation standards?

15. *Conclusion.* No, the so-called "litigation exemption" is provided for in the AICPA attestation standards and is further discussed in the attestation interpretations. The attestation standards do not apply to engagements in which a practitioner is engaged to testify as an expert witness in accounting, auditing, taxation, or other matters, given certain stipulated facts. This is clarified in the attestation interpretation, which states, in part, that the attestation standards do not apply to litigation services engagements when (among other requirements) the practitioner "has not been engaged to issue and does not issue an examination, a review, or an agreed-upon procedures report on the subject matter, or an assertion about the subject matter that is the responsibility of another party." (Interpretation No. 3, "Applicability of Attestation Standards to Litigation Services," of Chapter 1, "Attest Engagements," of Statement on Standards for Attestation Engagements *No. 10, Attestation Standards: Revision and Recodification*, as revised [AICPA, *Professional Standards*, vol. 1, AT sec. 9101.34–.42].) However, unlike the AICPA attestation standards, which do not apply in any capacity to litigation or controversy proceeding situations, as discussed above, the Statement's exemption for litigation or certain controversy proceedings is an exemption from the reporting provisions of the Statement (SSVS paragraphs 47–78).

## Illustrations Relating to Tax Engagements

16. *Illustration 6.* When does the Statement apply to members who determine values related to tax reporting and planning engagements?

17. *Conclusion.* The Statement applies when the member is engaged to estimate the value of a business, business ownership interest, security, or intangible asset (SSVS paragraph 1). The application of valuation approaches and methods and the use of professional judgment (SSVS paragraph 4) are required, unless an exception applies (SSVS paragraphs 5 through 10).

18. *Illustration 7.* If the sole purpose of an engagement is reporting a value in a tax return and the Statement applies to this engagement, are any separate reports (specifically, valuation reports) required to be issued? To whom are those reports required to be

provided? Is a report required to be attached to the tax return? Are any specific disclosures required?

19. *Conclusion.* The Statement requires the preparation of a written or oral valuation report (SSVS paragraphs 47–78) that is communicated to the client (SSVS paragraph 47) but does not require that any report be attached to the tax return or mandate any other tax-specific disclosures. In limited circumstances, a taxing authority may require its own report, which would obviate the need for a separate valuation report (SSVS paragraph 10 and *Illustration 18*). There is also a reporting exemption for certain controversy proceedings (SSVS paragraph 50 and *Illustration 4*).

20. *Illustration 8.* Are mechanical computations of value, for example, computations using actuarial tables, excluded from the Statement?

21. *Conclusion.* Mechanical computations of value are excluded from the Statement if they do not rise to the level of an engagement to estimate value, that is, if the member does not apply valuation approaches and methods, and does not use professional judgment, as described in the Statement (SSVS paragraph 9(a)).

22. Examples of services that do **not** rise to the level of an engagement to estimate value include: (*a*) computations of a remainder interest under a grantor retained annuity trust (GRAT) using actuarial tables; (*b*) determining the value of relatively small blocks (relative to the total amount of corporate stock outstanding) of publicly traded stock whose per share price is readily ascertainable; (*c*) preparing a tax return using the valuation of a business that was provided by a third-party appraiser, or by the client (SSVS paragraph 6); and (*d*) calculating cash "hold back" requirements for tax contingencies (SSVS paragraphs 1,4, and 9(a)).

23. Examples of services that rise to the level of an engagement to estimate value include: (*a*) valuing a block of publicly traded stock, if the analysis includes consideration of a discount for blockage, lockup, or other contractual or market restrictions such that valuation approaches and methods are applied, and professional judgment is used to determine the fair value, fair market value, or other applicable standard of value; (*b*) valuing stock that is not publicly traded; and (*c*) computing the fair market value of assets in a charitable

remainder trust (CRT), if the engagement requires the application of valuation approaches and methods, and the use of professional judgment to estimate the fair market value.

24. *Illustration 9.* Does the "jurisdictional exception" (SSVS paragraph 10) provide that an engagement to estimate value is not subject to the Statement if a member determines and reports values using procedures mandated or allowed by the Internal Revenue Code (IRC), Internal Revenue Service (IRS) regulations, court cases, or other published guidance and other sources of federal, state, and local law solely for purposes of tax return preparation and other tax services using these methods?

25. *Conclusion.* No, the "jurisdictional exception" would not exempt the engagement from this Statement, even if the engagement's sole purpose was to value a subject interest (SSVS paragraph 1) for tax reporting purposes. Only the portion of the Statement that differs from the published governmental or judicial authority is superseded for purposes of the engagement. The remainder of the Statement applies to the engagement.

26. *Illustration 10.* Is an interest in a publicly traded partnership whose shares are frequently traded considered a "security" under the Statement? Is an interest in a family limited partnership (FLP), or in another nontraded partnership, considered a "security" under the Statement?

27. *Conclusion.* Whether interest constitutes a "security" is a legal determination. However, where the value of a security is readily ascertainable, a valuation analyst does not need to apply valuation approaches and methods and use professional judgment. Accordingly, the valuation of such an interest would not be subject to the Statement (SSVS paragraphs 1 and 9(a)). An interest in a non-publicly traded partnership, such as an FLP, whether considered a security or not, is a business ownership interest. The valuation of such nonpublicly traded interest requires the application of valuation approaches and methods and the use of professional judgment, and, accordingly, would be subject to the Statement (SSVS paragraphs 1, 4, and *Illustration 6*), unless the exception under SSVS paragraph 9(b) applies (*Illustration 13e*). If the engagement requires the valuation analyst to consider and apply adjustments, for example, valuation discounts or premiums, then the engagement would be subject to the Statement.

28. *Illustration 11.* A client engages a member to provide advice for planning purposes (such as estate planning, personal financial planning, or merger and acquisitions planning). The client holds an ownership interest in a family business being operated as a limited liability company, an interest in a private real estate limited partnership, publicly traded stock, a personal residence, and a retirement account (not an IRA). Is this a valuation engagement subject to the Statement?

29. *Conclusion.* It depends. Providing technical advice, without reference to values for the various assets, is not subject to the Statement. However, if a member calculates a value to illustrate various planning options, he or she may fall under the Statement with regard to various assets. If one or more of the assets for which value is to be determined for purposes of the plan illustrations is a business, business ownership interest, security, or intangible asset, and the client or a third party does not provide the values for these assets, or the member does not use assumed or hypothetical values as part of the overall engagement, the member performing the valuation(s) is subject to the Statement with regard to these assets (SSVS paragraph 1 and *Illustration 6*). In this example, if the member applies valuation approaches and methods and uses professional judgment to determine the value of the ownership interest in the family business or the interest in the private real estate limited partnership in order to provide planning advice, the Statement would apply. In contrast, if the client or a third party provides the values for these assets, or the member uses assumed or hypothetical values, the Statement would not apply because the member would not be applying valuation approaches and methods and using professional judgment. In addition, the exception under SSVS paragraph 9(b), where it is not practical or reasonable to obtain or use relevant information, could apply (see *Illustration 13e*). The computation of the "estimated estate tax" or other taxes once the values have been determined, assumed, or provided is not subject to the Statement, as the computation is a tax computation but would be subject to the Statement on Standards for Tax Services (*Illustration 10* at paragraph 27 of this Interpretation).

30. *Illustration 12.* There are many instances where a tax engagement involves the need for a member to estimate value. The estimation of value may not be the primary purpose of the engagement, but rather a necessary task to perform or item to consider, when making

a tax determination concerning the reporting of a transaction on a tax return. Consider the following practice situations:

31. *Illustration 12a.* A member has been engaged to determine the deductibility of interest on a nonrecourse loan. Under applicable regulations, interest on a nonrecourse loan cannot be deducted if it is clear that the company will be unable to service the debt. For purposes of tax reporting, a conclusion must be reached concerning the ability of the company to service the debt. Is this considered a valuation engagement subject to the Statement?

32. *Conclusion.* This is not a valuation engagement covered by the Statement because it is not the valuation of a subject interest (SSVS paragraph 1). This example is a debt-service analysis.

33. *Illustration 12b.* There are compliance filings that require an estimate of the value of a company. For example, the "market value" of "intangible personal property," as defined by a state's taxing authority may need to be reported annually on an intangible personal property tax return. A client has a subject interest that is considered intangible personal property for purposes of the return. The member has been engaged to prepare the tax return. Is this a valuation engagement subject to the Statement?

34. *Conclusion.* It depends. If the state requires an estimation of the value of a subject interest, and the estimation of value requires the application of valuation approaches and methods and the use of professional judgment (SSVS paragraphs 1 and 4), the Statement applies. If, however, the client or a third-party appraiser provides the value of the subject interest to the member, the Statement does not apply (SSVS paragraphs 1 and 6). In addition, the exception under SSVS paragraph 9(b), where it is not practical or reasonable to obtain or use relevant information, could apply (*Illustration 13e*). Alternatively, if the state follows more informal rules where the application of valuation approaches or valuation methods are not necessary, the Statement does not apply (SSVS paragraph 4).

35. *Illustration 12c.* There are times when a member must allocate value among various assets. For example, IRC sections 1060 and 338 require the allocation to assets, based on relative values, of consideration paid. In partnership taxation, there may be allocations under IRC sections 754, 743, and 734 and special tax basis

adjustments for partnerships (sales or exchanges and transfers at or upon death) may require an allocation of value among various partnership assets. Are these types of allocations engagements to estimate value subject to the Statement?

36. *Conclusion.* It depends. If one or more of the assets to which value is to be allocated is a subject interest (that is, a business, business ownership interest, security, or intangible asset), and the client or a third party did not provide the member with a value for those assets, then the member performing the allocation would be subject to the Statement, and the member is required to apply valuation approaches and methods, and use professional judgment to value those assets (SSVS paragraphs 1, 4, and *Illustration 6*), unless an exception applies (SSVS paragraphs 5–10). For example, in an IRC section 1060 allocation, after the allocation of purchase price to cash, receivables, inventory, and depreciable tangible assets, there is a residual amount of value allocable to goodwill or going concern. The mechanical assignment of the residual amount to goodwill or going concern is not subject to the Statement. However, if the member allocates this residual amount to specific intangible assets (such as to various customer-based and supplier-based intangibles), such allocation is based on the assets' relative values. Because the member applies valuation approaches and methods and uses professional judgment to value those specific intangible assets, the Statement applies.

37. *Illustration 12d.* If the member does not apply any discount and simply computes the fair market value of an interest in a family limited partnership (FLP) for tax purposes, is this a valuation engagement subject to the Statement?

38. *Conclusion.* Yes, the Statement applies if the member determines the value of the FLP or an interest in an FLP. The application of valuation approaches and methods, and the use of professional judgment are required, unless an exception applies (SSVS paragraphs 5–10). The fact that the member does not apply a discount does not exempt the engagement from the Statement (SSVS paragraphs 1–4 and 9(a)).

39. *Illustration 12e.* Would the Statement apply to the computation of the fair market value of assets in, or the computation of the required distribution of, a charitable remainder trust (CRT)?

40. *Conclusion.* It depends on the underlying assets held by the CRT. The Statement would apply only if the member determines the value of a business, business ownership interest, security, or intangible asset (SSVS paragraph 1). To the extent that the CRT holds assets that, to be valued, require the application of valuation approaches and methods, and the use of professional judgment, such as an interest in a limited liability corporation (LLC), the Statement would apply. However, if the CRT only holds publicly traded stock with a readily ascertainable value, the Statement would not apply because valuation approaches and methods and professional judgment would not be needed in the computation (SSVS paragraphs 1 and 4, and *Illustration 6*).

41. *Illustration 12f.* In circumstances in which the value of assets contributed by partners to a partnership differ from their cost basis, each difference must be tracked for tax purposes under IRC section 704(c) so that amounts of gain or loss can be properly assigned to the contributing partners. Are these types of asset value assignments valuation engagements subject to the Statement?

42. *Conclusion.* It depends. If one or more of the assets for which value is relevant under IRC section 704(c) is a subject interest that is, a business, business ownership interest, security, or intangible asset, and the client or a third party does not provide the valuation, and the member applies valuation approaches and methods and uses professional judgment to value these assets for IRC section 704(c) tax purposes, then the Statement applies (SSVS paragraphs 1 and 6, and *Illustration 6*).

43. *Illustration 12g.* A member has been engaged to perform a cost segregation study. The study involves an analysis of the costs of building a structure and the allocation of such costs to the real and personal property components of the structure so that depreciation of those components may be properly computed. Is this a valuation engagement subject to the Statement?

44. *Conclusion.* No, none of the assets constitutes a subject interest (SSVS paragraph 1).

45. *Illustration 12h.* A member has been engaged to provide advice to a company regarding the tax planning for income from discharge of indebtedness under IRC section 108. The company has advised the member that the company will be able to negotiate a set-

tlement in complete satisfaction of an obligation at 30 cents on the dollar. Is this a valuation engagement subject to the Statement?

46. *Conclusion.* It depends. Under IRC section 108(a), gross income of the company excludes income from discharge of indebtedness only under certain circumstances. One of those circumstances is the insolvency of the company. Under IRC section 108(d) (3), insolvency results from an excess of liabilities over the fair market value of assets. If (*a*) the company must rely on the insolvency provisions of IRC section 108; (*b*) one or more of the assets for which value is relevant under IRC section 108 is a subject interest (that is, a business, business ownership interest, security, or intangible asset); (*c*) the company or a third party does not provide the valuation; and (*d*) the member applies valuation approaches and methods, and uses professional judgment to value the subject interest(s) for purposes of the IRC section 108(d)(3) insolvency determination, the Statement applies.

47. *Illustration 13.* An executor has engaged a member to prepare an estate tax return, which requires determining values for the following estate assets: (*a*) shares in a publicly traded company, "TI Corporation," whose shares are infrequently traded; (*b*) a large block of stock in "LB Corporation," a publicly traded company; (*c*) a brokerage account consisting of shares in various publicly traded companies; (*d*) "CHB Corporation," a closely held business owned by the decedent and the decedent's family; and (*e*) a 5 percent interest in "RP," a privately held rental real estate partnership. Does the Statement apply to any of the following assets owned by the estate? (See *Illustration 10* at paragraph 27 of this Interpretation regarding the valuation of a security.)

48. *Illustration 13a.* Does the Statement apply to shares in a publicly traded company, "TI Corporation," whose shares are traded infrequently?

49. *Conclusion.* It depends; although the price of a share of publicly traded stock is ascertainable from published sources, there are no definitive criteria that would indicate when the Statement applies to shares that are infrequently traded. A key consideration is the average daily trading volume of TI Corporation stock on or around the valuation date. The concept of fair market value incorporates the notions that (1) cash could have been received for the stock at the valuation date, and (2) the share price of an infrequently traded stock

could decrease if a relatively large block of the stock were to be put on the market on that date. If the subject shares held by the estate do not represent a significant percentage of the daily trading volume of TI stock on or around the valuation date, and the price of a share of the stock is readily ascertainable on the valuation date, then the resulting value (the quoted share price times the number of shares owned) represents a cash price that could have been received at the valuation date for the block, and the Statement does not apply because the calculation of value is mechanical (SSVS paragraph 9(a)). If, however, the subject shares held by the estate represent a large percentage of the average daily trading volume of the stock, the quoted market price for a share may not be adequate for purposes of determining the fair market value of the block of shares on the valuation date. In that case, the Statement applies because valuation approaches and methods need to be applied, and professional judgment needs to be used in determining the value of the block (SSVS paragraphs 1 and 4) (See *Illustration 10* at paragraph 27 of this Interpretation regarding the valuation of a security.)

50. *Illustration 13b.* Does the Statement apply to a large block of stock in "LB Corporation," a publicly traded company?

51. *Conclusion.* The answer depends on the amount of shares to be valued in relation to the average daily trading volume in LB Corporation on or around the valuation date. There are no definitive criteria that would indicate when the Statement applies to the valuation of a large block of publicly traded stock. The concept of fair market value incorporates the notion that cash could have been received from a sale of the block on the valuation date. A large block could decrease the share price if sold on the valuation date. The Statement would typically not apply to the valuation of a large block (for example, 200,000 shares) of a large and actively-traded public company. Even though the value of the estate's stock may be large in absolute terms, the daily trading volume in such stock on the valuation date may be sufficiently high that a sale of the block on the valuation date would not affect the market price of a company's shares. In such a case, the quoted market price of a share times the number of shares held by the estate may be considered to reflect the fair market value of the subject block of stock, and because it would not be the case that valuation approaches and methods would need to be applied and professional judgment used, the Statement would not apply. If, however, the large block of publicly traded shares repre-

sents a significant percentage of the daily trading volume, the Statement would apply because valuation approaches and methods would need to be applied and professional judgment used to determine the value (SSVS paragraphs 1 and 4).

52. *Illustration 13c.* Does the Statement apply to a brokerage account consisting of shares in various publicly traded companies?

53. *Conclusion.* The Statement would not apply to the determination of the value of a brokerage account consisting of publicly traded securities, except as discussed in paragraphs 49 and 51 of this interpretation. Absent certain scenarios involving infrequently traded securities or large blocks of stock, the application of valuation approaches and methods and the use of professional judgment are not necessary in that determination (SSVS paragraphs 1 and 4).

54. *Illustration 13d.* Does the Statement apply to "CHB Corporation," a closely held business owned by the decedent and the decedent's family?

55. *Conclusion.* The Statement would apply to the determination of value of CHB Corporation because valuation approaches and methods need to be applied, and professional judgment needs to be used to determine the fair market value of the ownership interest in CHB (SSVS paragraphs 1 and 4).

56. *Illustration 13e.* Does the Statement apply to a 5 percent interest in a privately held rental real estate partnership (RP)?

57. *Conclusion.* The Statement would apply to the determination of value of the 5 percent interest in rental real estate partnership (RP) because valuation approaches and methods need to be applied and professional judgment needs to be used to determine the fair market value of the ownership of a fractional interest in a privately held partnership (SSVS paragraphs 1 and 4). However, where it is not practical or not reasonable to obtain or use relevant information and, therefore, the member is unable to apply valuation approaches and methods, the Statement would not apply. For example, the member has requested from RP's general partner financial information the member needs in order to apply valuation approaches and methods. The general partner is not responsive to the member's requests, and the due date for filing the estate tax return is near. Given the small ownership interest, and given that RP is likely a relatively small percent of the total estate, unless prohibited by statute or

by rule, the member may then use the taxpayer's estimates if the member determines that the estimates are reasonable (based on the facts and circumstances known to the member) (SSVS paragraph 9(b)).

58. *Illustration 14.* Would the answers to *Illustration 13* change if the values were provided by the client or a client-engaged third party?

59. *Conclusion.* The Statement would not apply if the values were provided by the client or by a client-engaged third party because the member is not applying valuation approaches and methods and using professional judgment to determine value (SSVS paragraphs 1 and 4). However, the member would be subject to Statement on Standards for Tax Services No. 3, *Certain Procedural Aspects of Preparing Returns*, in providing appropriate due diligence with respect to the values provided to the member (see AICPA, *Professional Standards*, vol. 2, TS sec. 300). It is also recommended that the understanding between member and client in these circumstances include documentation of the fact that the member is not determining but rather is being provided with the value of the subject interest.

60. *Illustration 15.* Would the answers to *Illustration 13* change if the values were provided by an outside third-party specialist hired by the member?

61. *Conclusion.* If the member engages an outside third-party specialist to assist with the member's work, and it is the member expressing a conclusion or calculated value, the member will be applying valuation approaches and methods and using professional judgment; thus, the Statement would apply (SSVS paragraphs 1 and 4; SSVS paragraphs 20, "Using the Work of Specialists in the Valuation Engagement"). If, however, the third-party specialist is determining the value in his or her own name and providing that value to the client, and the member will not be applying valuation approaches and methods or using professional judgment (SSVS paragraphs 1 and 4, and *Illustration 6*), the Statement would not apply, but the member would be subject to Statement on Standards for Tax Services No. 3, *Certain Procedural Aspects of Preparing Returns*, in providing appropriate due diligence with respect to the values provided (AICPA, *Professional Standards*, vol. 2, TS sec. 300).

62. *Illustration 16.* The client and the member agree that the member will value a partnership interest and then apply an "average" discount that the member is to determine (based on the results of various studies and case law). Does the Statement apply? If so, is this a valuation engagement or a calculation engagement?

63. *Conclusion.* Yes, the Statement applies because the member determined the value of the partnership interest by applying valuation approaches and valuation methods and using professional judgment. This would be considered a calculation engagement because the member and the client have agreed on the specific valuation approaches or valuation methods the valuation analyst will use and the extent of valuation procedures the valuation analyst will perform (SSVS paragraph 21(b) and *Illustration 6*).

64. *Illustration 17.* Would the Statement apply if a member has an informal conversation or communicates in writing with a client regarding the alternative tax consequences of gifting versus selling a business using a presumption of a specific value of the business?

65. *Conclusion.* No, the Statement would not apply. The member is providing tax advice using an assumed or hypothetical value of a business and is not determining value, applying valuation approaches and methods, and using professional judgment to value a business (SSVS paragraphs 1 and 4, and *Illustration 6*).

66. *Illustration 18.* Would the Statement apply to a transfer pricing study (IRC section 482) that involves the use of specific methodologies, data, terminology, and documentation requirements that are provided in the IRS regulations and procedures, and whose methodologies and documentation requirements differ from those contained in the Statement?

67. *Conclusion.* No. To the extent that the transfer pricing study applies, for example, to the valuation of inventory or services, the Statement would not apply (see SSVS paragraph 1 and *Illustration 6*). To the extent that the transfer pricing study applies to the valuation of intangible assets, the Statement would normally apply. However, because the IRS regulations require that the taxpayer reasonably calculate an arm's-length price according to the best method that is determined using third-party comparable data under explicit IRS rules and documentation procedures, and to the extent these IRS rules and procedures differ from the Statement,

the jurisdictional exception (SSVS paragraph 10) would exempt the valuation of the intangible assets from the developmental provisions of the Statement (SSVS paragraphs 25–48). In addition, to the extent that the IRS regulations (such as IRS regulation section 1.6662-6(d)(2)(iii)) and procedures provide specific documentation requirements for avoiding potential penalties, and if a transfer pricing report is provided to a client according to such IRS documentation requirements, the jurisdictional exception would apply to the reporting provisions of the Statement (SSVS paragraphs 50–78) and thus a valuation report would not be necessary.

68. *Illustration 19.* In a situation where the Statement applies to members who determine value as part of tax engagements, would the member also be required to be in compliance with the Statements on Standards for Tax Services (SSTSs)?

69. *Conclusion.* Yes, the Statement would apply only to the valuation determination and reporting aspects of the engagement but the SSTSs would apply to all aspects of the engagement. For example, even though the Statement would govern the determination of value of an applicable asset reported on a tax return, the member would also have to be in compliance with SSTS No. 1, *Tax Return Positions,* for that valuation.

70. *Illustration 21.* Do settlements or negotiations of value in offers-in-compromise or tax disputes fall under the Statement?

71. *Conclusion.* No, settlements or negotiations of value in offers-in-compromise or tax disputes are part of a tax process. However, if a member prepares a valuation in preparation for a settlement or negotiation of value, and the valuation involves the application of valuation approaches and methods and the use of professional judgment, the valuation would fall under the developmental aspects of the Statement. The settlement or negotiation process itself is not a valuation and would not fall under the Statement. In addition, the Statement's reporting exemption for certain controversy proceedings would apply as the valuation was performed specifically for the administrative matter (SSVS paragraph 50).

— 

## Illustrations Relating to Other Engagements

72. *Illustration 20.* Does determining the value of accounts receivable fall under the Statement?

73. *Conclusion.* No, accounts receivable constitute **tangible assets** under the Statement (SSVS Appendix B), and do not constitute a subject interest (SSVS paragraph 1).

74. *Illustration 22.* In the course of performing a valuation under the Statement, if a valuation analyst prepares prospective financial information (for example, as part of a discounted cash flow or discounted earnings analysis within the income approach), does this require the valuation analyst to examine or compile such information in accordance with the Statements on Standards for Attestation Engagements (SSAEs)?

75. *Conclusion.* No, Chapter 1, "Attest Engagements," of SSAE No. 10, *Attestation Standards: Revision and Recodification* (AICPA, *Professional Standards*, vol. 1, AT sec. 101), as amended (AT sec. 101.01) states that the attestation standards apply when a practitioner is "engaged to issue or does issue an examination, a review, or an agreed-upon procedures report on subject matter, or an assertion about the subject matter..., that is the responsibility of another party." If the valuation analyst has not been engaged to examine, compile, assemble, review, or apply agreed-upon procedures to prospective financial information, and does not issue an examination, compilation, assembly, or agreed-upon report on prospective financial information, the SSAEs do not apply (SSARS 14).

76. *Illustration 23.* Under a valuation engagement, a valuation analyst is free to select any and all valuation approaches and methods the valuation analyst deems appropriate in the circumstances. Under a calculation engagement, the valuation analyst and the client agree to the specific approaches or methods the valuation analyst will use or the extent of calculation procedures the valuation analyst will perform. (SSVS paragraph 21.) Under SSVS paragraph 18, a restriction or limitation on the scope of the valuation analyst's work, or the data available for analysis may be present and known to the valuation analyst at the outset of the engagement, or may arise during the course of an engagement (and such restriction or limitation should be disclosed in the report). Is it possible to have a restriction or limitation

that is of such a degree that a valuation analyst engaged to perform a valuation engagement should propose altering the engagement to be a calculation engagement?

77. *Conclusion.* Although the two engagements represent two different types of service performed by valuation analysts, the possibility exists. If, in the course of a valuation engagement, restrictions, or limitations on the scope of the valuation analyst's work or the data available for analysis are so significant that the valuation analyst believes that he or she cannot, even with disclosure in the valuation report of the restrictions or limitations, adequately perform a valuation engagement leading to a conclusion of value, the valuation analyst should determine whether he or she has the ability to adequately complete the engagement as a calculation engagement or should consider resigning from the engagement.

78. *Illustration 24.* If a member employed in industry, government, or education "moonlights" doing engagements to estimate value, do the Standards apply?

79. *Conclusion.* Yes, the Standard applies. By moonlighting, the member is holding him or herself out as a certified public account and as being in public practice. The Standard would apply just as it would to any other member in public practice unless one of the exceptions applies.

80. *Illustration 25.* Does the Statement apply to an assignment from an employer to an employee member not in public practice to prepare a valuation for internal financial reporting purposes?

81. *Conclusion.* No, paragraph 7 exempts internal use assignments from an employer to an employee member not in the practice of public accounting. However, if the valuation is to be used for financial reporting purposes, the employer and the employee may wish to consider whether the work will be accepted by the employer's outside auditors if the statement is not followed.

# Illustrations for PFP-Specific Engagements

*These illustrations assume the member has not been engaged to perform a business valuation.*

82. *Illustration 26.* When does the Statement apply to members who determine values related to personal financial planning engagements?

83. *Conclusion.* The Statement applies to personal financial planning engagements when the member determines the value of a business, business ownership interest, security, or intangible asset (SSVS paragraph 1) and in the process of determining the value applies valuation approaches and methods and uses professional judgment (SSVS paragraph 4) unless an exception applies (SSVS paragraphs 5–10).

84. *Illustration 27.* If a member is engaged to provide personal financial planning services to a client and, in the course of the engagement, estimates the proceeds from a hypothetical future sale of the client's business interest, does the Statement apply?

85. *Conclusion.* No. The Statement does not apply because estimate of future sales proceeds does not in itself constitute a valuation engagement (SSVS paragraphs 1 and 4).

86. *Illustration 28.* A member is engaged to provide personal financial planning services to a client and, in the course of the engagement, estimates the proceeds from a hypothetical future sale of the client's business interest. As part of that engagement, the member shares general industry knowledge to assist the client in estimating the current value of the business interest. Does the Statement apply?

87. *Conclusion:*

(a) If, in the process of determining the current value from which the member estimates future sales proceeds, the member applies valuation approaches and methods and uses professional judgment, the Statement applies to the determination of the current value (SSVS paragraph 4). However, the Statement does not apply when the member shares general industry knowledge with the client instead of applying professional judgment.

(*b*) If the client or another party provides the current value, and the member does not apply valuation approaches and methods, the Statement does not apply (SSVS paragraphs 4 and 6).

(*c*) If the member uses a hypothetical or assumed value as the starting point for the calculation of future sales proceeds and does not apply valuation approaches and methods, the Statement does not apply (SSVS paragraphs 1 and 4). The Statement does not apply to a general discussion with the client of valuation concepts or industry price multiples based on the member's industry knowledge, which assists the client in determining a hypothetical or assumed value (SSVS paragraphs 4 and 6).

88. *Illustration 29.* The client has asked the member to prepare a personal financial plan that includes an estimate of future proceeds from a sale of the business interest at retirement. The member estimates the future proceeds based on an estimate of the business' current value by applying a rule of thumb for the business' industry, but the member does not consider the risk factors of the subject interest or exercise other professional judgment in applying the multiple. Does the Statement apply?

89. *Conclusion.* No, the Statement does not apply because the member did not use professional judgment (SSVS paragraph 4). If the member considers specific risk factors of the business interest in applying the price multiple, the Statement applies.

*This Statement titled* Valuation of a Business, Business Owner-ship Interest, Security, or Intangible Asset *was unanimously adopted by the assenting votes of the AICPA Consulting Services Executive Committee.*

### Consulting Services Executive Committee
### 2003–2007

Dominic A. Cingoranelli, Jr., *Chair*    Michael E. Mares
Lester Coffey    Paul D. Milne
Marianne Pulli Evashenk    Paul Richard Osborne
Dan H. Hanke    Robert F. Reilly
Bryan Eric Lundstrom

### Business Valuation Committee
### 2003–2007

Michael A. Crain, *Chair 2004–2007*    Rudolph L. Hertlein
Thomas E. Hilton, *Chair 2003–2004*    Yassir Karam
Melvin Haskell Abraham    G. William Kennedy
James A. Andersen    Michael E. Mares
Christine P. Baker    Bradley H. Minor
Richard S. Barnes    Robert F. Reilly
William J. Bavis    Sheri F. Schultz
Travis N. Chamberlain    Robin E. Taylor
Cindy Eddins Collier    Linda B. Trugman
Robert E. Duffy    Judith A. Wagner
John R. Gilbert    H.Joe Wells
Robert P. Gray    Carolyn J. Worth
Lindon A. Greene    Timothy W. York

### Business Valuation Standards Writing Task Force

Edward J. Dupke, *Chair*    Gregory Forsythe
R. James Alerding    James R. Hitchner

## AICPA Staff
### Specialized Communities & Firm Practice Management

James C. Metzler, *Vice President*
*Small Firm Interests*

Stephen L. Winters,
*Director*
*Specialized Communities*
*and Firm Practice*
*Management*

Thomas M. Miller, *Technical Manager*
*Business Valuation and Forensic &*
*Litigation Services*

*The AICPA gratefully acknowledges the contributions of Terry Jacoby Allen, James Feldman, Gretchen Fischbach, Nancy Gault, Michael N. Heaton, Joseph Lhotka, Debra Lockwood, Michael J. Mard, Richard I. Miller, Charles E. Landes, James S. Rigby, Jr., Marc T. Simon, James L. (Butch) Williams, Anat Kendal, Janice Fredericks, and Anthony Basile.*

# Index